Managing for Success

Managing for Success

Spotting Danger Signals
– And Fixing Problems before They Happen

Morgen Witzel

Bloomsbury Information
An imprint of Bloomsbury Publishing Plc

B L O O M S B U R Y
LONDON · NEW DELHI · NEW YORK · SYDNEY

Bloomsbury Information

An imprint of Bloomsbury Publishing Plc

50 Bedford Square	1385 Broadway
London	New York
WC1B 3DP	NY 10018
UK	USA

www.bloomsbury.com

BLOOMSBURY and the Diana logo are trademarks of Bloomsbury Publishing Plc

First published 2015

British Library Cataloguing-in-Publication Data
A catalogue record for this book is available from the British Library.

ISBN: HB: 978-1-4729-0496-6
ePDF: 978-1-4729-0498-0
ePub: 978-1-4729-0497-3

Library of Congress Cataloging-in-Publication Data
A catalog record for this book is available from the Library of Congress.

Design by Fiona Pike, Pike Design, Winchester
Typeset by Integra Software Services Pvt. Ltd.
Printed and bound in Great Britain

Contents

List of Tables

Acknowledgements

Three particular groups of people were influential in the making of this book. The first is my colleagues in the Professional Network of the Centre for Leadership Studies at the University of Exeter Business School, who listened to my outline ideas at a network day in March 2014 and gave me some excellent and highly useful feedback. The eighteen pages of notes I took that day helped reshape and reform the project and led directly to the present book. For your time and your ideas, thank you.

The second group is my academic colleagues at Exeter and elsewhere over the past twenty-five years. You've always known you harboured a cuckoo in your nest; none the less, you welcomed me in, shared your own thoughts and ideas and gave me inspiration. Some of what I say in this book will annoy the hell out of you. I hope some of it will also give you food for thought. To you also, thank you.

In the place of honour come the MBA and MSc students I have worked with at Exeter and other business schools. You too have been an unfailing source of inspiration. Through you, I calculate that in the fifteen years I have taught at business schools, I have had access to something like 7,000 years of professional experience, the sum total of the experience you brought to me. I have probably learned about 0.5 per cent of what I could have learned, but even that is pretty amazing. To all of you past and present, my thanks for welcoming me into your company and sharing your views with me.

It took a long time to find a publisher who was willing to take a chance on the subject of learning from management failure, but my agent Heather Adams believed in this project from the moment she first heard about it, and to her goes credit for its finding a home with a publisher. My thanks to Stephen Rutt and Alana Clogan for their support for it in the early stages, and to Alana and her team, especially Rosie Bick, for their encouragement and patience while waiting for me to write the book and then seeing it through production.

Marilyn Livingstone helped with the project in innumerable ways, from finding juicy articles to cite to talking through key concepts and generally providing her own brand of inspiration. To her, as always, my grateful thanks.

Chapter 1

Ludicrous, but unavoidable

At a conference a few years ago, I listened to a colleague's paper on the distinctions between successful and unsuccessful companies. She quoted Tolstoy's famous line from *Anna Karenina*: 'Happy families are all alike; every unhappy family is unhappy in its own way.' 'We can say the same thing about companies', my colleague concluded. 'Every happy company is alike, but each unhappy or unsuccessful company is unhappy in its own way.'

The more I thought about this idea, the less I agreed with it. Surely the success of companies is founded on their being able to do something unique and different from what other companies are doing? That is what the writers on strategy tell us when they talk about competitive advantage, and my own experience both as a business historian and a businessman seemed to bear this out. As for unsuccessful companies, is it possible that there are common factors that lead to failure? Don't failing companies follow certain patterns, certain paths? Again, experience seemed to suggest that this was so.

With this in mind, I turned to Norman Dixon's classic work *On the Psychology of Military Incompetence*. I found that Dixon had already reached the same conclusion. On military failures and disasters, he writes:

> *These moving, often horrific accounts evoked a curious déjà vu experience. For there was something about these apparently senseless goings-on which sent one's thoughts along new channels, making contact with phenomena from quite other, hitherto unrelated contexts; and then back again to the senseless facts, now not quite so senseless, until gradually a theme, continuous as a hair-line crack, could be discerned through the stirring tales of derring-do.*[1]

Dixon arrived at two main conclusions. First, by far the greater proportion of failures are the result of human agency. Disasters come about as a result of errors and blunders by those in charge, not because of environmental forces or so-called 'acts of God'. Dixon also argued that those who make mistakes are not necessarily stupid. He rejected the notion that the people in charge of disasters were fools; a little serious research shows that many of them were in fact highly intelligent. Incompetence is often highly situational. People who show great ability in one field may fall to pieces when thrust into another field and asked to make decisions. Dixon gives us examples of army officers who were both competent and courageous when commanding small units, but who turned into dithering incompetent wrecks when promoted to higher command.

Dixon's second point was that the reasons for incompetent behaviour are very often rooted in the organizations around us, not in ourselves. The culture of an organization – its norms, its values, its expectations in terms of attitudes and behaviour – often compel people to behave in ways that they *know* are wrong; yet they go ahead and make mistakes anyway. Peer pressure, the herd instinct and bullying combine with personal insecurity and lack of confidence to create a toxic mix that can force even highly intelligent people into making the wrong decisions. So powerful are these forces that surround us in most organizations that Dixon wondered whether people who achieve great things do so *because* of the organizations to which they belong, of *in spite* of them.

The more I reflected on these conclusions, the more I came to believe that Dixon was right. I examined many cases of business failure, businesses that had made big, game-changing, life-threatening mistakes and sometimes collapsed completely: Lehman Brothers, Royal Ahold, Swissair, Parmalat, Global Crossing, Marconi, BP, Time Warner, Royal Bank of Scotland, IBM, General Motors, Satyam, Motorola, Ratner's, Enron, Nortel and many others, and then further back in time too, British Leyland, ITT, Ford Motors, Harland & Wolff and even further back to the South Sea Company, the Medici Bank, the Society of the Bardi, even back into the ancient world to the tomb workers of Deir al-Medina in Egypt. I looked for common patterns and common threads of failure, and I found them. In every case there was a clear pattern of errors and blunders and poor judgement. Managerial incompetence ran through the whole saga, not so much like Dixon's hairline fault, but more like a great yawning chasm, into which value, jobs, hopes, dreams and lives had been sucked – and are still being sucked.

In these cases and many others, there are of course examples of poor decision-making by individuals, but it is rare to find cases where a single decision caused the disaster. Often it is not one big seismic event that leads to crisis, but rather a steady trickle of smaller ones, an accumulation of failures that builds up until the crisis point is reached. When things go wrong, it is fashionable to blame individuals: Richard Fuld has been held responsible for the crash of Lehman Brothers, Tony Hayward lost his job as chief executive of BP in the aftermath of the *Deepwater Horizon* disaster, Cees van der Hoeven was blamed for the crash of Royal Ahold: but were they and others like them solely responsible? In any properly functioning company, these men would have been surrounded by others who would have questioned the wisdom of their approach, urged a different strategy, insisted on more stringent health and safety procedures or the better auditing of accounts and so on. Junior executives would have realized that something was wrong and spoken up, or acted on their own initiative to prevent disaster.

Any of a number of things could have been done in these cases, but were not done. Why? Because as Dixon says, organizations build up *cultures of incompetence*, where it becomes customary and accepted to do the wrong thing, be it producing defective goods, operating dangerous workplaces, taking bad strategic decisions, turning a blind eye to financial irregularities, treating customers and workers with contempt or any of the other many things that companies do to get themselves into trouble. Henry Ford once remarked – with prescience, given what was to come for his own company – that he had never known a business problem that came from the market; problems arose thanks to internal defects within the company, things the company itself was doing wrong.

Whenever a big corporate crisis makes the news, the immediate reaction of the press is to hunt for a scapegoat? Who was to blame? They want to know, and usually also, when will that person resign? But the resignation of an incompetent leader rarely solves the problem on its own. Behind that leader lies a culture of incompetence that has to be broken down. It is those cultures of incompetence that I want to look at in this book. Where do they come from, how do they develop, and most of all, how can we prevent them from developing? If we are really are going to manage for success, as the title of this book suggests, then we need to learn how to eradicate cultures where failure is accepted.

Incompetence and failure

Before turning to where these cultures of incompetence come from, it is important that we define our terms. 'Incompetence' and 'failure' are big words, and potentially dangerous ones.

'Incompetence', in the context of this discussion, means a sustained failure to discharge one's duties. Anyone can make a mistake; the quality of a person can often be judged by how quickly and well they recover from that mistake. A single error is quite different from a sustained series of blunders, each compounding the last. A culture of incompetence is one where mistakes are frequent and, once made, are then left alone, swept under the carpet or not noticed at all.

A culture of incompetence does not always affect the entire company or its operations. There are some companies which are brilliant at operations but stumble when it comes to making strategy (with the result, as we shall see later, that they execute the wrong strategy exceptionally well), or which are superb at innovation but struggle to build relationships with customers. The truth is that in order to be effective, companies have to be good at *everything*. Finance, operations, marketing, supply chain management, innovation, human resources management, communications, leadership and so on are not a menu from which companies can pick and choose the things they like best and then set the rest to one side. It all has to be done, and done well.

'Failure', as implied above, here means systemic failure, the breakdown of a company at some point. It implies at the very least a major loss of value and reputation, and can include physical damage to assets, physical damage or death to customers, criminal charges and so on, and even total collapse and liquidation. It is impossible to avoid failure entirely, and indeed without failure there could be no innovation: an ability to engage in trial and error is very important for both personal and corporate development. But there are failures whose consequences are controllable and non-damaging, from which it is possible to learn, and there are failures which do massive damage, from which it is hard or even impossible to come back.[2]

Incompetence and failure have costs: financial, organizational and human. When a business fails, or when it suffers a serious setback, its entire mission is compromised. It can no longer serve its customers; it can no longer perform the social function for which it was created. That means lost opportunities and chances for the firm, its employees and its customers – at the least – and sometimes more broadly for societies too. Economists talk about 'opportunity cost', that is, if we choose one of several options, we should consider the cost to us of *not* picking one of the other options. What opportunities for benefit or profit have we forgone, and are they greater or less than the benefits or profits we expect from the option we have chosen?

I would like to propose an extension of this concept: *wasted opportunity cost*. When a company takes a significant hit, financially or otherwise, as a result of managerial incompetence, what opportunities are then lost forever? What are the costs of those lost opportunities, for the firm itself, for its employees, its customers and the governments and taxpayers that all too often have to step in and pick up the pieces?

When I set out to research this book, I was made aware at once of how difficult a subject this would be to tackle. Some colleagues recoiled in horror when I told them of my plan, and several tried dissuade me from writing it. 'We don't need to give people examples of failures', one declared. 'We need to give them examples of success, so that they can follow these and learn from them. Teaching people about failure is just horrible.'

Apart from this, I also found a kind of weary acceptance of failure as the status quo. Dixon commented that, 'by now most people have become accustomed to, one might almost say blasé about…incompetence. Like the common cold, flat feet or the British climate, it is accepted as a part of life – faintly ludicrous, but quite unavoidable', and that still seems to be true today.[3] There have been plenty of books written about management incompetence and management failure, and I will refer to these as we go on through the book, but

I have found no sense that business culture has changed its attitude to failure. People shake their heads over Enron and Lehman Brothers and the others, and click their tongues, and wonder how this could possibly have happened, and who was to blame, but there is no sense that the business world in general is in any way learning from failure.

This is a pity, because there is a great deal to be learned from failure. First, if we understand why things go wrong, then there is a chance that we can take preventive action so that they do not go wrong again. And, because many failures stem from very similar causes, paradoxically it is easier to learn from the failures of others than from their successes. We can watch other companies fall into the tiger trap, and thus we learn what a tiger trap looks like and how to avoid it.

Failure may indeed be 'horrible', a nasty yucky subject that makes us squirm and we would prefer to avoid. But we can still learn things by studying it. Roses bloom best when fed with well-rotted manure, and we can create something positive out of the refuse that failed managers and companies leave behind them, so long as we have the stomach for it and are able to confront the truth. But, most companies do not. Most companies hide their failures away and – with a few honourable exceptions – only admit to failings when they are exposed by whistleblowers or an outside agency. Most companies try to pretend that failures never happened. Very few – and I speak here from experience again, as a sometime historian of companies – are prepared to openly discuss their failures and learn lessons from them. There are various reasons for this, including legal reasons: in this litigious age, few companies are prepared to admit to anything that could get them involved in a lawsuit (which means that, to be on the safe side, they never admit to anything at all. John D. Rockefeller of Standard Oil and his executives routinely refused to answer even such basic questions as 'what is the business of your company?' and 'where is its head office located?').

When failure occurs, especially if it looks like there is a reasonable chance that the failure will not be made public, the first reaction in many companies is to hide the evidence. I have seen this happen myself, and I am willing to bet that many readers have seen it as well. I once argued to a group of senior executives that the best way to make a lot of money and then have time to enjoy it was not to rise all the way to the top, but to rise as quickly as possible to a position of considerable responsibility and then screw up massively, in a way that would embarrass the company if the news came to light though stopping just short of criminal behaviour. The resulting pay-off would set most people up for a life of leisure. The only response I received was the rather weak comment that 'companies are tightening up on that sort of thing nowadays'. Really? I have yet to see the evidence.

Incompetent behaviour is covered up, incompetent managers are paid off, redeployed or promoted sideways – or even upwards – and the failure is forgotten. As a result, these companies have no idea of what the wasted opportunity costs might be. They will never realize what they could have achieved had the incompetent behaviour been prevented in the first place.

Other writers before me have delved into the field of business failure, and there are some excellent works on the subject: Sydney Finkelstein's *Why Smart Executives Fail*, Jagdish Sheth's *The Self-Destructive Habits of Good Companies*, Stewart Hamilton and Alicia Micklethawyt's *Greed and Corporate Failure* and Donald Sull's *Why Good Companies Go Bad* are particularly outstanding examples. The works of psychologists such as Manfred Kets de Vries and Adrian Furnham have produced some valuable data on anti-social and deviant behaviour by managers. As noted above, though, very often these books – their authors no doubt urged by publishers who are equally convinced that failure is something nasty lurking in the woodshed – focus on the positive side, on how to recover from failure caused by incompetent managers.

Jeffrey Sonnenfeld and Andrew Ward's *Firing Back*, for example, has some excellent case studies of people losing their jobs for a variety of reasons, including personal managerial failures, but most of the book is devoted to showing how these individuals rebounded and rebuilt their lives. Memoirs by business leaders typically ignore failure altogether or concentrate on justifying their own behaviour. Rare and refreshing are memoirs such as those of former jewellery magnate Gerald Ratner, who acknowledge their own failings.

Five dangerous faults

Twenty-five centuries ago, the Chinese strategist Sunzi (Sun Tzu) listed five dangerous faults in a leader:

1. Recklessness
2. Cowardice
3. Reaction to provocation
4. Sensitivity to shame
5. Worrying over details[4]

Most of us are familiar with the problem of recklessness, but there is much more to recklessness than simply charging in like a bull in a china shop (though that problem certainly exists). What looks like reckless behaviour often turns out to be something quite different. The behaviour of bankers and traders in the run-up to the 2008 crash, for example, has been criticized as being 'reckless' and 'risky', but most bankers and traders would dispute this. As we shall see later, the bankers and traders took a number of steps to reduce risk, including introducing some very sophisticated mathematical models which were intended to predict market behaviour. Paradoxically, the very measures they took to reduce risk actually *increased* the level of risk they faced, often without their realizing that this was happening.

More generally, there is pressure on most managers most of the time to be seen to be doing things. The active manager gets noticed, gets the bonuses, gets promoted. The manager who does nothing is criticized for being idle, even if doing nothing is actually the best course of action at that moment. There is an old saying on trading floors that 'no one ever got promoted for tracking the index', even though statistically tracking the index is the safest course of action and also the one most likely to yield long-term profits. But the culture of most organizations pushes managers to take action, sometimes just for its own sake. And once that happens, levels of risk rise. Recklessness, then, manifests itself in the need for action at all costs.

Acting as a countervailing force is what Sun Tzu calls 'cowardice'. This could refer simply to indecision, the ability to choose between competing alternatives. Indecision in turn usually results from lack of knowledge. Without knowledge we cannot compare the opportunity costs of each option, therefore we have no way of knowing which is best. The 'reckless' manager will choose an option regardless of the risks, just for the sake of doing something. The 'indecisive' manager will hang back, debating, considering, tossing coins and then tossing them again, poised quivering on the brink of taking a decision but never quite taking it – until it is too late.

Fear plays a large part in many organizations, and sometimes this fear is deliberately induced. The culture of bullying described by the French courtier Eustache de Refuge in the seventeenth century had its exact counterpart at Enron in the late twentieth.[5] Dominant, powerful, macho figures bully their weaker colleagues into submission, so that the latter find that the best way to survive is to keep their mouths shut. Engineers at Morton Thiokol, which provided components for the space shuttle, were reportedly urged by their superiors to keep their mouths shut about what they knew of problems with the *Challenger*, which later blew up, killing all its crew. Even without bullying, there will be cases of managers who cannot make a decision because they are too frightened of the consequences. In such cases they will do all they can to pass the decision to a colleague or up the line to a superior – or just ignore it altogether and hope it goes away.

'Reaction to provocation' also manifests itself in a several ways. First, managers tend to be reactive rather than proactive. This was first noticed by Henry Mintzberg in his book *The Nature of Managerial Work*, where he challenged the conventional view of managers as rational thinkers who made plans and then proceeded to implement them in a deliberate way. In fact, said Mintzberg, managers spend most of their time firefighting, reacting to whatever events their colleagues and the environment and *fortuna* throw at them. Anyone who still believes that people in business always act rationally should read Satyajit Das's *Traders, Guns and Money*, a hilarious and horrifying description of the chaos, bitchery and backbiting that go on in the world of derivatives trading.[6]

Second, and probably as a result of this, managers tend to focus on the short term and leave the long term to take care of itself. This is in spite of ample evidence that a purely short-term approach is more risky and adds to the pressures on managers. Third, managers tend to follow what other managers are doing, sticking together with their colleagues. This of course can be a good thing, in that everyone pulls together and works for the good of the team, just as ants work together for the benefit of the anthill. But it can also lead to the herd instinct, groupthink and passive going along with the majority; again, just as ants will march blindly into an ant trap without noticing that the ants in front of them are all dying.

Why ants act in this way is not known, but one of the main reasons why managers indulge in formication (ant-like behaviour; we will discuss the other in Chapter 8) is related to personal self-image and self-respect. Like all human beings, managers desire the respect and esteem of others. For most of us, the image we have of ourselves is closely bound up with how others perceive us. If other people think of us as being weak, we begin to think of ourselves as weak. If others see us a stand-offish or egotistical, we tend to modify our behaviour so as to move closer to the herd. Fear is not the only factor that leads to groupthink. I have seen, many times, how people will scramble to align their opinions with the alpha male in the room (and it nearly always is a male) with a view to identifying themselves with the dominant power group. Often this behaviour is quite unconscious. In others, the pressure to align oneself with the alpha male is overt. People who insist on having their own view and standing apart are labelled as sociopaths. 'His face doesn't really fit in here', we are told, or else 'she doesn't believe in the things we believe in.' And so, in the name of teamwork and unity, dissenters are slid out until there is only one voice left, the voice of the alpha male.

The tendency for managers to get bogged down in details and fail to see the bigger picture will also be a familiar one. Mintzberg again alluded to this in *The Nature of Managerial Work*, and there is a view that the ends of organizations are best served by 'muddling through', taking a lot of small steps rather than a few big ones.[7] There is a lot to be said for this, but managers do still need to know where they are going and maintain a sense of forward motion. Instead, there can be drift towards 'analysis paralysis', the view that no action can be taken at all until every relevant piece of data has been analysed.

Again, analysing data in and of itself is a good thing. The problem is that managers use data much as drunks use lamp posts. Some use it for illumination, while others use it for support to keep them from falling over. (There is a third use, which I am sure you can work out for yourselves.) Managers need to get used to the fact that, most of the time, they will have to take decisions based on incomplete data. Intuition and experience must also come into play. And yes, there will be an element of risk.

Organizations and markets are open systems, so we cannot control all the variables. But instead there is a culture within management that insists on what my colleague Pablo Triana refers to as the 'unhealthy yearning for precision'. If we *can* identify every last variable, the belief goes, then we can write an equation which will account for every factor and yield a perfect solution. But, paradoxically, often these attempts actually *increase* the level of risk rather than decreasing it.

Another paradox: managers do need to analyse data and they do need to keep their eyes on the ground under their feet, looking out for signs of tiger traps. At the same time they also need to keep their eyes on the far horizon and keep thinking about the long term, trying to anticipate what may be happening down the road, just as Andrew Grove urges them to do. They need to be masters of the small brushstroke and the broad canvas, the fine detail and the big picture, simultaneously. There is only one problem. Our system of education and training has begun to discourage them from doing this. Management education itself has become increasingly fragmented and siloed, the focus moving away from general management towards ever-narrowing specialism.

One of the most dangerous consequences of this has been the growing separation of leadership from management. According to theory, and increasingly in practice, all things that leaders do – like long-term thinking, vision, innovation, determining strategy, motivating people to do, succeed and excel – are no longer the task of the manager. The manager's task is to attend to detail, to observe and monitor and report, create budgets, hire and fire people; in other words, to be a kind of self-aware robot.

The consequences of this approach are truly alarming. Managers who take this view become even more risk-averse than they already were. They feel reluctant to accept responsibility; indeed, there may be pressures for them *not* to accept responsibility. Buck-passing and 'above my pay grade' become standard responses. And again, this reluctance to accept risk – when we know that accepting risk is one of the things managers are there to do – results once again in the paradox of increased risk. On the other side of the coin, the failure of leaders to get involved in management carries its own serious risks. Ram Charan and Geoffrey Colvin, writing in 1999, estimate that 70 per cent of business failures were failures not of strategy or vision, but of execution.[8] Good ideas were executed badly. Why? Charan and Colvin offer several possibilities, but for me the answer is clear: the CEOs and chairmen who articulated these fine strategies failed to follow up on execution.

Prevention rather than cure

Everything said above about leaders, of course, can be equally applied to organizations as a whole. Again, I come back to the issue of culture. Leaders influence cultures, of course, and we shall see that as a running theme through this book, but on the other side of the coin, cultures also influence leaders. Toxic cultures constrain and subvert leaders, restricting their actions and altering their mindsets. Take for example the conservatism that sometimes sets in as fast-growing organizations begin to mature. They become more risk-averse, less flexible and less innovative, looking to their past successes rather than future opportunities. That conservatism is not just the leader's doing; it is part of the culture of the whole organization, and everyone feels it. This is not to absolve leaders from responsibility, by the way; they *can* change the culture, if they have the will and strength to do so, but the problem does not lie solely with them.

Often, too, the culture is broader than the organization. It can affect entire industries, even the entire business world. That, I have found, is the case with the failure to learn from failure. When failure is discussed at all, it is treated as something that happens, inevitable, and as Dixon says, unavoidable. The main thing, we are told, is to learn from failure.

Everyone seems to love this phrase; over the last twelve months I have heard countless politicians, civil servants, doctors, senior police offic- ers and bishops, as well as business executives, assure us that 'they will learn from this failure and move on'. (How many actually do learn, I wonder?)

Books about managerial incompetence and management failure also usually try to solve problem by looking at how to recover the failure. Take for example Donald Sull's *Why Good Companies Go Bad, and How Great Managers Remake Them*. It is a very good book, and I recommend it. But there is a problem. It is not always possible to 'remake' companies once incompetent managers have done their work. No one could remake Lehman Brothers; no one could rescue Royal Ahold, or Marconi, or Ratner's. Those companies went down, taking shareholders' money and employees' jobs with them, down into the chasm. Thus, while it is undoubtedly useful to study ways of recovering from near-death experi- ences, it is also important to try to stop these events from happening in the first place.

My aim in this book is prevention, not cure. I hope to show how incom- petence can be weeded out and the conditions that lead to incompe- tence can be avoided in the first place. Doing so may have its costs, but they are bound to be less than the costs of 'remaking' a failed company, assuming it can be remade at all.

The first step is to accept that failure is not, despite widespread belief to the contrary, inevitable. Just because systemic failure is an accepted part of business life now does not means it has to be. Businesses don't have to crash. Failure can be avoided, but first of all we have to believe that this is true.

Back in the 1970s, it was accepted that manufacturing processes would have defects. A certain portion of every batch would have to be sent back to the factory for re-work. Cars built on a Friday would never run properly. It wasn't a good situation, customers grumbled, but what could be done about it? Defects were a part of life.

Then came the Japanese, with zero defects and six sigma. The story is still told of an American company which ordered a shipment of a thou- sand components, and specified that the acceptable level of defects was ten per thousand. The shipment from Japan duly arrived, and someone noticed that in addition to the thousand components there was also a small box with a further ten. A phone call was put through to Japan: what was the meaning of this? 'Oh', came the reply, 'those are the ten defects you asked for.'

Today, zero defects and six sigma are commonplace in manufacturing. It is no longer acceptable to deliver shoddy goods to customers or clients. Failure in processes is no longer tolerated. Manufacturing processes have changed, of course, to become more efficient and effective, but what has really changed is the culture of business. Everyone, from the leader to the shop floor employees, is expected to play a part in ensuring that the zero defects philosophy is carried into action.

Similarly, until a few years ago (and in some parts of the world, still today), workplace accidents were considered as normal in industries such as construction and steel. Every year, some workers would be injured, some might even be killed. It was too bad, of course, very sad for them and their families, but nothing could be done about it. Then along came the concept of zero harm, the notion that workplace accidents were not acceptable and it was the duty of everyone in the company to ensure that accidents of all kinds were eliminated. Again, this was partly a matter of tightening up procedures, but colleagues in health and safety tell me that the real change is one of mindset and approach. Once again, everyone from the leader down to the shop floor employee, thinks about how to eliminate accidents, and thinking about eliminating accidents is the first step to actually doing so.

Part of the rationale behind both zero defects and zero harm, apart from keeping customers happy and employees alive, is cost. Producing faulty goods is expensive in terms of lost revenue, compensation paid to customers and reputational damage, and investments in quality nearly always pay back severalfold, leading quality guru Philip Crosby to coin the phrase, 'quality is free'. Similarly, industrial accidents generate huge costs in terms of work stoppages, compensation and, again, reputation. It is far, far cheaper to keep workers safe than it is to deal with the consequences of accidents.

I argue that the same is true of management as a whole. There are necessary investments, in training, education, organization structure and culture change if we are to reach a point where systemic failure is considered unacceptable, but when we consider the billions of dollars, pounds, euros, yen, rupees and yuan that have been wiped out in the past twenty years alone, we can count any investment along these lines as money well spent. If we can even get to the point where management cultures don't do actual *harm* to organizations, that would be a start; any further value added would count as a bonus.

We've done it with zero-defects manufacturing, we've done it with zero-harm health and safety; why can't we do it more broadly?

What about this for a concept? Zero-damage management?

Managing for success

In order to get to that point, though, we first need to look at where management incompetence comes from and why failures occur, and that is largely what this book is about. In the pages that follow, I present seven factors that lead to incompetence and failure; they are, if you like, the seven deadly sins of management, similar to but not identical to the list drawn up by Catholic theologians. They are as follows:

- Arrogance
- Ignorance
- Fear
- Greed
- Lust
- Linear thinking
- Lack of purpose

Although the book discusses the implications for individual managers and executives, the main focus is on corporate cultures, where these things can take root. For example, there are arrogant managers and leaders, but provided the rest of the organization identifies them and takes steps to deal with them, there is a limit to the amount of damage they can do. Far more dangerous are cultures of arrogance, where companies believe blindly in their own brilliance. These *cultures of mindless superiority* lead companies into several traps, chief among which are overconfidence, complacency and a belief that they are invincible. There is also what I refer to as the arrogance of good intentions, which happens when companies believe in their mission so fanatically that they are prepared to let the end justify the means.

Ignorance, or literally 'not knowing', starts off as a personal issue, but when a large number of ignorant people are gathered to gather, they create in effect an ignorant organization. I want to be clear that I am not using the word 'ignorant' in a pejorative sense. There are many reasons why people and companies lack knowledge, including inexperience, lack of opportunities to learn and lack of imagination. The inability to learn from the past is a particularly dangerous form of ignorance, highly prevalent among executives who believe that 'the only constant is change'. Ignorance leads to *cultures of unthinking action*, where companies do things without knowing why, and without understanding what the consequences will be. Like a blind person on the edge of a precipice, they are not aware of danger until it is too late.

Fearful companies are aware of danger but don't know how to manage it. Fear of uncertainty, fear of the unknown, fear of people and things outside their own experience or that are different to themselves all create a kind of straitjacket that inhibits action and thinking. Fearful companies don't know how to manage risk; they seek options which they think will reduce risk, but which sometimes have the opposite effect and increase risk to unacceptable levels. Fearful companies are desperately seeking certainty, not knowing or refusing to know that uncertainty in business is impossible. These are cultures of *anxious precision*, where no one will make a move unless they can pretend that they know what will happen next.

Greedy companies are those that privilege growth and competition over all else. Driven by numbers, they grow at rates that are unsustainable. Some go on buying sprees, acquiring more and more subsidiaries until their financial and operating systems collapse. Some become obsessed with scale, others with profits and still others with 'winning' and beating the competition. These *cultures of conspicuous acquisition* are so focused on growing and winning that they forget their true goals and purpose.

Lust can mean sexual lust, and more than one company has been damaged by the sexual behaviour of its executives, but in this book lust also means the lust for control and power over others. In *cultures of selfish domination*, what matters most is that others should do our bidding; our self-esteem, personally and in a corporate sense, depends on the authority we can exert over others. The lust for power often asserts itself in the form of bureaucracy, where those at the top of the bureaucratic pyramid gather more and more power to themselves, simply for the sake of having power.

The presence of linear thinking on this list may come as something of a surprise, but excessive reliance on linear thinking is a dangerous trap into which entire teams and companies are only too likely to fall. In *cultures of linear logic* people believe that so long as they do the right things in the right order, success will surely follow. These cultures focus on the short term, because short-term results are easier to control. They are wedded to targets, rather than purpose or mission. They cannot make a move without spreadsheets or PowerPoint, those two indispensable tools of linear thinking in the modern day. Their thinking is blinkered, narrow, constrained and, again, dangerous.

Lack of purpose manifests itself in *cultures of emptiness*, in which the organization forgets its purpose. No one cares any more. Executives go through the motions. Leadership is weak, or absent. Teams fall into patterns of groupthink and social loafing. No one is willing to take responsibility. Of all the sins of management, this is the most deadly, for it opens an easy door into a world of corruption and ethical collapse.

In the chapters to come, we will take a look at two classic examples of management failure and see how these 'sins' impact on companies in practice. We will then look at each of them in turn and, at the end of each chapter, discuss what the cures might be. The cures are often simple in nature, though implementing them will not always be easy. Each chapter also has a series of warning flags,

the symptoms of potential failure which need to be watched out for. Most organizations will have one or two of these, but it is when large clusters of warning flags start to appear that managers need to sit up and take notice, and start thinking about the cure. I append a list of all fifty warning flags at the end of the book.

Business academia has a role to play in the cure too, and in Chapter 11 I look at changes that are badly needed in that world too. Finally, in Chapter 12 I offer a summary of the key lessons and some steps to be taken if we are to move towards a philosophy of prevention of failure, rather then relying solely on cure.

A personal note

So that there should be no confusion, I would like to make my own purpose clear. I have run my own business for more than twenty years, and have been involved in studying and researching business around the world for nearly as long. For the last dozen years I have taught MBA students at a business school in the United Kingdom. I am emphatically *not* a management basher. The good men and women who work hard every day to create value, serve customers and help even if only in a small way to make the world a better place have my great respect. My critique is aimed at the few, the dangerous few, the incompetent people who undermine the efforts of the others, and the rigid, dysfunctional and toxic organizations that force even the good managers down the road to failure. The damage that they do sickens me.

I believe absolutely in business as a force for good in the world. Forget Ivan Boesky's nonsense about 'greed is good' or Milton Friedman's utterly misguided view that the only duty of a business is to return value to its shareholders. When it comes to business and management, my household gods are philosophers, not economists, and I call on a tradition of thinking which goes back to Confucius, Plato, Ibn Khaldun, Ishida Baigan and St Thomas Aquinas which tells that business is an integral part of society. Businesses exist because society needs things; businesses flourish when they provide the things society needs; businesses fail when they stop providing what society wants. If I had my way, I would paint that mantra on the wall of every office of every manager in the world.

Look at any business today which has been successful over the long term, and you will find this concept right at the core of their thinking and their values. Remember that basic principle, and you cannot go too far wrong.

But incompetent managers lose sight of this principle. Incompetent managers, for a variety of reasons that we shall come to shortly, make decisions that are not in the best interests of their customers or of society, very often in the naive belief that these decisions *are* in the best interests of the organization, or themselves. This is a myth. As Peter Drucker famously said, 'there is only one valid purpose for a business – to create customers'.[9] No business will survive, at least for very long, if it neglects its customers. Yet managers persist in ignoring this fact. They set out on expansion programmes that they cannot afford. They cut costs in the wrong places. They invest in uninvestable projects. They gamble on new products without ever determining whether the market wants them. They create mergers between entirely unsuitable organizations which then fail. They abuse their positions of power in ways which are often unethical, sometimes even illegal. All of these and many other things are the symptoms of managerial incompetence.

And the result? You could say that managerial incompetence is less serious than the military incompetence. After all, the latter kills people. Business is not so serious a matter as war. But is that really true? Think, again, of the billions in value that has been destroyed by the actions of incompetent managers and companies. Think of the damage done to national economies. Think of the jobs lost, the homes repossessed, the educations cut short, the poverty and deprivation that have resulted. And yes – think of the dead, drowned on the *Titanic*, burned to death on the *Deepwater Horizon*, smothered by toxic gas at Bhopal, dying a slow death from mercury poisoning at Minamata. Managerial incompetence is not consequence-free. It kills companies. And sometimes, too, it kills people.

---

[1] Norman Dixon, *On the Psychology of Managerial Incompetence*, London: Jonathan Cape, 1976, p. 17.

[2] A further note on terminology is also in order. I refer variously to managers, leaders and executives; I am in fact referring to the same people in each case because, as I make clear later in the book, managers also lead and leaders should also know how to manage. I also refer to companies, corporations, firms,

businesses and organizations. These terms too are used synonymously. This will offend purists, but I made this deliberate choice for two reasons: (1) to encompass as many types of organization large and small as possible, and (2) to avoid wearying repetition of the same term.

3 Dixon, *On the Psychology of Military Incompetence*, p. 17.

4 Sun Tzu, *The Art of War*, Oxford: Oxford University Press, 1976, Chapter 8, full reference to follow.

5 *Treatise on the Court*, reference to Enron.

6 Satyajit Das, *Traders, Guns and Money: Knowns and Unknowns in the Dazzling World of Derivatives Trading*, London: FT-Prentice Hall, 2006.

7 Charles Lindblom, 'The Science of Muddling Through', *Public Administration Review* 19 (1959), pp. 79-88.

8 Ram Charan and Geoffrey Colvin, 'Why CEOs Fail', *Fortune* 21 June 1999, http://archive.fortune.com/magazines/fortune/fortune_archive/1999/06/21/261696/index.htm

9 Peter Drucker, *The Practice of Management*, New York: Heinemann, 1954, p. 37.

Chapter 2

No defects but our own:
Ford Motors[1]

Through all the years that I have been in business I have never yet found our business bad as a result of any outside force. It has always been due to some defect in our own company.

–Henry Ford

There are few more extraordinary stories in the history of business than the story of the foundation of Ford Motor Company. It began like the embodiment of the American dream, the rags-to-riches story of a self-made man who rose to become America's foremost business leader, a man who remade an entire industry and changed the world in doing so. It ended like a Shakespearean tragedy, in disaster, madness and death.

Looking back at Ford's rise and fall, many modern writers have concluded that Ford's decline was a result of its failure to meet the competitive challenge posed by its main rival, General Motors. GM, the story goes, was more agile, more flexible, more responsive to customer needs. True – but why was Ford unable to respond to the GM challenge? Why did a firm whose name had once been a byword for innovation and vision fail to adapt to changing times? Why did the company that invented the concept of the mass-market motor car not see off this young pretender to its crown?

Pride and arrogance, not external competition, brought about Ford's downfall. Ford failed to respond to the GM challenge because, for many years, the company refused to recognize that any challenge existed. Henry Ford and his senior managers believed that they were supreme, that no rival could touch them, and this arrogance effectively blinded them to what was happening in the world around them. Their case is not unique, of course. The tragedians of ancient Greece had recognized this syndrome long ago. They called it *hubris*, the overweening pride that comes before a fall, the arrogance that leads to divine retribution. Henry Ford and his managers had hubris, in abundance.

The rising star

Where did it come from, this pride and arrogance? There are few clues to be found in Ford's background. He came from humble beginnings, born near Dearborn, Michigan in 1863 as one of eight children of the farmer William Ford and his wife Mary. He attended his local village school, but apparently was barely literate when he finished school in 1879. Leaving the family farm, the sixteen-year-old Ford found work as an apprentice mechanic in a machine shop in Detroit, and later took on a part-time job repairing watches. He became fascinated by cogs and gears, and even considered going into business as a watchmaker, but lacked capital to start a business.

It became apparent that Ford had a natural talent for engineering. At nineteen he set up his own machine shop. A few years later he sold this business and took a post with the Westinghouse Corporation, servicing and maintaining steam engines. He married around this time, and he and his wife, the long-suffering Clara Bryant Ford, had a single child, a son whom they named Edsel. The year of Edsel's birth, 1893, saw a breakthrough when Ford was hired by the newly formed Edison Illuminating Company, rising rapidly to become its chief engineer for the Chicago area. Electric lighting was in its infancy then, and Ford found himself at the cutting edge of an entirely new industry. He got to know Thomas Edison well, and the great inventor took an interest in Ford and they became good friends. For years thereafter, Ford, Edison and Harvey Firestone, another self-made man who founded a company making rubber tyres for carriages and then for automobiles, used to go off every summer on camping and fishing expeditions to northern Michigan, during which they habitually went naked. Given the mosquitoes and black flies of the Michigan forests in summer, this must have taken some courage.

Ford's fascination with watches and gears continued. One of the problems that beset early automobile designers was how to transmit the power generated by a steam or internal combustion engine into drive through the wheels. Ford came up with a simple design for a transmission, and to test it built his first automobile, a skeletal affair that ran on four bicycle wheels; indeed, he called it a 'quadricycle'. Ford later recalled that at the time he had no interest in designing more automobiles, and it was Thomas Edison who encouraged him to carry on.

In 1899, with capital provided by a Detroit timber dealer, William Murphy, Ford established the Detroit Automobile Company and resigned from Edison to become the new firm's superintendent in charge of production. This venture was a complete failure, largely because Ford knew nothing about production and managed to make only a handful of cars in the first year; certainly not more than twenty, and possibly as few as three. Undeterred, Ford and his backers tried again, setting up the Henry Ford Company in 1900. One of the designs this company produced was a successful racing car, and suddenly Ford had found another enthusiasm. He became so involved in racing cars that his partners fired him from the firm named after him for dereliction of duty (ironically, the Henry Ford Company was later renamed the Cadillac Motor Car Company and went on to become part of General Motors). Ford and the former racing car driver Tom Cooper together designed the 999, which broke the world land speed record. But racing cars proved in the end to be only a passing fancy.

Automobiles, in 1900, were still very much luxury items. They were very expensive and available only to the wealthy. Many car makers had been carriage makers before converting production, and they continued to sell to the same elite clientele. Production followed the craft-working model, with only a few high-value units produced each year; that indeed was the production model Ford himself had followed in his earlier companies. But there were signs that the demand for cars from the middle classes was rising. A few car makers had tried to respond to this demand, and all had failed. No one, it seemed, could make reliable cars cheaply enough to cater to this new market.

Ford resolved to succeed where others had failed. But, he now realized, to do so he would have to come up with two things: a product to meet market needs, and a production system that would enable him to produce cars cheaply. The latter in turn meant volume production in order to achieve economies of scale and drive costs down. In 1903 he founded another company, the Ford Motor Company, with backing from the Detroit merchant Alexander Malcolmson. From Malcolmson's company came a clerk named James Couzens, who just a few years before had been a railway ticket collector. Now he became company secretary, and within a few years had risen to become general manager, running Ford's marketing and commercial operations. He and Ford complemented each other perfectly, Couzens's talent for management matching Ford's genius as an engineer.

A few years later Ford Motors purchased one of its main suppliers, the steel maker John R. Keim. From Keim, Ford recruited his new produc-tion manager, William 'Big Bill' Knudsen, who completed the group of top-level talent. A dozen years ago, I descried the combination of Ford, Couzens and Knudsen as 'one of the greatest management teams the world has yet seen'.[2] I still stand by that judgement.

After several experimental models had failed, in 1906 Ford launched the Model N which went on sale for $600, much cheaper than most of the cars then on the market. Despite its simplicity and defects the Model N did well, proving Ford's view that there was a big middle-class market waiting to be tapped. What happened next is part of the stuff of business legend.

Ford wanted a car that would appeal to the masses. He built one. He and his design partner, the improbably named Childe Harold Wills, created one of the most iconic automobiles of all time, the Model T. Known affectionately as the 'Tin Lizzie', the Model T had a 22-horse-power engine and improved chassis and steering design. It was techno-logically advanced when first launched, yet its design was so simple that interchangeable parts could be easily mass produced. It was an attrac-tive car, too, by the standards of the time; it may have come off an assembly line, but it looked like quality. It was probably Wills who designed the calligraphy for the equally iconic Ford badge, which still adorns Ford cars today. Ford never uttered the phrase attributed to him, that 'a customer can have a car painted any colour he wants, so long as it is black'. Model Ts were originally marketed in a range of colours, but black proved most popular; for young people of the time, a black Model T was the epitome of cool. The initial price, at $875, was higher than Ford intended, but over the years he drove costs down until by the 1920s a new Model T could be purchased for $225.

Between 1908 and 1927, 17 million Model Ts were sold, more than every other make of car put together during that time. Ford had been absolutely right; the demand for cars was there, and growing. Possession of an automobile, for young middle-class Americans, meant more than just access to transport. It was a symbol of freedom. The car gave people the ability to move about, to seek work in other parts of the country, to migrate in search of the opportunities that the American dream promised them. The car became a social leveller, too, giving the middle classes and even more prosperous working people the ability to travel once enjoyed only by their betters. Among the main beneficiaries were young women, for whom the car offered chances of escape and opportunity once denied them. Preachers denounced the Model T as a corrupting influence on the morals of women, but to little avail. America's long love affair with the automobile had begun.

To make this automotive marvel, Ford and his team developed an equally radical production facility. They drew on the techniques of mass production and standardized parts already in use by companies such as Colt and International Harvester. They also drew on the principles of organization at work known as 'scientific management', developed by Frederick Winslow Taylor and his colleagues in the steel industry. The young architect Albert Kahn was brought in to design the new production facility at Highland Park, near Detroit. Opened in 1910 and covering sixty-two acres, Highland Park was the largest assembly line production facility in the world. It revolutionized the mass production of cars. Prior to the opening of Highland Park, it took Ford's workers between 12 and 14 hours to assemble a single car from finished parts. At Highland Park, the process now took an hour and a half.

A seismic shock ran through the business world. Leaders from around the USA and Europe rushed to Highland Park to see the marvel Ford had created, and try to figure out how it worked so they could copy it at home. One thing which would not have escaped the notice of these visitors was the keenness and enthusiasm of the workers. Ford and Couzens and Knudsen paid their men well, very well. In 1914 Ford began offering workers a rate of $5 per day, five times the going rate in other Detroit plants. As a result, he could recruit the cream of mechanics and engineers. It was estimated that there were around a thousand applicants for every job going at Ford. Another innovation, the Sociological Department, headed by the Episcopalian minister Samuel Marcus, was tasked with studying the working conditions and practices and recommending improvements. Ford was the first company to actively and continuously conduct research into worker motivation, and lessons learned from this research were fed back into employment policy.

This was not just a matter of self-interest. As someone who had come up through the engineering ranks, Ford knew that the hard work of his people was the key to the company's success. The workers were, in modern parlance, creating value, and like other enlightened managers and leaders, Ford believed it was right that they should share in the profits. As well as high wages, Ford workers received a share of profits and generous benefits. 'The company was an institution in the sense that it existed not to make money, but to make jobs and goods', commented Allan Nevins in his magisterial history of Ford.[3]

By 1916, Ford and his managers had achieved success beyond their wildest dreams. In that year the company produced more than 500,000 cars – all of which were sold – and made a profit of just over $57 million.[4] They dominated the category of mass-market automobiles, a category they had largely created in the first place. They had a powerful brand which was not just a byword for quality but had tapped into the American psyche, become part of the American dream and in doing so changed American society itself. They had a state-of-the-art production facility, a loyal and committed workforce, a track record in both product and process innovation that was the envy of the world. They had every opportunity to go on to further and greater success.

And they threw it all away.

Pride before the fall

Quite when things first began to go wrong is hard to say. The cracks had certainly begun to appear by 1915. In the early days Ford had been very much part of a team, but now he began to gather more and more control to himself and became increasingly intolerant of rivals and critics. He seems to have resented the authority and influence of James Couzens, who had been a founder member of the company and played a very important role in its commercial success. Disagreements between the two men became more frequent, and in 1915 Ford forced Couzens's resignation.

Others followed. James and Horace Dodge, the designers of Ford's engines, were forced off the board of directors. Samuel Marcus the humane head of the Sociology Department quit in 1921. Willis, the co-designer of the Model T, resigned in 1919, followed soon after by production supremo 'Big Bill' Knudsen who quit after a violent argument with Ford. His replacement was his deputy Charles Sorenson, known to his workers as 'Cast-Iron Charlie'. Sorenson maintained the nickname was derived from his advocacy of the use of cast iron for chassis and other components. Others have suggested that the name stemmed from his management style.

Cast-Iron Charlie was emblematic of the new breed of manager rising to the top at Ford. He was, by his own account, a 'yes man'. Even when he disagreed with Henry Ford, he never challenged him, nor did he tolerate dissent or disagreement by his workers. The once powerful culture and work ethic at Ford began to decline. Sorenson himself never saw this; he believed that the workers respected him and loved him. In his memoirs he recalled how during a visit to Soviet Russia in the late 1920s he visited a car assembly plant and was greeted with shouts of 'Hiya, Charlie!' by workers on the line who had once worked at Highland Park.[5] It never occurred to Cast-Iron Charlie to ask why workers would leave the five-dollar a day wage and the benefits of Highland Park to go to work in increasingly autocratic Soviet Union. Had he been told that one of the reasons might be he himself and the culture he had created, he would have refused to believe it.

It seems too that Henry Ford's attention had begun to wander. One of the sources of discontent between Ford and Couzens was that while the former had been very keen on the design of Highland Park, he did not seem very interested in running it. He developed other ventures such as a plant to make tractors; significantly, he kept this very much to himself and refused to let any of his colleagues at Ford Motors be involved. Another source of dissent between the two men was Ford's pacifism. In 1915 Ford chartered a 'peace ship', a liner that carried Ford and other peace activists including the pacifist Rosalka Schwimmer and the socialist Jane Addams to Europe with the stated intention of negotiating an end to the First World War. When the American and European newspapers learned of the venture they responded with derision. Ford, publicly humiliated for the first time in his life, abandoned the venture and sailed home.

Other signs of hubris followed. In 1919 President Woodrow Wilson told Ford that the country needed his enormous talents and persuaded him to stand for election as a US senator. Ford was narrowly defeated, and the experience seems to have disillusioned him; from this time forward he began to turn against the US government. Another telling sign came when Ford took a mistress, his secretary Evangeline Cote. In public, Ford was a puritan about sex and did not tolerate affairs among his colleagues and employees, so this was hypocrisy of a high order. To keep the affair secret, he insisted that Evangeline marry his chauffeur and installed the couple in a house where he continued to pay her visits for another twelve years. Ford refused to acknowledge paternity of Evangeline's son, though he did provide financial support.

Why is this significant? Because Ford was increasingly living in a world of his own making. He believed what people such as President Wilson said about him: that he was a giant, a titan, a man of vision. He believed that he was right, that his views were the correct views and that those who disagreed with him were wrong. He did not have to obey the rules that governed ordinary people – even the rules he had made himself – because he was above the common herd. During the 1920s he wrote a series of books in collaboration with the business journalist Samuel Crowther, philosophizing on society, culture, democracy and business. The last of these books, *Moving Forward*, published in 1931, contains a telling statement:

> *Through all the years that I have been in business I have never yet found our business bad as a result of any outside force. It has always been due to some defect in our own company, and whenever we located and repaired that defect our business became good again – regardless of what anyone else might be*

*doing. And it will always be found that this country has nationally bad busi-
ness when business men are drifting, and that business is good when men take
hold of their own affairs, put leadership into them, and push forward in spite
of obstacles. Only disaster can result when the fundamental principles of business are disregarded and what looks like the easiest way is taken.*[6]

Yet Ford and his managers had disregarded the fundamental principles of business, and there were defects in the company. And disaster
was waiting.

While Ford flirted with politics and dallied with his mistress and set
himself up as the philosopher-king of American business, the yes-men
and sycophants who had risen to command after the departure of
Couzens and Knudsen let the company drift. The Model T that was
being built in 1920 was exactly the same as the one built in 1910; there
had been no innovations or improvements bar the drop in price to the
customer. Production facilities had increased greatly, and Ford was
now building cars in Britain and Canada as well as the USA. But scaling
up brought its own complications, and the firm was now increasingly
bureaucratic and top-heavy. Ford had fallen victim to what Harvard
professor Clayton Christensen calls the 'innovator's dilemma'. Having
created dazzling innovations in process and product, the company
became wedded to these. It could not bear or tolerate deviation from
that original successful recipe.

Meanwhile, hungry competitors waited. The first serious challenge to
Ford had been mounted by Willys Overland in the late 'teens. Its leader,
John North Willys, was a brilliant marketer who had some excellent
designs, but the company expanded too fast and then collapsed. Then
General Motors appeared on the scene. At first, few observers were
inclined to take General Motors seriously. This company had been
created by the entrepreneur William Crapo Durant, his middle name
serving as adequate commentary on his managerial skills. Acquiring
several small firms including Cadillac and Chevrolet, Durant tried to
weld these into a single company, General Motors. He failed. His board
ejected him and recruited Pierre du Pont as the new chairman. Du Pont
was already well known for having effectively restructured the family-
owned gunpowder maker, E.I. du Pont de Nemours, before quitting its
board after a spat with his cousins. Taking over as chairman of General

Motors, du Pont turned this ramshackle business into a smoothly functioning organization.[7] He hired top talent, including the legendary Alfred Sloan as chief executive. And at least as significantly, in 1921 du Pont hired Big Bill Knudsen to take over production at Chevrolet with the specific brief of knocking the Model T off its perch.

Knudsen responded with alacrity. The thought of wiping the eye of his former boss was motive enough, and he took all the skills and ideas he had learned at Ford and put them into practice in the service of the opposition.[8] The Chevrolet Model D was superior to the Ford Model T in terms of comfort, speed, horsepower, and under Knudsen, cost savings meant it was soon also competing on price. The Model T's market began to erode. Now was the moment for Ford to respond with innovations of its own, but instead the only response that Ford's managers could think of was to cut costs and drive prices down still further in an attempt to grab back market share.

The atmosphere in Ford factories changed dramatically as wages were cut by nearly half and worker education and many other benefits were done away with. Strict discipline was enforced which prevented workers from whistling or even talking during shifts. Ford's famous sociological department which had studied worker motivation was closed down and replaced with the Ford Service Department, which was tasked with enforcing conformity.

The Model-T's market share continued to fall. Belatedly, Sorenson and Ford's son Edsel, now running the company on a daily basis, realized that they needed to innovate. But instead of incremental changes in response to market demand, they decided to recreate the successful recipe of 1908–10, going for a radical new car and a radical new production facility to build it. But the designing and engineering geniuses who had created the Model T and Highland Park were no longer there, nor was the instinctive understanding of the car market – which in any case had moved on a long way since 1910. The Model T's successor, the Model A, took too long to come to market and cost too much to design. It was a good car, an improvement in many ways on the Model T, but it was not radical and did not catch the imagination of the public in the same way as the Chevrolet Standard Six, which came out a few years later. And the new production plant at River Rouge, Michigan, was gigantic – at its height it employed 120,000 workers – but there were long delays in achieving full production speed and the efficiencies of Highland Park were never matched. The changing culture inside Ford almost certainly played a part in this.

Ford lost its position at the top of the market. Chevrolet became the best-selling car by volume, and General Motors took over from Ford as the largest car maker in the world, a position Ford was never able to regain. And still the decline continued. Henry Ford came back into the business much more directly, and much more autocratically, than before. He had delegated many powers to his son Edsel, but now he seems to have blamed Edsel for the failures and systematically humiliated and insulted him in public. Edsel, already in poor health, suffered under the barrage of insults and criticism heaped upon him by his father. Cast-Iron Charlie Sorenson records that the only time he ever stood up to Ford was over his treatment of his son, but he was unable to sway the old man. Edsel died in 1943, and Sorenson was convinced that it was Edsel's own father who had hounded him into his grave.

But Sorenson did not speak up about the rest of Ford's policies. No one did, because a culture of fear ruled now at Ford. Workers and managers alike were now under the thumb of the Ford Service Department, now run by Harry Bennett, a former prize-fighter with alleged connections to the Chicago mafia. His thugs used verbal threats, backed up with violence when needed, to make certain that no one stepped out of line. According to Sorenson, even Ford's wife Clara lived in fear of Bennett. Signs of mental illness were also creeping in. Ford was becoming increasingly paranoid, and he relied on Bennett as one of the few people he could trust. When the Second World War broke out and orders were given to convert factories to war production, Ford at first denied government agents access to his factories, believing that they were assassins sent by President Roosevelt to kill him. Eventually Ford gave way and the company did engage in war work, building heavy bombers at a new plant at Willow Run, Michigan.

The Second World War – both for the war work it generated and because the domestic car market effectively ground to a halt – probably saved Ford from the brink. The company had run out of new products, run out of talent and run out of ideas. Its brand still inspired respect, but General Motors with its diversified product strategy now dominated the car market. Yet still Henry Ford would not relax his grip, and still his managers kow-towed to him. In 1943 after the death of Edsel, Ford insisted on taking full control of the company only to face a revolt from the most unlikely of sources; his wife and daughter-in-law, Edsel's widow, threatened to sell their own shares in the company to General Motors unless Ford retired. This would have denied Ford a controlling interest in his own company. Reluctantly he complied, but he lingered on like a malevolent ghost in the background until his own death in 1947.

Edsel's son Henry Ford II was released from military service and sent home to take over the company, and following the war he began the long and painful process of rebuilding. Ford went on to have more successes; it recruited a new generation of talented managers including Robert McNamara and Lee Iacocca, and developed another iconic brand, the Mustang. But Ford never regained its old position in the world of car making.

Our Ford

Were Ford and his managers incompetent? On a technical level, no. There were some brilliant engineers among them, including Sorenson, whom I have criticized harshly above but was undoubtedly technically very good at his job. But they all fell – and Ford himself fell first and foremost – into the trap of believing that technological excellence was a guarantee of success. James Couzens had an intuitive understanding of the market and its needs; so for that matter, in the early days, did Ford. But after Couzens's departure, Ford's managers stopped thinking about the market. They developed what a later critic of management, Theodore Levitt, described as 'marketing myopia'.[9] They believed that if they made products excellently and cheaply, those products would somehow mysteriously sell themselves. They were not the first company to fall into this trap, and not the last. In the 1980s, British car maker Austin Rover made exactly the same mistake when it embarked on a strategy of 'production-led recovery', building cars that the market did not want, at least not in sufficient volume to make their production profitable.

So, there were technical and strategic mistakes. But it is hard to escape the feeling that those mistakes could have been avoided, some of them easily, had the culture at Ford been different.

Ford himself must bear the brunt of the blame. Of the seven deadly sins, he exhibited at least three: pride, an overweening arrogance that comes across with breath-taking force in his books; lust for power and domination over others, as witness his bullying of his son and his treatment of his secretary; and greed, the desire for more and more growth instead of concentrating on the needs of his customers. Of the three, arrogance is the most obvious. Ford believed he was supreme; he was a Master of the Universe. Did he even know that the British novelist Aldous Huxley had satirized him in *Brave New World* as 'Our Ford', the deity worshipped instead of 'Our Lord'? Did he read the more sober condemnation uttered by another British novelist, John Buchan, who described him as a remote, cold genius to be admired but not emulated?[10] Probably not. By 1930 if not earlier, Ford had become immune to criticism. He demanded sycophancy. The contrast with his successful rival Alfred Sloan, famously intolerant of 'yes men', could not have been more acute.

But Ford was not the only culprit. All of these flaws were reflected in his managers in later years. The company went from being a closely bonded team to an adversarial organization in which people fought for power, following the example set by the father and son who led them. Macho figures like Cast-Iron Charlie and Harry Bennett took over from more human-centred managers such as Couzens and Wills and Marcus. Management lost touch with those early ideals of value creation and service; instead it became about the naked exercise of power, usually for its own sake, for self-gratification. And the prevailing culture also meant that talent could no longer find a place. Good managers soon departed. The mediocre remained, and gradually floated to the top. And as they rose, the company declined.

Incompetence nearly killed the Ford Motor Company. The amount of value destroyed at Ford between 1915–16 and 1943 has never been calculated. It is probably impossible to calculate the wasted opportunity costs, for we cannot know what Ford might have done had the company and its managers continued as they began. Contemplating on those later years, the dead son, the beaten and cowed workers, the disappointed customers, the unhappy wasted years and most of all, that terrible paranoid old man living alone with his delusions, one is conscious of a sense of tragic futility and waste. One would hope that the lessons of this experience were learned and that other companies were able to steer clear of the pitfalls that Ford fell into. And yet...

---

[1] The most important source for the history of Ford is the three-volume history by Allan Nevins, which is detailed and reliable. Steven Watts, *The People's Tycoon: Henry Ford and the American Century*, New York: Alfred A. Knopf, 2005, is good and readable, and Ford's own books are sometimes still available.

[2] Morgen Witzel (ed.), *Biographical Dictionary of Management*, Bristol: Thoemmes Press, 2001, vol. 1, pp. 315-20.

[3] Allan Nevins, *Ford: The Times, the Man, the Company*, New York: Scribners, 1954, p. 576.

[4] Nevins, *Ford*, p. 568.

[5] Charles Sorenson, *My Forty Years With Ford*, London: Jonathan Cape, 1957.

[6] Henry Ford and Samuel Crowther, *Moving Forward*, New York: Doubleday, 1931, pp. 2-3.

[7] Alfred DuPont Chandler and Stephen Salsbury, *Pierre S. du Pont and the Making of the Modern Corporation*, New York: Harper & Row, 1971.

[8] Norman Beasley, *Knudsen: A Biography*, New York: McGraw-Hill, 1947.

[9] Theodore Levitt, 'Marketing Myopia', *Harvard Business Review*, 1960; reprinted with a retrospective commentary, *Harvard Business Review* September–October, 1975, pp. 1–14.

[10] John Buchan, *The Courts of the Morning*, London: Hodder & Stoughton, 1929.

Chapter 3

How the mighty fell:
Lehman Brothers[1]

Let's recognise that this is a once-in-a-half-century, probably once-in-a-century type of event.

—Allan Greenspan

At a quarter to two in the morning of 15 September 2008, Lehman Brothers, the fourth largest investment bank in the USA, declared bankruptcy. There had been rumours about the bank's solvency for a while, and since the earlier crisis of January 2008 there was no doubt that Lehman Brothers was in trouble, but few had expected the bank to actually fail. Several rescue plans had been mooted, and there had been confidence – particularly at Lehman Brothers itself – that a solution would be found. Surely an institution of this size and importance would not be allowed to fail.

But Lehman Brothers did fail. Its collapse was the equivalent to throwing a stone into a smooth pond. The ripples spread, first through the American financial sector, then to Europe and Asia, then to the world economy in general. The USA and much of Europe slipped into recession, and growth slid to a halt around the world; even the new economic powerhouses, China and India, stuttered and slowed.

In the aftermath of the crash people began to look for reasons, and such is human nature that they also looked for someone to blame for their economic woes. Not surprisingly, they blamed the banks and the bankers, and Lehman Brothers chairman and CEO Richard Fuld was one of those singled out for criticism and abuse. One American magazine named him 'the worst CEO of all time'; others branded him as one of the prime culprits not only of the fall of Lehman Brothers but of the financial crisis itself.

But is that entirely fair? Was Fuld alone responsible for the failure of Lehman Brothers? Or had there been something deeper, a time bomb buried inside Lehman Brothers and its culture, waiting to explode?

A century of service

Certainly there is nothing in Lehman Brothers' early history to suggest the manner in which the company met its end.

The origin of Lehman Brothers can be found in the city of Montgomery, Alabama, where in 1844 a Bavarian immigrant named Hayum Lehman founded a general store and changed his first name to Henry. He was joined a few years later by a second brother, Emanuel, and then a third, Mayer, who had to make a hasty exit from Bavaria after taking part in the failed revolution of 1848. The retail business they owned and ran was called Lehman Brothers.

America in the 1840s and 1850s did not really have a banking system. Thanks in part to the bitter opposition of early presidents such as Thomas Jefferson and Andrew Jackson, who believed that big banks were a threat to America's liberty and way of life, there was no central bank; the Federal Reserve system was only established decades later. Attempts by men like Stephen Girard and John Jacob Astor to found a national bank met with bitter resistance and ultimately failed. Instead, the Free Banking Act of 1838 opened up the market to small local banks, many of which were poorly capitalized and badly managed. Every bank printed its own notes, and bank notes issued by banks rumoured to be in trouble were often exchanged at lower than face value. Bank failures were frequent.

The city of Montgomery's only bank had failed not long before Henry Lehman settled there. With no bank, there was no system of credit and no institution to issue bank notes or coins, and as a result the cotton farmers around Montgomery were perpetually short of cash. To ease the situation, Lehman Brothers operated its own credit system, but it also began to barter goods for cotton. The brothers then transported the cotton to markets in New Orleans, where they sold it for cash. Realizing that there was both an important service to be provided and money to be made, they set up a cotton brokerage business. By the end of the 1850s this was making more money than the retail store.

Henry Lehman died of yellow fever in 1855, but his brothers carried on expanding the business. In 1857 Emanuel Lehman moved to New York and established an office there; New York was the centre of the cotton-broking industry, and this move signalled that Lehman Brothers had ambitions to grow. Mayer remained in Alabama. The outbreak of the American Civil War in 1861 put the business in a difficult position, for New York was part of the Unionist north while Alabama was part of the Confederate south. A Union blockade of Confederate ports led to a depression in the cotton industry. But the firm survived intact, and after the war Mayer Lehman contributed heavily to the rebuilding of the Alabama economy, even lending money to the state government. Then, possibly concerned about the rise of racist movements such as the Ku Klux Klan in the south, he joined his brother in New York.

There, despite their Jewish faith, the Lehmans became pillars of New York society. They helped found the Cotton Exchange, and Mayer Lehman was one of the exchange's first governors. They began to trade in other products such as coffee, sugar and a rising new commodity, oil. The financial crash of 1873 and the longer term decline of the cotton market caused the Lehmans to branch out in new directions, investing in steel mills and railways, particularly in the investment-starved south-ern states. In *The Last of the Imperious Rich*, Peter Chapman credits the Lehmans with founding the railway network in the American south. In a move far ahead of its time, the firm even invested in a company making electric-powered automobiles.

As the twentieth century dawned, a new generation of the Lehman family took charge, led by Emanuel's son Philip. Philip had a summer home in New Jersey, where his next-door neighbour was a trader named Samuel Sachs. He introduced Lehman to his partner, Marcus Goldman. Peter Chapman rather curiously describes Goldman and Sachs as 'crea-tures of the swamp', referring to their business dealings in the area around the East River in New York known as 'the swamp'.[2] Goldman and Sachs had established a small-scale merchant bank. Now they teamed up with Lehman Brothers in an effort to break into merchant banking and underwriting share issues.

Philip Lehman had spotted an opportunity. The New York Stock Exchange and the banking community around it was very much oriented towards 'big business' and especially big industrial business: steel, railways, manufacturing and the like. No one was paying much attention to smaller businesses; or to retail, and thanks to the USA's rapid population growth, the retail sector was flourishing. Catalogue retailers and chain stores were appearing, with companies such as Sears Roebuck and Woolworths growing rapidly. The entrepreneurs who founded these firms were interested in floating them. When the mainstream financial community ignored them, Lehman and his new partners stepped in.

Their first joint venture was underwriting the share issue of United Cigars, a retailer with a chain of about 300 stores around the country. The underwriting of Sears Roebuck followed, and then came the big one, Woolworths, where founder entrepreneur Frank Woolworth needed capital to bring his huge chain of retail outlets together. Lehman Brothers and Goldman Sachs underwrote the successful flotation, making a profit and their reputation in New York financial circles at the same time. (Ironically, the Woolworth company was one of the casualties of the same 2008 crisis that brought down Lehman Brothers.)

More successes followed, including the share issues of department stores Macys and Gimbels, and then a move into traditional industry with the flotations of car maker Studebaker and tyre manufacturer B.F. Goodrich. Now the Lehman family (and Goldman and Sachs) were wealthy. Philip Lehman and his son Robert, generally known as Bobbie, both became noted art collectors and connoisseurs. Philip Lehman's cousin, Mayer Lehman's son Herbert, served as an infantry officer in the First World War and then went into a career in politics. He served as lieutenant-governor of New York from 1929, working with state governor Franklin D. Roosevelt, and after Roosevelt became president was elected governor in his place.

Philip Lehman retired in 1925 and was succeeded by Bobbie. Around this time Lehman Brothers and Goldman Sachs parted company; henceforth they would be competitors. This did not disturb Bobbie Lehman, a talented leader with a sharp eye for an opportunity. Among the companies he backed in the late 1920s were United Fruit Company and the fledgling airline Pan Am. A strategy of prudent management and smart investment strategies that kept risk down to acceptable levels meant that Lehman Brothers did not join in the investment frenzy of the late 1920s, and came through the Wall Street crash of 1929 with only minor bruises. During the Great Depression of the 1930s, there were many fewer share issues to underwrite; Lehman Brothers instead developed a venture capital arm, helping new businesses get off the ground in a credit-starved economy. Many of the companies the bank supported, like Pan Am, would probably not have survived without Lehman Brothers support.

Through all of this period, Lehman Brothers was doing what a bank should do. In the short term, it provided capital to companies that needed it. In the long term, it helped to contribute to national prosperity. From rebuilding the Alabama economy after the Civil War to backing companies that could create jobs, Lehman Brothers was a positive social force. Today in the non-smoking age we might be tempted to see its support for General Cigars as reprehensible, but that is take the event out of context. Few at the time thought there was anything wrong with smoking cigars. The same applies to Lehman Brothers' support for distilleries after prohibition was repealed; a legalized and regulated alcohol industry strong enough to stand up to the bootleggers was a good thing.

It is also interesting to note that Bobbie Lehman, though a Republican (unlike his uncle Herbert, the governor of New York), was in favour of regulating the financial service industry. He believed that more and better regulations might have prevented the crash of 1929, and said as much to the Securities and Exchange Commission in 1936.

After the Second World War, Lehman Brothers played an important role in the long American economic boom of the 1950s and 1960s. Cautious but far-sighted, softly spoken but acute, Bobbie Lehman guided the ever-expanding partnership onto the international scene, opening an office in Paris in 1960s and investing in films and television as well as traditional industries. American Express, Getty Oil and General Motors were among the companies supported by Lehman Brothers invested in during this period. Importantly too, Lehman

Brothers had learned a lesson from its rivals in 1929, and always maintained large cash reserves in case it ran into trouble.

Lehman Brothers was now no longer just a family firm. Non-family members had been taken on as partners in the 1920s, and now there were dozens of partners with no direct connection to the firm. Bobbie Lehman was the person who acted as the firm's sheet anchor, the custodian of its values and the reminder of the bank's purpose and why it existed.

Change of culture

Bobbie Lehman died in 1969. No other member of the Lehman family was involved with the bank; all had moved on to careers in other fields. The partners chose one of their own members, Frederick Ehrman, as chairman and CEO. It often happens that when an iconic leader moves on, his or her successor has trouble living up to expectations, and so it happened with Ehrman; he was unable to cope with the demands of managing and leading the firm through the economic downturn following the first oil shock in 1973.

Ehrman was fired and replaced by Pete Peterson, formerly CEO of a photographic equipment company but most recently Secretary of Commerce in the administration of President Richard Nixon. During the Watergate scandal Nixon became convinced that a member of his government was leaking secrets to the press, and his suspicion fell on Peterson. What happened next is not entirely clear, but in February 1973 Peterson resigned and joined Lehman Brothers, being appointed chairman and CEO despite his having no previous banking experience. It proved to be a fateful decision.

At first all went well. Peterson had a clear vision for the bank and drove it down a policy of expansion both domestically and internationally. An internationalist himself, Peterson sold a stake in Lehman Brothers to Banco Commerciale Italiana in order to strengthen its presence in Europe. He guided Lehman through the first of its big takeovers of other banks, culminating with the acquisition of Kuhn, Loeb & Co. in 1987. Lehman Brothers was now the fourth largest bank in the USA.

Thanks in part to these acquisitions, Lehman Brothers made steady profits through the 1970s.

Slowly but surely, Peterson changed the culture of the bank. Bobbie Lehman was not a target-driven man; he looked for long-term performance and profitability, of course, but he was above all interested in opportunity. A connoisseur of art, he saw markets and investments too with a connoisseur's eye. Peterson was more interested in quantity than quality. Rapid growth was his goal; he wanted to propel Lehman Brothers into the top league alongside Goldman Sachs and Salomon Brothers. He got his wish, but it cost him his job and changed the destiny of the bank.

Much of the growth during the 1970s came not from investment banking but from trading activities. The trading division, headed by former trader Lew Glucksman, was much more aggressive and even more short-termist in outlook. Glucksman's senior trader, the young Richard Fuld, set the tone for much of the division. Driven and intense, Fuld worked fifteen-hour days, coming into the office long before his colleagues and remaining there after they had gone home. Other traders saw him as an example to live up to, especially as Glucksman obviously favoured him.

Increasingly, Glucksman and Peterson began to clash. The high profitability of the trading division meant that Glucksman had more power in the firm, and he knew it. His first victory came when Peterson was forced to appoint him as co-CEO. Tensions increased, and factional strife broke out within the company. The traders mostly supported Glucksman; the bankers were largely behind Peterson. There were unpleasant scenes during which members of the two factions abused each other openly. In 1983 Glucksman's supporters staged a coup d'etat. Peterson resigned, leaving Glucksman in command of the company.

Almost at once, Glucksman opened negotiations with Shearson/ American Express, a division of the American Express financial services group. In 1984 Lehman Brothers was sold to Shearson, the new entity taking the name Shearson Lehman. One senior partner later recalled that he wept at hearing the news. 'To me, investment banking was a noble undertaking, whereby capital was used for social purposes as well as personal gain.'[3] No longer; what had been Lehman Brothers was now just another money-making machine.

'There is no Lehman anymore', claimed one senior executive, and the last remnants of old culture were swept away.[4] The new culture was one of growth and competition. In pursuit of targets and personal gain, people began to cut corners. Shearson Lehman got caught up in one of the major scandals of the decade, the insider trading ring centred around the investment bank Drexel Burnham Lambert and one of its vice-presidents, Ira Sokolow, joined more famous names such as Ivan Boesky and Michael Milken in jail. In Britain the firm became involved with the corrupt businessman Robert Maxwell, and ended up having to pay $90 million in compensation to the people Maxwell had defrauded.

Meanwhile, American Express had begun to feel the ill effects from its badly planned foray into mainstream financial services and began a slow process of withdrawal. In 1990 the Shearson name was dropped and the firm returned to its old name, Lehman Brothers. (Many Lehman Brothers staff had never stopped using name.) Then in 1994 AmEx spun off Lehman Brothers entirely, setting it up as new firm but with a significant difference; it was now a limited company, not a partnership. Even though most senior executives owned shares, they no longer faced the same risks; in other words, they could indulge in more risky trades and investments without fearing for their own financial futures. At the head of the newly independent firm was its former head trader, a man who had opposed the sale of the firm in the first place and who had made Lehman Brothers his life: Richard Fuld.

Fuld remained at the helm of Lehman Brothers for the next fourteen years. Beneath him, his deputies fought each other for power and control. Christopher Pettit, another former trader, served as president and chief operating officer, effectively the number two person in the bank, for two years until his colleagues found out that Pettit was having an extramarital affair. Fuld had strong views on family values and insisted his executives remain faithful to their wives; Pettit was forced to resign (there were rumours that Fuld also suspected Pettit of intriguing against him and going after the top job). Bradley Jack and Joseph Gregory were then appointed co-COOs, an arrangement that increased the tension between them almost at once; Jack was later demoted and Gregory served as sole COO until he too was demoted in early 2008.

The story of Lehman's final decade has been told many times and does not need to be repeated in detail here. In its constant pursuit of growth and income – between 1994 and 2007 net revenue increased from just under $3 billion to over $19 billion – Lehman Brothers pursued the investments and deals that offered the highest returns. It cut the last tie with its roots, abandoning commodities trading altogether and focusing instead on speculative instruments such as mortgage-backed securities including the now infamous collateralized debt obligations (CDOs). Lehman Brothers took a significant position in this market, increasing its leverage ratio to frightening heights. In 2007 it was estimated that a decline in value of its assets of just 4 per cent would wipe out the book value of the bank's equity.[5]

Downfall

And by 2007 the world banking system was beginning to stagger. By now even Wall Street bankers were beginning to realize the danger, as the US subprime housing market bubble burst and the chickens of all those risky investments started flying home to roost. Other banks began reining in, but Lehman Brothers ploughed on almost recklessly. One trader who urged caution was rebuked; it was implied that his concerns about risk stemmed from cowardice.[6] Even more than Fuld, COO James Gregory seemed to observers to be obsessed with risk and risk-taking.

In theory, the activities of Fuld and Gregory and the rest of the executive team were scrutinized by the board, especially the independent directors responsible for governance and oversight. But, whether by accident or design, Lehman Brothers' board had become increasingly weak. The non-executive directors were big names and had imposing CVs; but only a few had any banking experience and many had been retired and out of senior management for a long time. The board should have rung the alarm bells long before Lehman Brothers moved into

danger, but for whatever reason – lack of confidence? lack of experience? an unwillingness to challenge the status quo? – it did not do so.
The board sat quietly like so many nodding dogs while Lehman Brothers
moved closer and closer to the edge of the precipice.

In June 2008 Lehman Brothers opened an office in Dubai – itself about
to suffer its own economic downturn – and Fuld himself flew out to
prospect for new investments there. Convinced that the property
market would come back, Lehman Brothers spent $15 billion acquir-
ing a property company, the Archstone-Smith Trust, which consumed
three-quarters of Lehman's available capital. The company had now, in
the words of Peter Chapman, 'thirty-two dollars borrowed for every
one dollar of its own'. The situation, he adds, was 'very delicately
poised'.[7]

That is an understatement. Credit was drying up, so was inter-bank
lending. Already two British banks, Northern Rock and Bradford &
Bingley, had collapsed under the strain. The writing was on the wall, for
those who cared to turn their heads and read it.

In March 2008 came the collapse and sale of Bear Sterns in New York.
Some in Lehman Brothers were delighted by this; Bear Sterns was a rival
that was now out of the way. But observers of Wall Street now openly
predicted that Lehman Brothers could be the next failure; its leverage
position was insanely out of kilter and a puff of wind would now bring
the house down. Desperate to keep up appearances, the bank resorted
to accounting dodges to inflate profits, but even so it was forced to
report a quarterly loss of $2.8 billion in June 2008.

Now, a sure sign that the buffalo was wounded and the hyenas were
waiting for the kill, short sellers moved in. Fuld reacted in a fury. 'When
I find a short seller, I want to reach down, tear his heart out and eat it
before his eyes', he said. Peter Chapman comments drily: 'Bobbie
Lehman would never have spoken like this.'[8]

Fuld now realized that the bank was in trouble and began looking for
foreign buyers. Several expressed interest, but no more. By 10 September
Lehman Brothers' creditors were closing in. Fuld now pinned most of
his hopes on a bailout by the Federal Reserve, and counted on his relationship with Treasury Secretary Henry Paulson – himself a former

CEO of Goldman Sachs – to save Lehman Brothers. Instead, Paulson took the view that Lehman could be allowed to fail; there were other firms, especially the insurance company AIG, whose importance to the economy was greater.

On 13 September the possibility of a takeover by Barclays Bank emerged, but the deal would take time to arrange; too much time. Lehman Brothers' stock was down to $4 a share, and falling. Then on 14 September Paulson made his final ruling. There would be no bail-out for Lehman Brothers. There was nothing left for its lawyers to do except file for bankruptcy.

What went wrong?

I was in the air between Tokyo and New York when the news of the collapse of Lehman Brothers broke. I landed in New York to find a city in mourning. The taxi driver who brought me into the city from JFK, the concierge at my hotel, the bellman who took me to my room, all had no other topic of conversation. 'All those people', the bellman kept saying, 'all those jobs, all those people', as if they were dead rather than merely unemployed. My colleagues next day were equally gloomy. 'This will start a downturn as bad as the Great Depression', one said. The only response I could make was, 'It doesn't have to be.'

In light of what happened next my words sound rather foolish, but I still believe it was possible even then to have avoided the worst of the downturn. Had the rest of the banking world sucked in its breath, swallowed its losses and concentrated on what could still be saved, the downturn need not have been nearly as severe as it was. Hank Paulson thought the same, at least in public; his statement after the fall of Lehman Brothers commented that 'what we are going through in the short term doesn't make things any easier, but in the long term it is going to make things better, because we've got excesses we need to work through'.[9]

But no one was in the mood to listen to Paulson, who in any case was already being blamed for the crisis. What they wanted to hear was the storm crows like Allan Greenspan, the former Federal Reserve chairman who commented darkly that 'this is a once-in-a-half-century, probably once-in-a-century type of event'.[10] It was a little like being in Europe on the eve of the First World War. Everyone knew war could have been prevented, but no one wanted to prevent it; everyone wanted a fight. Now, everyone knew a recession could have been prevented, but they had been predicting disaster for so long and waiting for it so long that, now it had arrived, they felt compelled to embrace it.

And Greenspan was right, because people's thinking made it right. New Yorkers regarded Lehman Brothers as part of their landscape; bankers regarded it is a powerhouse, and Fuld was one of the wise old men of Wall Street, the longest-tenured CEO of any financial services firm. Despite his outbursts of aggression, he could also be intelligent, thoughtful and perceptive; he had won plaudits for his speech the previous year at the World Economic Forum, in which he suggested that some sort of financial crisis was on the way. His reflections on the fall of Lehman Brothers after the event are quiet and thoughtful.[11]

The problem was that Wall Street, New York, the world had put Lehman Brothers and Fuld on a pedestal, and Fuld and the company had started to believe in their own greatness. They looked at the numbers, the growth, the steeply rising revenues and profits up to 2007, and they were dazzled by their own success. Their arrogance merely fuelled the public myth of their superiority. The fall, like the assassination of Franz Ferdinand, was an event whose symbolic significance was far greater than its real consequences.

The fall of Lehman Brothers did not happen overnight between the 14th and 15th of September 2008. It was an event thirty-nine years in the making. It began with the death of Bobbie Lehman and the change in culture of the firm that came about when outsiders took over, men with little understanding of or interest in Lehman Brothers' values. It continued with the internal rupture between traders and bankers and the baronial warfare that developed between the two divisions. The sale to Shearson and the wiping out of the last vestiges of the old culture applied an accelerant. The high-risk strategies that began in the 1990s lit the match, and finally the decision to increase the leverage ratio by investing in mortgage-backed securities lit the flame. So long as the market kept rising, the bank would survive, but some sort of failure, some sort of damage was inevitable. The financial crisis hastened Lehman Brothers' end; it did not cause it.

Blaming Richard Fuld for the fall of Lehman Brothers is a bit like blaming Captain Edward Smith for the sinking of the *Titanic*. Both are responsible, because both were in command, and both took actions which contributed to the disaster. But Smith was not responsible for the arrogant assumption that the ship was unsinkable, nor was he responsible for the failure to fit enough lifeboats to hold all of her passengers and crew. Fuld was not solely responsible for the risk culture at Lehman Brothers; if accounts are reliable, his deputy James Gregory was equally keen to take risks, but Jared Dillan's memoir also suggests that risk-taking was embedded in the culture throughout the bank. In *Traders, Guns and Money*, Satyajit Das reveals that a culture of risk-taking was endemic throughout the world of financial services. People were rewarded and promoted for taking risks; no one got a bonus for doing something safe.

Lehman Brothers fell because over the course of forty years it moved away from its roots and its purpose and became 'just another bank', a place for making money for traders, bankers and investors. Profit and growth became goals in their own right. Lehman Brothers forgot what it was for.

Managerial incompetence, in the form of greed and arrogance and linear thinking and above all that fatal lack of purpose, killed Lehman Brothers. It crashed the world economy, creating an economic whirl-pool that sucked down hundreds, thousands of other businesses large and small as the credit crunch deepened and sucked the oxygen from the lungs of firms that desperately needed short-term credit. It is ironic that Lehman Brothers was founded in the aftermath of a bank failure in part as a way of giving short-term credit to Alabama farmers. In 2008, small businesses around the globe began going bankrupt as a result of Lehman Brothers' failure.

Yes, I believe the disaster could have been prevented; but it was not prevented, and the management of Lehman Brothers over four decades must bear their share of responsibility for what happened: wasted opportunities, failed businesses, wrecked careers, poverty, hunger and suicides. Those are the consequences of management failure. That is why failures must be prevented, stopped from happening before the damage is done.

---

[1] Peter Chapman, *The Last of the Imperious Rich*, London: Portfolio/Penguin, 2010, is an excellent history of the foundations of Lehman Brothers, and also recommended is Ken Auletta, *Greed and Glory on Wall Street: The Fall of the House of Lehman*, New York: Putnam, 2001. On the early period, see Allan Nevins, *Herbert H. Lehman and His Era*, New York: Charles Scribner's Sons, 1963. Lawrence McDonald, *A Colossal Failure of Common Sense: The Inside Story of the Collapse of Lehman Brothers*, New York: Crown Business, 2009, is a colourful account of the last days of the firm, and Jared Dillan, *Street Freak: Money and Madness at Lehman Brothers*, New York: Simon & Schuster, 2011, offers a personal perspective.

[2] Chapman, *The Last of the Imperious Rich*, p. 53.

[3] Chapman, *The Last of the Imperious Rich*, p. 200.

[4] Chapman, *The Last of the Imperious Rich*, p. 200.

[5] Robin Blackburn, 'The Subprime Crisis', *New Left Review* 50, March–April 2008, http://newleftreview.org/II/50/robin-blackburn-the-subprime-crisis

[6] McDonald, *A Colossal Failure of Common Sense*.

[7] Chapman, *The Last of the Imperious Rich*, p. 263.

[8] Chapman, *The Last of the Imperious Rich*, p. 266.

[9] http://news.bbc.co.uk/1/hi/business/7616037.stm

[10] http://news.bbc.co.uk/1/hi/business/7616037.stm

[11] http://dealbook.nytimes.com/2011/02/14/a-different-side-to-dick-fuld/?_php=true&_type=blogs&_php=true&_type=blogs&_php=true&_type=blogs&_r=2&

Chapter 4

Masters of the universe

Sherman McCoy, the hero of Tom Wolfe's satirical novel *Bonfire of the Vanities*, has everything. A successful New York bond trader, he has all the trappings of power: money to burn, a flash car, a show-off office, an expensive apartment, a wife, a family, a mistress. Surrounded by the evidence of his own success, McCoy has convinced himself that he is no ordinary man. He is superior to everyone around him. He describes himself jokingly as a 'Master of the Universe' (a reference to a television cartoon series of the 1980s), but as the story goes on, it becomes clear that he really does believe in his own greatness. He thinks he can do anything he wants, without fear of consequences.

Of course, it all goes horribly wrong. His arrogance brings about his own downfall. By the end of the book McCoy has lost everything – and he cannot understand why.

Arrogance is one of the main reasons why so many executives and companies suffer from what Margaret Heffernan refers to as 'wilful blindness', deliberately denying the existence of certain facts.[1] Unlike ignorance, which is genuinely *not knowing*, wilful blindness means *choosing not to know*, or at least to behave as if one did not know. Heffernan first encountered the term while reading a transcript of the trials of Enron bosses Jeffrey Skilling and Kenneth Lay. Blinded by the light of favourable publicity, its corporate ego stroked by academics and consultants who praised its innovative business model and wrote and taught case studies about it, Enron stopped believing in reality and started instead to believe in its own myth. From that moment, as with Sherman McCoy, there could be only one result.

This raises an important point. We think of arrogance and wilful blindness as being conditions that affect individuals. In fact, they can also permeate the culture of an entire organization. In effect, the organization – or, at least, the people who make the key decisions in it – becomes infected with a kind of *corporate arrogance*. The organization believes it is superior to its rivals and to the world around it. And, because of that belief, the organization and its executives are not bound by the normal rules of the game. They can do whatever they want.

The results of corporate arrogance manifest themselves in several ways. One is rule-breaking, deliberate flouting of the law such as happened at Enron, WorldCom, Parmalat and many others over the years. Another is detachment from the real world, where executives lose touch with not only the business environment but the organization itself. A third is complacency, a kind of intellectual arrogance that comes with success; if enough people tell a company how wonderful it is, sooner or later the company will start to believe it. A fourth, which follows on from this, is the belief that the company is bulletproof and nothing can touch it. A fifth is contempt, looking down on those who are not part of the company and treating them as being of lesser importance; the company's needs come first, everyone else's a long way second. And finally, there is what I call the *arrogance of good intentions*, in which the company is so convinced of the rightness and morality of what it is doing that it believes the ends justify the means (Table 4.1).

Table 4.1 A Typology of Arrogance

Type	Manifestation
Personal arrogance	*I am superior to you, therefore I can do what I like*
The arrogance of Olympian detachment	*We are far above the ordinary; what happens down on the ground is of no interest to us*
The arrogance of past success	*We are the best in the world; just look at our track record*
The arrogance of invulnerability	*Nothing can touch us; we are unbeatable*
The arrogance of contempt for others	*Our needs are all that matters. The rest can look after themselves*
The arrogance of good intentions	*So long as the end is good, the end justifies the means*

Arrogant companies make the crucial mistake of thinking that the business is all about *them*. Everyone and everything else – including the customer – is less important. That belief, once it becomes ingrained, is a primary killer of companies.

Think of all the scandals that have affected the business world over the past five, ten, twenty years – I won't list them all, it would take too long – and think too of the lesser business failures, the once great companies that suddenly staggered, stumbled and fell. Analyse what happened, and you will find that personal and corporate arrogance was a major factor in a great many cases.

We must be careful, when discussing arrogance, not to confuse it with self-belief or confidence. Both are necessary, and as we shall see later, fear and lack of confidence can be dangerous too. It is good for a company to be proud of what it *does*. The tipping point comes when it no longer cares much about what it does and instead becomes proud of what it *is*; its own reputation, its own self-image. A culture of *mindless self-belief* forms which effectively traps the company like a fly in amber, imprisoned in the cage of its own corporate ego.

We will begin our tour of arrogance with a brief look at personal arrogance. This is rarer than some might think, but it can be very damaging when it does occur.

FIGJAM

Australians have a useful term for anyone seems to be too full of themselves: FIGJAM, an acronym for 'Fuck, I'm Good – Just Ask Me'.

Sherman McCoy was a classic FIGJAM character; so too, if we accept the evidence presented by biographer Joe Haines, was the British media entrepreneur Robert Maxwell.[2] Bernie Ebbers, the entrepreneurial founder of WorldCom, reportedly claimed that he had been chosen by God.[3] Football manager José Mourinho has also described himself as 'the special one' and 'the only one'.[4]

FIGJAM characters can also be found at lower levels of organizations. I have worked with several over the years, in India, Germany, Britain and the USA, and found them all to be pretty much alike: overconfident, cocky, loud, domineering and generally unpleasant to be around. Also, none of them were anywhere near as good as they thought they were. Most of the ones I knew have sunk without trace; one crashed and burned spectacularly, doing considerable damage within his own organization as he did so.

To start with, we take it for granted that arrogant people are arrogant because of some quality or defect within them, what Adrian Furnham describes as 'malignant charisma'.[5] But that is not necessarily so. To paraphrase an old saying, some are born arrogant; others achieve arrogance; and still others have arrogance thrust upon them.

The first group, those who are born arrogant, are comparatively easy to identify. Adrian Furnham, Manfred Kets de Vries, Sydney Finkelstein and others describe in detail the psychology of the pathologically arrogant mind.[6] It requires courage and resolution to stand up to these people and either freeze them out or throw them out of the organization, but it can be done. Much more insidious and dangerous are the people who start out as perfectly ordinary human beings but then grow into monsters of ego. Often, those around them do not see the warning signs until it is too late.

There is nothing in Henry Ford's early life and career to suggest that he would turn into a bullying tyrant. Even in the years after the launch of the Model T, there are few hints about the tragedy to come; to all appearances he was a highly successful business leader, with a stronger social conscience than most.

Two factors contributed to the change in Ford's character. First, he began to believe his own publicity. Indeed, it must have been hard not to do so; the avalanche of laudatory praise that flooded the American and world press must have been impossible to escape. Ford was not just admired in the early days; he was idolized. Other business leaders came to see his factories and went home and tried to emulate him. Heads of state humbly asked his opinion on important matters of the day.

Second, Ford was surrounded by yes-men who did their best to stoke his ego still further. This was especially true after the departure from the firm of James Couzens and William Knudsen, two blunt-spoken men who could be relied on to keep Ford in touch with reality and tell him when they thought he was wrong. Knudsen's successor Charles Sorensen, by his own admission, never contradicted his boss. Roman emperors had slaves whispering in their ear, reminding them that they were mortal. Ford had no one to do the same.

British jewellery entrepreneur Gerald Ratner fell into the same trap. There is much to admire about Ratner; he took a small family retail chain and turned it into the world's first global jewellery business in a matter of a few years. He also did one of the hardest things any European retailer can do; he cracked the American market. At the height of its success, Ratner had more than a thousand stores in the USA alone, trading under several different brands. Like Ford, Ratner was the subject of a barrage of red-hot publicity, extolling his virtues as a self-made man and a business leader for his times. British Prime Minister Margaret Thatcher was amongst his admirers.

And then, in a speech to the Institute of Directors in London in April 1991, Ratner destroyed most of what he had worked for. In the speech, he told two jokes about his company's merchandise, and just in case you missed them, here they are:

> We do cut-glass decanters with six glasses on a silver tray... all for £4.95. People say, 'How can you sell this for such a low price?' I say, 'Because it's crap'.

and

> We sell earrings that are cheaper than a Marks & Spencer prawn sandwich. But the earrings probably won't last as long.

The speech was reported in the media around the world. The conclusion to which nearly everyone jumped was that Ratner was sneering at the tastes of his customers. Within days, a reported £500 million was wiped off the value of the company, and Ratner himself was thrown out of the firm he had built. The remnants of the group were eventually sold for a knock-down price. Seldom has so much value been destroyed in so short a space of time.

Why did he do it? In his memoirs, Ratner describes the event with a candour that is almost painful.[7] It turns out that this was not the first time Ratner had made these jokes. He had repeated them before to colleagues and friends, and even used them in earlier speeches, in closed venues with no press present. Yet neither he nor – and this is the important part – anyone around him seems to have realized what would happen if these remarks were made in public. Far from questioning his wisdom, his staff and colleagues egged him on. 'Tell some of your jokes, Gerald', said one person when asked for suggestions for the speech. 'Everyone loves your jokes.'

 Leaders who are surrounded by people who are too afraid or too syco-phantic to challenge them.

Henry Ford and Gerald Ratner did not start off as arrogant men. But, as they became more successful, they were surrounded by people who thought that their own jobs depended on stroking the boss's ego. I find it hard to blame either man entirely for what happened. Yes, they were the leaders, and yes, they should have taken personal responsibility (as Ratner did, and Ford did not), but they were not solely to blame. The people around them, their staff and executives and advisors failed in their own duty of care to their leader. For their own reasons, fear, self-interest or whatever, they pushed their leader down the path towards arrogance. They too are culpable.

Look on these works, ye mighty, and despair

The culture at Ford was one not so much of mindless self-belief as mindless belief in the leader. The same was true at Lehman Brothers, not least in the boardroom where inexperienced and unconfident directors effectively gave Richard Fuld and his executive team permission to do what they liked. But, at the same time, there was also a belief in the strength and power and size of the organization. Ford was the largest car maker in the world, one of the largest companies in the world, and had led the way in revolutionizing not only an industry but American society itself. Lehman Brothers was one of the largest, most successful, oldest and certainly the most iconic of the merchant banks. Both had gone from success to success. Surely it was impossible that they could fail?

Ford and Lehman Brothers both suffered from *Olympian arrogance*, the detachment from the real world that comes with being too big and too successful (yes, I know what you're thinking; I'll come back to this at the end of the chapter). Sometimes this detachment manifests itself in a feeling that the company is above or beyond law, and in these cases mindless self-belief quickly evolves into a culture of corruption. Often, this first manifests itself in one division or department of the company (for example, the bribery scandals affecting Wal-Mart's international division or GlaxoSmithKline's China operations in 2014[8]), and if the rest of the company moves fast, the infection can be cut off and isolated before it spreads. It is important, particularly for large firms operating across many geographies, to be alert to the signs of corruption, but an even better idea is to create a culture where corruption cannot take root in the first place.

More dangerous, and more likely to kill a company outright rather than simply damaging it, is the division that opens up between the upper and lower levels of the company. The problem comes when the people at the top fail to realize this division exists. They *think* they are still in touch with their junior managers and staff, but in fact they are not. IBM in the 1970s and 1980s was one such company. Top executives prided themselves on the fact that theirs was the most innovative company in the sector, perhaps in the world. In speeches they sometimes talked about the people who made it all possible, the 'wild ducks', free thinkers and free spirits who roamed around the company sowing creative ideas and driving the innovation process forward. 'Treasure the wild ducks' was a favourite phrase of IBM chairman Thomas Watson.

What Watson and others at the top did not understand was that in reality IBM had become a bureaucratic cage, where conformity was everything and freedom was no longer tolerated. Creative thinking had largely become a thing of the past. 'What happened to the wild ducks?' ran the bitter joke at lower levels of the company. 'They all got shot.' The disconnect between top management and the rest of IBM was so severe that it nearly brought down the company, and it took several bitter years of struggle by new chairman Lou Gerstner to change the culture and free people to become creative once again.[9] (Interestingly,

IBM still refers to its creative people as 'wild ducks'; presumably there has been a successful breeding programme.)

Olympian arrogance also deepens the fissure between leadership and management. From the majestic heights of the boardroom, leaders look down and see their followers scurrying ant-like to do their bidding; but after a while, like the gods themselves, they become bored with this and start staring out into the wider distance, taking their eyes off the ground at their feet. In time, they come to believe that it is neither right nor proper for them to intervene in matters of mere management.

Again, as Ram Charan and Geoffrey Colvin pointed out, most corporate failures are not failures of strategy, they are failures of execution. But the message doesn't seem to be getting through. How many times have we seen a company, or a leader, apparently setting off on the right course and then coming unstuck through a failure of execution? Bob Diamond was a much admired chief executive of Barclays banking group until he was engulfed in the Libor scandal. Pressed to resign, he refused at first, claiming that he was not responsible: Barclay's was a huge organization, and he could not be expected to know what was going on everywhere in the bank (he did step down several days later).

 Top executives who are invisible to the rest of the organization.

This attitude is widespread. Ask company chairmen or chief executives whether they know what is going on everywhere in the companies they lead. If they are being candid, they will tell you no, they don't. Most will also tell you that they lose sleep over this. The others, the Olympians, will tell you very seriously that it is not their job to worry about these things. Their job is to create vision, give direction to the company, chart a course into the future. Execution is someone else's job.

The signs of Olympian arrogance are easy to spot. They come in two forms, *physical signs* and *behavioural signs*. Behavioural signs include chairmen's statements in annual reports that begin with phrases like, 'As we look back on yet another year of unparalleled growth', or 'As

chairman of the dominant firm in our industry, I would like to congrat-
ulate you all on another year of success.' Self-congratulatory speeches
and statements to the press by chairmen and/or CEOs are another.
Also, look twice at any business whose leaders spend a large portion of
their time sitting on government panels and inquiries or giving evidence
to policy think tanks. When companies start believing that they can
influence governments, they are well on the road to Olympian
arrogance.

The physical signs include large and grandiose office buildings, statues
and paintings of the company founder, fountains in the lobby of the
headquarters building, company flags and severely restrictive dress
codes for non-contact staff. (It should be added that on their own these
aren't necessarily signs of danger; the Tata Group displays images of its
founder J.N. Tata in most of its offices worldwide as a reminder of
values of this very humble man. But Tata's main headquarters in
Mumbai, Bombay House, is a quite ordinary building – and there is no
fountain.) In *How They Blew It*, Jamie Oliver and Tony Goodwin compare
business leaders who built such monuments to monarchs like Henry
VIII who built grandiose palaces in an attempt to ensure their own
immortality.[10] They, like Henry Ford, would do well to read Shelley's
'Ozymandias':

> *And on the pedestal these words appear:*
> *'My name is Ozymandias, king of kings:*
> *Look on my works, ye Mighty, and despair!'*
> *Nothing beside remains. Round the decay*
> *Of that colossal wreck, boundless and bare*
> *The lone and level sands stretch far away.*

We've always done it this way (part 1)

The *arrogance of past success* is a classic trap which has been remarked
upon by many writers. In *The Innovator's Dilemma*, Clayton Christensen
describes how some firms become prisoners of their own past. A spectacularly successful innovation that propels a firm into a position of
market leadership can, a few years later, turn into an intellectual

straitjacket. So wedded is the firm to that technology that it cannot conceive of any challenge or change to it.[11] An example is Wang Laboratories, which had a technological advantage over other computer makers, and knew it. Wang engineers used to laugh at the primitive designs put out by rival IBM; until IBM, revitalized by its new boss Louis Gerstner, cut the ground from under Wang's feet. In 1992 Wang went bankrupt.

Examples of firms falling into this trap are legion. Kodak was for years the leader in the film and camera market, until the emergence of digital cameras. Kodak stuck to its tried and tested products, and was duly swept away by the revolution. Motorola, famous for its mastery in analogue technology mobile phones, stuck to that technology in the face of the challenge from digital, and lost much of its market share as a result. Nokia, which took over the dominant position from Motorola, failed in turn to adapt to the rise of the next generation of phones. Motorola survived the transition in diminished form, and so far Nokia has too. Kodak did not.

Some companies become dependent on key technologies; others are reluctant to give up on established brands. Few executives have been more stubborn in their defence of past success than those of the Dep Corporation, which manufactured a diet candy containing an appetite-suppressing drug and marketed it with the brand name Ayds. In 1987, when the AIDS epidemic began to gather force in the USA, it was suggested that this name might be, to say the least, a turn-off for consumers. 'We've been around for fifty years', replied one executive. 'Let the disease change *its* name.' Eighteen months later the company did reluctantly change the name to Diet Ayds, which made no difference. In the end, this once highly successful brand had to be withdrawn.[12]

Both the innovators' dilemma and diehard loyalty to brands that have run their course is part of a more general problem of complacency that creeps into many highly successful companies. There is a quite natural tendency to think that, having made it to the top, the company can now rest on its laurels. But that way danger lies. In *The Self-Destructive Habits of Good Companies*, Jagdish Sheth writes at length about the causes and nature of complacency, which he describes as the illusion that 'bad things can't happen here'. Complacency, he says, 'breeds in the assumption that the future will be like the present and past, that nothing will change. Complacency likes blindness and inertia; it likes the status quo'.[13]

 The belief that just because the firm has been successful in the past, it will go on being successful in the future.

One of the most interesting examples Sheth cites is De Beers, which during the twentieth century controlled about 85 per cent of the world diamond market. Grown fat on success, De Beers could not imagine a situation in which its hegemony would be challenged. But then within the space of a few years, new diamond producers emerged in Russia and Canada and new cutting and polishing houses in Israel and India began to undercut De Beers on price. The Indian diamond industry in particular developed into a potent competitor, with De Beers unable to do a thing about it.

At least De Beers developed a response strategy and fought back strongly. Delta Airlines, another of Sheth's examples, was also a very good company, famous for its reputation for good customer service. But it failed to notice the changes that deregulation was imposing on the airline market until its revenues began to suffer. The response, a series of cost-cutting measures that badly affected staff morale, simply made the position worse and Delta went from being one of America's most admired airlines to bankruptcy in 2005 (the company has since been turned around).

I say that the tendency to complacency is quite natural because, deep down, most human beings are uncomfortable with change. Growth and change of direction and risk taking all imply uncertainty, and we don't like uncertainty. Doing things the way we have always done them makes us feel comfortable and secure, and we don't recognize – or are wilfully blind to the fact – that not changing actually makes us *less* secure. Also, creating a successful innovation or building a successful brand makes us feel good. We can sit back and admire it, and remember how clever we were in the old days when we first came up with the idea, and then made it happen. It strokes our egos. But, again, this is also very dangerous. As Andrew Grove says, every organization needs a sense of paranoia, a realization that nothing good will last forever and that somewhere out there, someone is waiting to get you.[14]

 People saying, 'But this is how we've always done it.'

But, it can be argued, if we find a successful recipe, a business model that works, we would be foolish to keep re-inventing it. As they say in poker, never throw away a winning hand. Quite so; but this is true only so long as the business model *still* works. Clayton Christensen argues that each time a company commercializes a new innovation, it should start looking at the next step, the next evolution, the next technology to come along, and that on the whole this is what companies like Apple and Microsoft do. The same principle applies to business models more generally. We need to keep thinking about change, keep thinking about what might happen next and be ready to shift position when the time comes.

Nothing lasts forever; no business model is sustainable indefinitely. In poker, you hold a winning hand for only a few minutes; then the cards are shuffled and a new hand is dealt.

So long as it is black

Unlike the arrogance of past success, which can be so subtle that for a long time it goes almost unnoticed, the *arrogance of contempt for others* is visible and deliberate. It manifests itself in disdain, open or covert, for other groups of people. A classic example of an organization with a strong vein of contempt for others is the Mafia. Gang members are treated as family and given protection and support, but anyone outside the organization is expendable. Ironically, investigations into corruption in police forces have uncovered similar behaviour: officers close ranks to protect each other, sometimes against the interests of the victims of crime and the public they are meant to protect and serve.

As well as being unpleasant in its own right, the arrogance of contempt for others is symptomatic of a narrowness of outlook and unwillingness to change. Scores of scholars and consultants down through the years have argued the necessity of a strong corporate culture.[15] The benefits are said to include higher levels of motivation at work, a greater commitment to innovation and adherence to the company's values, among other things.

All this is so, but there is also an inherent danger. Cultures can become exclusive: they can start to see the world in terms of *us* and *them*, and then there creeps in gradually the belief that *we* are in some way superior to *they*. We are very successful because we are very good, the belief goes; it follows that people who are not as successful as us must also not be as good as us. Over time this superiority becomes unthinking, handed on from person to person as part of a corporate cult that has little or no basis in reality.[16] The culture becomes an intellectual and emotional straitjacket.

Contempt for customers

As noted in Chapter 2, Henry Ford never made the infamous remark about customers being able to choose the colour of their car so long as it is black, but ask most people to quote something Ford said and that is what they will come up with. And whatever he may or may not have said, Ford *was* contemptuous of his customers. In the early days he regarded them with a kind of benevolent paternalism; he was 'giving' them the goods they wanted. In later life his attitude to customers was that they should be grateful for what they got.

Sometimes contempt for customers is simple arrogance, with the company believing that it knows better than they do. As Sydney Finkelstein puts it, 'they [the companies] don't just claim, "We know what customers want." They go further, claiming, in effect, "We know what our customers want better than they do, because we know what's best for them, and eventually they'll see it too."'[17] He cites Motorola as an example, continuing to design phones that it thought customers wanted rather than finding out what customers really did want. This is relatively benign arrogance, which in the end hurt no one but the company and its shareholders.

Rather more toxic were the actions of Lululemon, the Canadian fashion company that in 2006 launched a brand of garment bags under the brand Vita-Sea. The bags, it was claimed, were made with seaweed fibre which had health-giving properties that would benefit consumers. They were, of course, sold at a high premium. Tests then showed that there was no seaweed at all in the bags, which were made of ordinary cotton.[18] Confronted with the test results, Lululemon refused to apologize for the deception, though it did eventually drop the health-giving claims for its product. Lululemon went on to develop a line of expensive women's trousers that customers complained were see-through. Chip Wilson, the founder of the Lululemon, blamed the problem on the size of his female customers' thighs. In the end he was forced to leave the company.

Of course mistakes happen, and any company no matter how well-intentioned can screw up when delivering products or services to customers. Most customers know this, and will be satisfied with an apology and reparation. They grow annoyed when they feel that the company is deliberately treating them with disrespect or condescension. In the Lululemon case, Wilson's derogatory remarks about his customers backfired with spectacular results. Gerald Ratner probably intended no disrespect to his customers, but he managed to upset them all the same, and killed his company.

There are borderline cases here: for example, budget airlines around the world treat their customers like cattle and still remain in business. But, most people who fly with budget airlines know what to expect, and still believe that they are getting value for money. Where customers really do draw the line is when it becomes clear that they are being milked, that the company doesn't care about them at all but only wants to relieve them of as much money as possible. In these days of social media, where customer retaliation can spread widely and quickly, such a business strategy is not only morally questionable but also financially dangerous.

I was amused to read of a New York businessman who maintained that deliberately treating customers badly was part of his growth strategy. Each incident resulted in more publicity and more hits on websites criticizing his company. This in turn increased the visibility of the company during Internet searches. This peculiar form of search engine optimization can only have one ending.

Rule: annoying your customers is seldom a good idea; ripping them off is never a good idea.

Contempt for employees

Employers have been treating employees with contempt since time immemorial, but the problem grew worse during the Industrial Revolution when a new generation of employers, self-made men who were full of the FIGJAM attitude, emerged on the scene. Men like Richard Arkwright and Samuel Oldknow saw their workers not as people but as a commodity to be exploited (Arkwright later ameliorated his views). When mill owner Robert Owen discovered that cutting the working day from fourteen hours to ten resulted in an overall increase in productivity, he communicated this news to his fellow entrepreneurs and urged them to follow his example.[19] The other owners rounded on him as a traitor to his class. The workers were common people; what right had they to expect good hours or a decent standard of living? The mill owners felt they had not just a right, but even a duty to exploit the workers.

Confrontational attitudes to employees persist to this day, and the 'us' and 'them' approach to human resources management remains a very common one. Often, too, individual groups of employees are singled out for discrimination. Women, ethnic minorities and the disabled are particular targets. In theory, these groups are protected by legislation, which ensures equal rights. In practice, abuse continues with little abatement. In some countries, notably China, the position of women in the workplace is actually getting worse, not better. Everywhere, women are denied access to some jobs, paid at lower rates and subject to verbal and physical harassment. To some extent, though, this contempt for women is also based on ignorance, fear and sexual desire, so I shall reserve further treatment of this issue for later chapters.

Treating employees with contempt is, in the long run, completely counterproductive. Study after study, beginning with the Hawthorne experiments in the 1920s and continuing up to the present day, has shown that motivating people makes them work harder.[20] It has been pointed out that there is no empirical link between motivation and higher productivity; maybe so, but there is plenty of evidence that demotivating people makes them work *less* hard. It is nearly a hundred and fifty years since the economist Henry Carey showed that a single willing free worker will outperform four slaves. Some executives still haven't figured this out.

History's first recorded industrial action took place around 1100 BC, at the Valley of the Kings in Egypt, when workers building a pharaoh's tomb walked off the job in protest because they had not been paid. Their incompetent managers continued to mess the workers around, the quality of their work declined, and eventually a once-highly effective work team had to be disbanded. Who says you can't learn from history?

Rule*: treating your employees with disdain will not motivate them to work harder.*

Contempt for suppliers

Contemporary supply chain management theory suggests the notion of building partnerships along the value chain, alliances that benefit every member of the chain and result in efficiency and good working relationships. Some companies prefer instead to view the supply chain as a series of gladiatorial contests, in which the winner takes the spoils. The dominant concept is not partnership, but power.

Several inquiries have been held into the grocery retail business in the United Kingdom, which is dominated by a handful of large supermarket chains which have tremendous buying power. Many food producers, especially in fresh produce and dairy, are small in scale. The supermarkets are accused of driving down prices paid to wholesalers, who in turn pass these cuts on in the form of lower prices paid to farmers. The inquiries have exonerated the supermarkets; the farmers still ask why they are making less money (they say) than they were thirty years ago. An adversarial relationship exists, which benefits no one. The farmers continue to supply the supermarkets at the moment because they have few alternative markets, but when a better opportunity appears, and it will – see the arrogance of past success, mentioned earlier – they will be off to greener pastures and the supermarkets will suddenly find themselves in trouble.

Rule: *what goes round, comes round. Respect your suppliers and treat them well and they will reward you with quality and service. If you fail to do so, don't be surprised if both deteriorate, and if they defect to your rivals at first opportunity.*

Contempt for shareholders

The separation of ownership and control, a concept pioneered in Germany and developed to its fullest extent in the USA, holds that the owners of businesses, the shareholders, should step back from day-to-day management and hand over control to salaried professional executives. In theory, this separation ensures that businesses are run in the best interests of all concerned, not just for the benefit of the owners themselves, thus ensuring protection for other stakeholders. In reality, as James Burnham pointed out in *The Managerial Revolution*, executives began running companies as if they owned them, and bitterly resented any attempt by shareholders to interfere or question their authority.[21]

Seventy years on from Burnham, not much has changed. Executive directors look down their noses at non-executive or independent directors who are nominated by shareholders, believing – sometimes, with cause – that the latter know nothing about the business and are not competent to comment on its management. Companies share information with shareholders because they are required to do so by law, but they give that information grudgingly and often in such obtuse formats that it takes a combination of a mathematical genius and a lexicographer to make sense of it. And then, when the shareholder undervalues the company and sells stock, causing the share price to fall, executives become even more resentful and blame shareholders for their ignorance.

In Asia and parts of Europe, the situation is different. Here, the separation of ownership and control is less pronounced, and individual owners often retain majority control and take a direct role in management. Under this system, contempt for shareholders is even stronger. No outside shareholder has enough power to influence strategy or governance. The role of the shareholder is to hand over money in return for shares and then go away and wait for the quarterly dividend payments, without making any fuss about how the company is actually run. There again, owner-executives wonder why shareholders pull their money out as soon as the market begins to slow down.

Common sense suggests that executives and shareholders should make common cause and pursue profit and growth to the benefit of both, and sometimes they do. But such cases are not the norm, and in most companies the relationship between management and shareholders is founded on mutual dislike, misunderstanding and contempt. There is no sign of this situation ending soon.

> **Rule**: *whatever you do to your shareholders, they will do to you. And they're better at it.*

Contempt for government and regulators

One article of faith in business communities the world over is that governments don't understand business. Government intervention in markets is always seen as interference, and that interference always has a negative outcome. Government is a necessary evil, and laws and regulations are a barrier and a cost. Get rid of regulation, the belief goes, and everyone would be better off: customers would pay lower prices, companies would receive higher profits.

As Jagdish Sheth has shown, though, deregulation can be a two-edged sword. Not every company profits in deregulated markets, and as passengers on British railways will know, prices do not always go down. Even more interesting is the view of George Siedel and Helena Haapio in their book *Proactive Law for Managers*.[22] They advance two propositions: (1) that most laws and regulations are there to protect companies, and the absence of these laws would expose companies to more risk, not less, and (2) that prompt compliance with the law can be a source of strength, creating both cost savings and reputational advantage. Most successful of all, they say, are those companies that engage with the regulatory process and help make the law, rather than simply sitting back waiting until the last minute to comply.

Actually, when you stop and think about it, both of these propositions are simple common sense. But many executives *don't* stop to think; they merely carry on with their ingrained contempt for government, which makes it anathema for them to even consider working with regulators.

Rule: it is nearly always cheaper and easier to work with regulators than to fight them. If you're going to take on the establishment, make sure it is a fight you can win.

At the heart of the matter is the belief that the company's needs come first, and those of stakeholders only second. In fact, of course, the opposite is true. Without stakeholders, the company would not exist. That truth needs to be remembered, always. And even if you do feel a genuine contempt for some or all of your stakeholders, for heaven's sake, don't let them know it!

 Executives speaking about stakeholders, especially customers, in derogatory terms.

Titanic syndrome

Q: What do RMS *Titanic*, Singapore, the Greek hero Achilles, the German battleship *Bismarck* and Lehman Brothers have in common?

A: Two things. First, during their lifetimes all were described by terms such as 'unsinkable', 'impregnable' or 'invincible'. Second, they all (metaphorically or literally) sank.

Famously described as 'unsinkable' by an executive owner of White Star, the *Titanic* sank on her maiden voyage. The British claimed Singapore was an impregnable fortress, able to hold out against an enemy forever; but in 1942 the Japanese captured Singapore after a siege of just one week. Achilles could not be harmed by a weapon unless it struck him in the heel; which is exactly where the Trojan prince Paris shot him with an arrow. The *Bismarck* was sunk by the Royal Navy on its first foray into the Atlantic in 1941. Chapter 3 showed what happened to Lehman Brothers.

The *arrogance of indestructibility* has its origins in the arrogance of past success, and perhaps a little in the arrogance of contempt too. In the popular press it is sometimes referred to as the 'too big to fail' syndrome, but smaller companies can also be victims of the belief that they are bulletproof. Many things can contribute to this belief, including a dominant position within an industry, a very large customer base, a superior production system, a superior product, possession of large amounts of intellectual capital and a personal belief on the part of senior executives, at least, that the company has been somehow 'chosen' or 'destined' for greatness (perhaps we should be calling this Mourinho syndrome).

Ford, in Henry Ford's day, had all these qualities; Lehman Brothers had most of them. In the early 2000s, in the aftermath of another rash of banking scandals, the CEO of Britain's Co-operative Bank gave an interview in which he claimed that the Co-op Bank was proof against scandal. The bank's values and ethos, he said, were defence against corruption. Other banks might stumble and fail, but the Co-op's high moral principles would see it through. I thought at the time he was giving a hostage to fortune, and memories of this interview came flooding back in 2014 when news broke of a huge financial scandal at the bank, a black hole in its finances and a chairman who stood accused of drug use. Hubris in action, again.

 People saying, 'That can't happen here.'

Every company has an achilles heel, a place where it is vulnerable. Attempts to proof oneself against disaster are bound to fail. Why? Because, inevitably, all one does is proof oneself against events that have happened in the past. We cannot foresee the future; we don't know what will happen next; so how can we expect to defend against it?

Readers will by now have spotted a problem. In the introduction I said that the purpose of this book was to spot the signs of management failure and eliminate failures before they occur. But if we cannot predict the future, and don't know what will happen next, how we can we prepare for future events? The answer is to spot the warning flags, the storm warnings, and then to take action against the *causes* of failure.

In other words, instead of preparing to fight a war, take steps to prevent war from breaking out in the first place.

The road to corporate hell

The road to hell, it is said, is paved with good intentions, and the path of business history is littered with the wreckage of companies that thought good intentions were enough. The Co-operative Bank, discussed earlier, is just one such casualty. But, it turns out that doing good is not the same as doing well.

Entrepreneurs are particularly susceptible to this form of arrogance. They come up with ideas that will change the world, and then don't understand why the world is not grateful. I once worked with a small company in the renewable energy market that had a very clever idea, and was convinced that the idea was *so* clever that other companies would generously donate, for free, the parts it needed to build its products which it would then sell. Needless to say, I did not work with this company for very long. At time of writing, the sustainability sector is full of starry-eyed entrepreneurs who believe that the world will beat a path to their door once it knows about their invention; and also, that in this new era, the ordinary rules of business no longer apply.

The first thing that these entrepreneurs need is a dash of humility. Their world-changing, world-saving inventions have to be financed, and they have to have a business model that will work. The principles of economics have not changed in 4,000 years, and they are unlikely to change now. Supply and demand, opportunity cost, the exchange of labour, all these things still exist, no matter how pure one's heart might be. The dotcom entrepreneurs, who also had dreams of changing the world, learned this the hard way, and today's sustainability entrepreneurs could learn from their failures.

 Any manifestation of the belief that, so long as intentions are pure, the end justifies the means.

The arrogance of good intentions can also tip people, and companies, over the edge into corruption. Research into how corruption begins has shown that many people engage in corrupt activities because they actually want to do good. Executives will pay a bribe because they fear that if they do not, the company will lose business and jobs could suffer. Corners are cut on health and safety in order to save the company money and help it keep a valuable contract. The executive promises himself or herself that 'this will happen only once', but then it happens again, and again, and after a while rule-breaking becomes normalised.

My concern is that this will happen, sooner or later, in some of the new sustainability industries where the eagerness to save the planet will start to trump the need to behave ethically towards one's fellow human beings. I have yet to hear of a recycling business employing child labour, or a wind farm company bribing local officials to get planning permission to build wind turbines, but I expect it is only a matter of time.

Cultures of mindless self-belief

What brings an entire group of managers, even an entire company, to adopt a culture of mindless self-belief? It starts with the view that the company and its people are in some way superior to others: to other companies, rivals and competitors, and also to stakeholders. At first, that belief may well be justified. Maybe the company really does have a highly advanced technology, or a superior business model, or smarter executives and employees. Whatever special competencies or assets the company has that make it stand out become a source of pride. And there it begins.

Some parents are proud of their children's achievements, but are aware too of their frailties and limitations. Others are mindlessly proud, and believe their children can do no wrong. One group understands reality; the other creates an alternative reality in which it sees the world the way it wants it to be. The same principle applies to corporate pride. We can be proud of our company and its achievements, but at the same time we have to ask: is our pride realistic? Are we seeing our company clearly, warts and all? Or are we wilfully blind, ignoring weaknesses and failings, concentrating on the strengths we can see, imagining other strengths where none exist? If the answer is yes to the latter, then we have the beginnings of a culture of mindless self-belief.

These cultures are incredibly easy to establish because, at heart, many of us want to believe that the companies we work for and manage are good and that our work has some meaning. (Companies where people don't care much about the business and simply turn up to do a job are never arrogant. They have other problems instead.) If a few of our peers or people we respect start to insist on the company's superiority, it is tempting to along with them and believe without questioning what they tell us. There is the crucial difference. *Questioning* self-belief can be a positive force, because it encourages us to re-examine ourselves and question our assumptions about ourselves. *Mindless* self-belief, on the other hand, does not admit questions or dissent. Like members of a cult, or football fans, we go on believing in our idols until they collapse in ruins.

The paradox of pride and humility

Earlier in this chapter, I referred to companies being 'too big and too successful'. Surely, it is not possible to be 'too successful?' Well, yes, it is, if you let yourself be so dazzled by your own success that you can no longer see the company clearly. We saw earlier how individuals can have their heads turned by success, and this is true of organizations as well. Once the idea of 'greatness' – and there are few more pernicious ideas in business than the idea of 'great leaders' or 'great organizations' – gets into a corporate culture, it exercises a subtle distorting effect on how the company sees itself, and the rest of the world.

I am *not* saying that growth and success are things to be avoided. I *am* saying that they have to be handled carefully, and the business needs to continue to live by its values and remember why it was created in the first place. Sydney Finkelstein speaks of 'protecting companies from their own excellence', ensuring that successful companies do not take their success so seriously that they become blinded by their own reputation and self-image. This is a danger that needs to be taken very seriously. At all costs, the company must retain the ability to analyse itself rationally and see the flaws as well as the successes.

The antidote to arrogance is humility, and it is my belief that every organization must have an element of humility about it, whether it is

McKinsey's 'insecure overachievers' or Tata's executives who look beyond profit to the social impacts of their business and constantly ask themselves why they are doing what they are doing.[23] I have cited Tata earlier in this chapter, and I hold them up again as an example of how pride and humility, concepts that would seem to be the opposite of each other, can coexist in an organization. The Tata Group is India's largest business group with operations on every continent except Antarctica, and its corporate brand is one of the fifty most valuable in the world. As a business entity it is incredibly proud of its reputation, its history and its achievements. At the same time, there is also a deep understanding of why the group was founded, its mission and its purpose, which are to contribute to the communities where it operates. As R. Gopalakrishnan, deputy director at Tata Sons, once told me, 'profit is a by-product of what we do'. And what they do is, provide service.

Pride and humility coexist elsewhere too. As a contrast to the exalted Olympians, consider Data General Corporation, the American computer maker that had its headquarters in a plain brick building in an industrial park, away from the public eye. The only adornment to the spartan lobby of the building was Data General's first computer, which printed out regular updates on the company's stock price.[24] That is quiet confidence; it is not arrogance.

In fact, pride and humility probably need each other. Pride without humility leads to arrogance, while humility without pride leads to lack of ambition. Humility enables us to be proud and at the same time gives us leave to doubt; we know we must question ourselves from time to time. Pride enables us to ask those questions clearly, and to confront the answers squarely and do something about them.

How do we breed more humility into organizations? Selection has to be one of the keys to this. FIGJAM types should be identified and weeded out; psychometrics can be valuable here, experience and intuition even more so. Leaders also need to set an example; their humility will be imitated by the rest of the organization. Finally, all staff need to be gently reminded of what the company is for, why it exists. Mechanisms need to be put in place – seminars, values days, breakouts, social events, it doesn't matter – which will allow them to ask questions about the company and itself and receive honest answers. And above all, everyone from top to bottom needs to remember: it is not who you are that makes you successful, it is what you do, and how well you do it.

We have been talking about cultures, but if we come back to where this chapter started, with individuals, I think the same principle applies to us as people, too. We need to remember why we do what we do, and do it with humility and a sense of purpose that goes beyond ourselves. It could be argued that I myself am guilty of a double standard here – there are few things more arrogant than writing a book, telling other people how to run their businesses – but in mitigation I would plead that I have written this book not to gratify my own ego but because I really do care about how businesses are run.

And, if you are still reading by this point and have not thrown the book at the wall, then I assume so do you.

---

1 Margaret Heffernan, *Wilful Blindness: Why We Ignore the Obvious at Our Peril*, London: Simon & Schuster, 2011.

2 Joe Haines, *Maxwell*, London: Futura, 1988.

3 Jamie Oliver and Tony Goodwin, *How They Blew It: The CEOs and Entrepreneurs Behind Some of the World's Most Catastrophic Business Failures*, London: Kogan Page, 2010.

4 http://www.mirror.co.uk/sport/football/news/real-madrid-boss-jose-mourinho-1260409

5 Adrian Furnham, *The Elephant in the Boardroom*, Basingstoke: Palgrave Macmillian, 2010, p. 73.

6 Furnham, *The Elephant in the Boardroom*; Kets de Vries, *Leaders, Fools and Impostors*; Sydney Finkelstein, *Why Smart Executives Fail*, London: Penguin, 2003.

7 Gerald Ratner, *The Rise and Fall... and Rise Again*, Oxford: Capstone, 2007.

8 http://fortune.com/2013/12/27/11-most-scandalous-business-events-of-2013/;   http://www.huffingtonpost.com/tag/walmart-bribery-scandal/

9 Louis V. Gerstner, *Who Says Elephants Can't Dance? How I Turned Around IBM*, New York: HarperCollins, 2003.

10 Oliver and Goodwin, *How They Blew It*, p. 19.

11 Clayton Christensen, *The Innovator's Dilemma: When New Technologies Cause Great Firms to Fail*, Boston: Harvard Business Review Press, 1997.

12 'Diet Firm in Dilemma', http://articles.latimes.com/1987-06-24/business/fi-6279_1_diet-product

13 Sheth, *The Self-Destructive Habits of Good Companies*, p. 75.

[14] Andrew Grove, *Only the Paranoid Survive: How to Exploit the Crisis Points that Challenge Every Company and Career*, New York: HarperCollins, 1996.

[15] A good accessible treatment is Edgar H. Schein, *Organizational Culture and Leadership*, New York: Wiley, 2010, but there are many other works out there.

[16] Margaret Heffernan is particularly emphatic about the danger of what she calls 'the cult of cultures'; see Heffernan, *Wilful Blindness*, p. 161 ff.

[17] Finkelstein, *Why Smart Executives Fail*, p. 173.

[18] http://www.nytimes.com/2007/11/14/business/14seaweed.html?pagewanted=all

[19] Robert Owen, *A Statement Regarding the New Lanark Establishment*, Edinburgh: Molendinar Press, 1812.

[20] On Hawthorne, see Elton Mayo, *The Human Problems of an Industrial Civilization*, New York: Macmillan, 1933. More recent studies of motivation in the workplace are far too numerous to mention.

[21] James Burnham, *The Managerial Revolution*, London: Putnam.

[22] George Siedel and Helena Haapio, *Proactive Law for Managers: A Hidden Source of Competitive Advantage*, Aldershot: Ashgate, 2010.

[23] http://www.businessinsider.com/mckinsey-hiring-policy-2013-9; Morgen Witzel, *Tata: The Evolution of a Corporate Brand*, Delhi: Penguin India, 2010.

[24] Tracey Kidder, *The Soul of a New Machine*, New York: Random House, 1998.

Chapter 5

Deer caught in the headlights

The title of this chapter comes from Kenichi Ohmae's *The Mind of the Strategist*. In this book, Ohmae observes that executives who lack experience of strategy making are often very bad at dealing with crises. When a threat appears, they behave like deer caught in the headlights of a car at night. They see danger coming, but don't understand the nature of the threat and don't know how to react.[1] Paralyzed by not knowing what to do, they continue to stand in the middle of the road until they are run over and killed.

Many of my academic colleagues dislike *The Mind of the Strategist*, claiming that it is not rigorous or based on empirical data. That is a bit like hating a salad because it doesn't have meat in it. The book was never meant to be empirical; it was intended as a reflection on the art of strategy making by someone who had been there and done it. Ohmae's argument is that much of the formal strategic planning so beloved of academics (in his own day, and to a lesser extent still today) is a waste of time. Rather than indulging in long-winded strategic planning exercises, Ohmae says, executives should instead *think* about strategy, all the time. Strategy is not something that happens once a year; it goes on constantly around us. Ohmae believes that executives should train themselves in strategic thinking. Boxers practise daily in the gym before a fight, symphony orchestras spend hours in rehearsals before a performance, and so by the same token executives should devote substantial portions of their time practising the arts of strategy, getting ready for the real thing.

In reality, most executives don't do this and strategic thinking is not something that occupies large portions of their time. As a result, the people who are responsible for strategy often don't know very much about making strategy, and even less about implementing it. The last is particularly important. Anyone can think up a strategy, but making it work, as Lawrence Hrbeniak reminds us in *Making Strategy Work*, requires knowledge, insight and skill.[2]

This brings us to the second deadly sin of management, which is ignorance. The word 'ignorance' often has a derogatory connotation, but that is to misuse the word. Ignorance, says the *Oxford English Dictionary* simply, is 'the lack of knowledge', which in a business context also includes lack of skill. Some people may be ignorant through no fault of their own, they may lack essential training or the experience which gives them insights. They should not be blamed for this.

However, promoting people who lack knowledge into positions of power, giving them control over assets and people that they have no idea how to manage, and asking them to make decisions which they are not equipped to make are wrong, and the people who knowingly sanction those promotions deserve our condemnation.

As with arrogance, there are several kinds of ignorance. Inexperience is a common cause of ignorance; the more we do, the more we learn, but some managers are promoted too far, too fast, too soon before they have time to acquire the knowledge they need. If too many managers are promoted in this way, the inexperience of the company can be exposed with fatal results.

Lacking knowledge, some managers become deer trapped in the headlights. Others go the other way and become overconfident, trusting in their own ability to carry them through. They are unaware that there are important gaps in their knowledge that will likely cause them to fail, no matter how clever or well intentioned they are. Sometimes they get lucky and succeed; much more often, they do not.

Another common form of ignorance is narrow-mindedness, the deliberate shutting out of knowledge. Narrow-minded people adopt mental blinkers that make them incapable of seeing or understanding the world around them; it is, if you like, another form of wilful blindness.

A special form of ignorance is ignorance of the past, which can take two forms. First, there is the simple lack of knowledge of anything before the present day, which can lead companies into the trap of path dependence. Knowledge of the past is essential if path dependence is to be broken. Second, there is the denial of the importance of the past, where executives and companies refuse to learn lessons from the past on the grounds that it is supposedly irrelevant.

Then finally there is the *ignorance of ignorance*, also known as sheer stupidity, which is more common than it should be (Table 5.1).

Table 5.1 A Typology of Ignorance

Type	Manifestation
The ignorance of inexperience	*We have no idea what to do next*
The ignorance of overconfidence	*Don't worry, we can handle anything they throw at us*
The ignorance of narrow-mindedness	*We don't recognize this situation, therefore we refuse to deal with it*
The ignorance of the past	*(1) We're not sure why we're doing what we're doing, but we can't think of anything else to do (2) The past is irrelevant. Only the future matters*
The ignorance of ignorance	*Huh?*

Ignorance, like arrogance, starts with individuals but can quickly become a culture infecting an entire organization. Ignorant companies lack critical types of knowledge. They can do some things quite well, but others are beyond their competence. In his famous article in *Harvard Business Review*, 'Marketing Myopia', Theodore Levitt also used the metaphor of blindness.[3] Companies fail to see what is going on around them, and because they cannot see they cannot understand. Instead of proceeding with deliberate steps towards a carefully identified goal, as strategic planners like to think they do, most companies actually spend most of their time groping in the dark.

Ignorance leads to bad decisions, and bad decisions kill companies: sometimes quickly, sometimes very slowly and painfully. It is rare, in cases of business failure, to find that a single decision is responsible for the crash. More commonly it is a series of decisions, a concatenation of mistakes, that brings the company to its knees. Very often too, we find that any one of those bad decisions could have been avoided and the chain of events halted, if only the company and its executives had known what they were doing. The problem lies not in the mistakes themselves. It lies in the culture that allows them – even encourages them – to be made.

Black swans and inflection points

In *The Black Swan*, Nassim Nicholas Taleb unwittingly threw a lifebelt to ignorant managers and leaders.[4] Taleb's thesis is that the world is full of uncertainty, and 'black swans', or 'highly improbable events' can emerge at any time to throw a strategy off course. Black swan events are outside our previous experience; we cannot imagine the possibility of them occurring, and thus we have no way of predicting them. Taleb argued that we should put less effort into trying to predict the future, and instead embrace uncertainty and be ready for the unexpected.

The book's intention was to get people thinking about and preparing for the unexpected, but unfortunately the law of unintended consequences has kicked in and the opposite has happened. I now hear, almost as a matter of routine, managers refer to almost any crisis – particularly one where they failed to react in time – as a 'black swan event'. 'It was one of those black swan events', they say, 'so of course we could do nothing about it.' 'Losing that client came completely out of nowhere, a real black swan event.' This is often accompanied by a shrug of the shoulders. Too bad it happened, but there you are. Black swan event. What could we do?

 People describing even relatively minor failures as black swan events.

This is a massive intellectual cop-out which rests on several fallacies. First, just because *I* failed to predict something would happen doesn't mean that *no one* could have predicted it. A more intelligent, more experienced and better educated person in my position might well have done so. Second, just because an event is unpredictable doesn't absolve me of responsibility for dealing with it. And finally, even with genuine black swan events, while it may be impossible to predict exactly what will happen, there are nearly always warning signs that show us that *something* is about to happen. If we can read the warning signs, we can at least brace ourselves for the impact, giving us a better chance of riding out the shock.

In *Only the Paranoid Survive*, Andrew Grove also talks about the impact that big unexpected events – he terms them 'strategic inflection points' – can have. Grove says that adaptable, flexible companies are better able to meet these challenges, while those that are inflexible and slow to change are more likely go under. One of the essential prerequisites of flexibility is knowledge, and I would argue that conversely, inflexibility is often a direct result of ignorance. We cannot be flexible because we don't know how to do so, and have no experience of doing so.

Not knowing what to do in a crisis is part of the *ignorance of inexperience*. The other part is the tendency by inexperienced managers and leaders to set off blindly in the wrong direction and do the wrong things. Sometimes, often even worse, companies set off blindly in the wrong direction and do the *right* things, what Sidney Finkelstein refers to as 'strategic misintent'.[5] Some would argue that this is preferable to doing nothing at all, but I disagree. A bad strategy, brilliantly executed, is still a bad strategy.

One of the classic cases of a bad strategy well executed is Long-Term Capital Management, the now infamous hedge fund founded in 1994. Its strategy was based on a complex mathematical model which showed how the hedge fund could hypothetically make money out of trading government bonds. Convinced that the model would work, LTCM ploughed billions into bonds. Initially it invested in fairly low-risk deals but as time passed and the supply of low-risk bonds dried up, the fund began making higher risk investments as well. There was only one problem; the model was flawed. It worked well when markets were stable, but when the Asian financial crisis of 1997 struck, the model began to come apart at the seams. LTCM racked up losses of more than $4 billion, and after a massive government bailout the fund was wound up in 2000.[6]

What went wrong? LTCM relied on its model and its theory of how markets *should* work. It lost touch with the reality of how markets *do* work. What makes this more surprising is that LTCM had a core of executives with many years of experience and also had two Nobel Prize-winning economists on its board. But this model had led them into new territory, and no one quite knew how it would work because no one had tried it before. Somewhere along the line, someone should have said: hold on, everyone, what happens if the model doesn't work? But that doesn't seem to have happened.

The Swiss national airline, Swissair, is an example of a potentially good strategy that failed through poor execution. In the 1990s, Swissair set out on an ambitious expansion strategy with the intention of strengthening its position in the increasingly competitive European airlines market. Many other airlines were merging, but Swissair rejected merger in favour of a growth strategy which would help it to keep pace with its rivals. Instead of embarking on full acquisitions, Swissair chose instead to take minority shareholdings in other airlines, including crucially a large stake in the troubled Belgian airline Sabena. Swissair thus invested large – ultimately, unsustainably large – sums in other firms, but without gaining control over those firms. In many cases those other airlines had severe problems of their own, problems which, thanks to its minority position, Swissair was unable to influence. The inevitable happened; losses mounted, and Swissair went into liquidation in 2001.

The growth strategy was a complex one, but it should have been possible to make it work had the right investments been made in the right companies (i.e. not Sabena). Lack of knowledge played a crucial role in the failure. Examining the disaster afterwards, Stewart Hamilton and Alicia Micklethwayt concluded that the board of Swissair weren't up to the job.[7] 'We got overwhelmed with so-called analysis', complained one executive; presumably it was 'so-called' analysis because he didn't understand it. Hamilton and Micklethwayt refer to the board of directors as 'distinguished but ineffective', and that 'none of the directors had any airline experience to speak of'.[8] Like Lehman Brothers, Swissair had attempted a strategy that was beyond the competence of its directors to carry out.

 Significant numbers of people in senior positions who have no prior experience of that role.

One of the odd things about the ignorance of inexperience is that very few managers are prepared to admit that it exists, at least in public.

There seems to be a kind of weird pseudo-masonic fraternity, especially in certain sectors, which leads managers to try to cover up for other managers, even when they work for rival firms. A few years ago I worked on a book in which my co-authors and I opened the story with some notable examples of recent business failures: Société Générale, Lehman Brothers and BP. When one of the co-authors showed the draft to his colleagues, they reacted with consternation. These could not be considered business failures! These were bolts from the blue, something which no company could anticipate! These were black swan events! How could we blame managers for failing to foresee the unforeseeable?

I encountered something similar in 2014 when I wrote a short article for *The Conversation* about Malaysia Airlines in the aftermath of the MH370 disaster, when an airliner was apparently hijacked, veered off course and was never seen again. The airline was criticized for its apparent neglect of the relatives of passengers – messages of condolence to the bereaved were sent out late, and in some cases were delivered by text message – and its share price tumbled. I suggested that a better grasp of disaster management would have helped boost the airline's reputation and its financial position. After publication I received a fair amount of feedback, the great majority of it hostile. How dare I criticize Malaysia Airlines? The situation was unprecedented, nothing like this had ever happened before! How should the airline know what to do? Black swan event!

In fact, most of these so-called 'unforeseeable' events are perfectly foreseeable had anyone bothered to look. Barings' rogue trader Nick Leeson was only able to continue to carry on his fraudulent trades because the managers to whom he reported failed to exercise due supervision over him. The idea that the *Deepwater Horizon* explosion, fire and oil spill were 'unforeseeable' is nonsense; these are exactly the kinds of events that managers engaged in deep-water drilling *should* be foreseeing, it is what they are *paid* to do. And as we saw in Chapter 3, the problems at Lehman Brothers were absolutely apparent – provided managers and directors pulled their heads up out of the sand and looked around them. It really is time that managers stopped defending colleagues who are not able to discharge their duties and started acknowledging that ignorance is a killer of companies – and people.

Where angels fear to tread

Overconfidence, as noted, often derives from inexperience. Experience tends to bring wisdom, and though it can also bring arrogance – see the discussion on the arrogance of past success in the previous chapter – if deployed properly it can help us towards a more realistic picture of the world.

For entrepreneurs, the *ignorance of overconfidence* is almost an occupational hazard. It is interesting to watch contestants on the television programme *Dragon's Den* – not exactly a scientific sample, I know, but an useful cross section all the same – and see how many come before the panel with vastly inflated expectations of their business and its prospects. The most realistic entrepreneurs are nearly always ones with prior business experience – and especially, experience of success.

In *A Culture of Purpose*, Christoph Luenenburger talks about the Dunning-Kruger effect, which leads people to overestimate their own abilities. 'It's a cognitive bias of not knowing what one doesn't know', says Luenenburger, 'and wrongly assuming that one knows quite a bit.'[9] The presence of enough overconfident people can lead to an entire culture of overconfidence in which the company believes its ability to innovate or grow or influence the market to be much greater than it actually is.

Overconfidence leads companies to reach for the stars, only to discover too late that their arms aren't nearly long enough. The idea of a 'blue ocean strategy' is very seductive; the subtitle of Kim and Mauborgne's book of that name is 'how to create uncontested market space and make the competition irrelevant', and who wouldn't want that?[10] The desire to get ahead, get out in front, get on top is so great that companies start investing in areas where they have little or no competence, hoping that they if they throw enough money at the problem something will happen. But, as Patrick Barwise and Seán Meehan have pointed out, very often all that happens is that you lose a lot of money. Most attempts at breakthrough innovation end in failure.[11]

This does not mean you should not attempt to innovate, far from it; Barwise and Meehan see innovation as essential to growth. But innovation needs to be *realistic* and grounded in what the company can do. Polaroid was a wonderfully inventive company that created dozens of new products and several breakthrough technologies, but Polaroid was a unique company with a culture and business model that supported blue skies research. Most companies do not have such a model, but some behave as if they do.

In fairness, Wang Laboratories was a knowledge-rich organization which grew out of research conducted at Harvard by a brilliant scientist, An Wang. When he established his company, Wang announced that his goal was to be as big as IBM, and he carried in his pocket a chart showing how this goal would one day be realized. In fact, he had only a fraction of the resources available to IBM, in part because IBM had annual sales more than fifteen times those of Wang. We can applaud An Wang for his ambition, but he was not being realistic. A more focused ambition on an achievable goal might have helped Wang Laboratories to survive. Instead, obsessed by growth, unable to fund expansion at the pace desired and losing its technological edge, the company declined. Wang Laboratories went bankrupt in 1992.

    Unrealistic plans and expectations.

Overconfidence also comes from arrogance and the detachment from reality that the latter brings. Marconi embarked on an ambitious expansion strategy in the late 1990s confident that its great reputation would soon make it a major player in the technology sector. But Marconi's executives failed to read the market. Unrealistic targets for growth were set, and when the bottom fell out of the market during the bursting of the dotcom bubble, Marconi crashed too. By 2003 its share price had slumped to almost nothing, and the remnants of the company were eventually sold.

As the old saying goes, 'fools rush in where angels fear to tread'. But overconfidence is not necessarily folly (even though it might look like it at the time). Overconfidence is born out of not knowing, of being unaware one of one's own limitations and just how hard it will be to execute a given strategy. Remember, once again, that most failures are failures of execution. Overestimating one's own abilities and what can be accomplished in a given time frame is one of the major causes of execution failure.

The poverty of imagination

The world of management includes some nasty, narrow-minded and shallow people, and when they cluster together they create nasty, narrow-minded and shallow company cultures. In the last chapter I referred to the arrogance of disdain for others and the treatment meted out to women and minorities in some workplaces. It is clear, however, that a good deal of this disdain is rooted in the *ignorance of narrow-mindedness*. Let us look at treatment of women as an example.

Masculine ignorance of women is hardly a new subject for discussion, but the scale of it still remains breath-taking. Consider the history of women in sport. At first it was held that women should not play sports at all, as they were too delicate and fragile (a view still held in boxing until a few years ago). Then women began to play sport anyway, and survived. Next it was argued that women should give up competitive sport once they got married, as they needed to concentrate on their primary role as homemakers. But married women started playing sports and society did not break down. Then it was ordained that women must retire from competitive sport after having children, as the stresses of childbirth would render them physically incapable of competing. However, some women who had children took up sport again, and guess what? They were just as good as they were before.

For every activity that women might want to undertake, from riding in railway carriages to voting in elections to managing large and complex organizations, there has been a body of opinion (sometimes backed up by 'scientific evidence') saying that women should not/could not/must not do these things. Rare indeed has been the man who, like Vietnamese president Ho Chi Minh, was willing to proclaim that 'women are half of humanity' and decree that they were to be considered fully equal to men. Common even now are people like Sepp Blatter, president of football's international governing body FIFA, who suggested that women's football would be more popular if the players wore tighter shorts.

The stereotyping of women in business is just as strong as elsewhere. Even efforts to support women in business are sometimes tinged with sexism. I have on my desk an otherwise excellent book, *Beyond the Boy's Club*, which offers advice to women on how to build a career in the man's world of management.[12] But the cover writing and motifs are in a pretty, girly pink, presumably because that is the colour women are supposed to like. I am willing to bet that whoever approved the cover was a man.

Women in management are often damned if they do and damned if they don't, and the higher they climb on the corporate ladder the worse it gets. They are deemed too 'feminine', too 'soft' to handle the hurly-burly of management life; yet if they do prove themselves by standing up to their male colleagues, they are castigated for not being feminine enough. Carly Fiorino, during her stint as CEO of Hewlett-Packard, was described by male colleagues as being thrusting, competitive, feisty and sometimes abrasive. These are qualities that, in a male manager, would be seen as virtues. Presumably Fiorino was expected to run a global company while making cupcakes at the same time, just to prove how feminine she was.

Lynda Gratton reminds us how female managers are stereotyped by their family circumstances and described as 'mothers' or 'wives' as if that were their primary identity.[13] Even the left-wing British newspaper *The Guardian* recently described a newly appointed female chairman as a 'mother of three'. If there was a league table for the ignorance of narrow-mindedness, that should get some sort of prize.

What goes on in the minds of men – and some women – who take this attitude is hard to say. Probably, it is not very much. Ho Chi Minh was of course incontrovertibly right: women are half of humanity, and by refusing to take advantage of their skills, talents and experience, executives might as well try to manage with one arm cut off. The same goes for ethnic minorities, people of different gender orientation and the disabled. Each represents a pool of possible talent that cannot and must not be overlooked.

The dangers of recruiting boards and executive and managerial teams from people who look like us are well known. There is every chance that they will also *think* like us, and thus there will be no challenge and nothing to keep us from sinking into the cocoon of complacency. Studies of organizational culture show almost universally that companies with a diverse mix of people in their workforce perform better and are more innovative than those run exclusively by heterosexual white guys. This not just a Western problem; enlightened business leaders in India are starting to learn the value of recruiting more women and outsiders onto their boards, and even those fossils of yesterday's grandeur, Japanese boards, are beginning slowly to open up. But, for the most part, the dinosaurs still rule.

 Intolerance of or prejudice against 'people who aren't like us'; casual sexism and/or racism.

The reason why I have talked about this issue at such length is that it also signals narrow-mindedness in other ways. People who refuse to consider the idea of women on boards of directors or in senior finance posts, for example, are equally likely to challenge anything new that is thrust at them. These people are not flexible in their thinking. They cannot understand any view other than their own. I cite again the example of Chip Wilson of Lululemon, mentioned in the last chapter, whose response to a crisis involving his products was to disparage his customers. His words were offensive, but they also showed a refusal to engage with the business problem. The sexist FIFA chief Sepp Blatter is also known for his refusal to engage with innovations such as goal line technology, making football the only major world sport not to offer technological assistance to referees.

Narrow-minded thinking is a form of ignorance because it deliberately excludes not only some kinds of people but also some kinds of knowledge. Narrow-mindedness refuses to see that there might be more than one solution to a problem, or that to make a strategy work, some previously held notions might have to be challenged and jettisoned. Narrow-mindedness sticks to the same old routines, preferring to drive the ocean liner into the iceberg rather than change course. Ford filled his company with yes-men, and nearly ruined a powerful business. Lehman Brothers failed to acknowledge the reality around it, and fell.

Path dependence

Ignorance of the past manifests itself in two principal forms. The first is a simple lack of knowledge of what has gone before, where the company has come from and what key decision have been made that shape the company today. Without this knowledge, there is a serious danger that the company will fall into what economists call *path dependence*, a kind of intellectual lock-in that affects many companies to a degree, and is particularly common among large, highly successful ones.

The basic premise of path dependence, or path dependency, is that any decision we take, whether we know it or not, is constrained by previous decisions that we or others have taken. Suppose we are in the car business, and we detect a surge in the market for, say, cars with hybrid engines. We take a decision to invest a large sum in developing our own hybrid cars and marketing them. That commits us to a strategy in this direction. Any future decision we then take about the strategy of the company must take into account the consequences of that earlier decision. We can try to change or reverse that decision at a later date, but that decision will have consequences of its own, and it too will constrain later thinking.

Path dependence creates a kind of snowball effect, and the more decisions we take to steer the company in a particular direction, the harder it becomes to change direction. Most organizations, once they have started down a particular path, will choose to follow it through to the end rather than turning away in a new direction because that is the easiest option. Businesses become *dependent* on decisions made years or even decades earlier about strategy – and perhaps especially dependent on early decisions about values and goals.

A famous example is the American railway industry. As Levitt describes in 'Marketing Myopia', the railway companies were founded and led by engineers and railway men. Their thinking was accordingly path dependent; they saw themselves as being in the *railway* industry, and that is how they behaved and thought. In reality, says Levitt, they were in the *transportation* industry and their real competitors were not other railways, but airlines and road haulage companies. The railway companies could have diversified and tried to compete with their transportation rivals but their path dependence, their mental lock-in to the railway industry was such that they did not know how to do so.

The problem, Levitt went on to say, affects many companies to some degree, especially those which are led by technologists and engineers. These leaders concentrate 'on what they know and what they can control, namely product research, engineering and production. The emphasis on production becomes particularly attractive when the product can be made at declining unit costs. There is no more inviting way of making money than by running the plant full blast'.[14] Ford certainly fell into this trap, and his devotion to building ever larger and ever more complex production facilities such as River Rouge was one of the proximate causes of the company's eventual downfall and near collapse.

 No one ever questions the efficacy of a strategy once it is set in motion.

Is it possible to break out of path dependence? Yes, of course. Nokia transformed itself from a forest products company to a technology company. IBM managed a sideways shift from being known primarily as a computer maker to a new operation with an emphasis on software and consulting. In *Rejuvenating the Mature Business*, Charles Baden-Fuller and John Stopford showed how companies can effectively reinvent themselves and extend their lifespan.[15] But in order to make these changes, one first has to be aware that path dependence exists, and what factors caused the company to follow the road it is now on. Once the full nature of the constraints is known, a realistic view can be formed about changing direction and the resources and effort that will be required to manage this strategic change successfully.

However, many executives never realize the extent to which they and their organizations are path dependent. They believe that their decision-making is free and unfettered, that they have a wide choice of options before them. They don't even feel the chains that time has wrapped around them; until, suddenly, they face seismic crisis and realize that the real options available are hopelessly limited and inadequate, thanks to choices made years or even decades earlier.

Path dependence manifests itself in little ways too, for example in the procedures that we use in the workplace for reporting and control. How many consultants over the years have gone into an organization and asked why things are done in a particular way, to receive the answer: 'We've always done it this way.' No one knows the real reason, which is lost in the mists of time. Somewhere, someone decided this is how things should be done, and thus that is how they are done. And then, when everything breaks down, no one knows why. (*Black swan event!*)

Here again, most path-dependent organizations are not aware that they are dependent. They carry on with their established routines because they believe that how they do things is the best way to do it, not because this is how it has always been done. When, like crack smokers who suddenly wake up to the realization that they are addicts, they notice they are doing things wrong, it still requires a major effort of will for them to change. Revising procedures requires the effort of devising new ones, and then training staff to follow the new procedures. Most of the time it is easier just to keep on with the old ways.

 Set routines and procedures, the purpose and utility of which are never questioned.

The past is a foreign country

'History is bunk', said Henry Ford, which is quite amusing, given that he is now part of it.

Path dependence leads to an unthinking complacency, getting stuck in a mental and intellectual groove. The other side of ignorance of the past is denial: the view expressed by Ford and many others that the past is not relevant, and only the future matters.

Proponents of this view point out that the past cannot be reliably used to predict the future. This is quite true, but two points need to be remembered. The first is that although it cannot predict the future, the past is extremely important when it comes to explaining the present.

Second, as Taleb says, predicting the future is impossible anyway, so why do we waste so much time trying?

'The past is a foreign country', wrote L.P. Hartley in his novel *The Go-Between*, 'they do things differently there.' True, but as we know from our own experience of going to foreign countries, they also do many things the same way, and we see much that is familiar and recognizable as well as much that is different. In business, much has changed and is still changing, but we must not forget that there are also some things that remain the same and always have. For example, businesses have always relied on customers to buy their products and services, and the simple fact is that if there are no customers there will soon be no business. Smart businesses for the last several thousand years have known this and adopted what the gurus call 'customer-focused strategy', or what I refer to as 'strategy'.

Not everyone gets this. A colleague recalls giving a lecture on the importance of creating satisfied customers and putting the customer at the centre of the business model. A puzzled marketing executive button-holed him after the lecture. 'I found your talk really interesting', he said, 'but I must say, this idea of putting the customer first is completely counter-intuitive.'

That was the mistake, or one of them, made by the dotcom entrepreneurs of the late 1990s, the first wave of Internet retailers who put technology first and customers somewhere further down the line of priorities. They developed splendid marketing pitches and excellent interfaces allowing customers to buy goods, but having relieved customers of their money they forgot about one important thing: how, after purchase, to send goods promptly and swiftly to their new owners. Errors and delays in fulfilment killed off many of these companies, especially the infamous fashion retailer Boo.com.[16]

Had they been less convinced of the superiority of their 'new' model and looked back at their ancestors, the pioneering cataloguing retailers Montgomery Ward and Sears, the dotcom retailers could have learned some useful lessons. Both Sears and Montgomery Ward put customers first, and invested in systems for getting goods to customers quickly and reliably. Both survived and prospered, while Boo and others like it did not. This is just one example of learning from the past; there are many, many others.

But the cult-like belief in change is strong, and some like Tom Peters have even argued that there should be change for change's sake. In *Thriving on Chaos*, Peters says that the mantra 'if it ain't broke, don't fix it', should be replaced by 'if it ain't broke, fix it anyway'. This attitude leads to a great deal of unnecessary reinvention of the wheel. In particular, it is responsible for much corporate restructuring, every chief executive's fallback position when he or she can't think of anything else to do. The passion for restructuring that began in the 1960s shows no sign of ending. The damage done to morale and the value destroyed by failed restructurings have been incalculable. 'We trained hard', as one bitter screed says,

> but it seemed that every time we were beginning to form up into teams, we would be reorganised. I was to learn later in life that we tend to meet any new situation in life by reorganising; and a wonderful method it can be for creating the illusion of progress while producing confusion, inefficiency and demoralisation.[17]

Restructuring does however make consultants very happy. 'We love to see companies attempt restructuring', one confided in me. 'Four times out of five they make a mess of it, and then call us in to help them have a second bite at the cherry.' And sometimes a third, and a fourth.

 Constant churn and reorganization; a belief in change for change's sake.

Directed, purposeful change with a clear goal in mind is essential, and the ability to make such changes smoothly and quickly can be a huge source of strength. But there is no merit in change for its own sake. Change without focus or direction very often destroys value rather than creating it. And continuity is always with us, whether we recognize it or not. Some things do *not* change. Next time someone tells you pompously that 'change is the only constant', point out that this was first said by British Prime Minister Benjamin Disraeli in 1867, and see if they get the irony.

The ignorance of ignorance

There isn't really much to be said about the *ignorance of ignorance*, or stupidity, except to repeat the point that there is far too much of it in management. Once again the management confraternity will doubtless take umbrage: 'how dare Witzel suggest that managers are stupid?' Well, some are, and here is an example.

In 2014, someone at fashion retailer Zara thought it would be a good idea to market a children's T-shirt with dark and light horizontal stripes and a yellow star on the chest. The T-shirt bore a disturbing resemblance to the uniforms worn by Jewish concentration camp prisoners during the Holocaust. There was an immediate outcry and Zara withdrew the offending T-shirts at once, but its public statement suggested that the company didn't really know what the fuss was about. The T-shirt was meant to have a Wild West theme, a Zara spokesman said, and the star was not a Star of David but had eight points like a sheriff's badge. Where was the harm in that?

The *Financial Times*, reporting the story, slapped Zara lightly over the wrist (although it did note that a few years earlier Zara had been forced to withdraw a handbag decorated with a swastika) and commented, 'Designing children's clothes and costumes can be fraught with difficulty.'[18] Well of course it can, if you are a bloody fool. How many people in the western hemisphere are genuinely unaware of those potent, haunting images of gaunt, half-dead people in striped uniforms and yellow stars that Allied troops found when they liberated the death camps? And how does someone so ignorant and uneducated as to have *not* seen those images rise to a position of responsibility? For it is not just the designer who was at fault here; someone in management must have seen that design and approved it.

 The presence of large numbers of people who clearly aren't up to their jobs.

As it happens, Zara's prompt recall and apology probably did the company little harm. But customers will remember this, and another such incident will be harder to wriggle out from under. Zara has penalty points now: another offence could result in punishment.

Adrian Furnham is kinder than I, and refers to 'cognitively challenged' leaders and managers.[19] I'm Canadian and blunt, so I will say instead: some leaders and managers are idiots. Quite how they get promoted to these positions of power is not always certain, though nepotism usually plays a part somewhere along the line. If you find people like this in an organization, there must be no room for sentimentality or personal loyalty. Get them out. Do it as gently, kindly and sensitively as possible, but above all, do it quickly before they have chance to cause damage.

Cultures of unthinking action

The ignorance of individuals, such as happened at Zara (which is otherwise quite a smart company), causes damage but for the most part it can be contained. Real danger comes when cultures begin to privilege ignorance. They act either without knowing why they do so, or without full knowledge of the position they are in, or both. The result is *unthinking action*, blind, clumsy and slow.

The *ignorance of inexperience* is found in companies where there are not enough experienced people at senior levels and there is a genuine uncertainty as to what to do next. (Many of Enron's senior finance people, for example, had little experience of working at this level in a large and complex company.) Managers and directors either do not understand what is going on around them and do not see the signs of danger or else they do see the signs but misunderstand them. In time this leads to a culture where mistakes are considered acceptable: defects in manufacturing, shoddy goods delivered to consumers, accident and death in the workplace are considered the norm. A health and safety consultant tells me that one of the hardest issues he faces is getting clients to realize that work-related accidents are not just a cost of doing business.

In these cultures, people make mistakes without realizing they are doing so, and fail to take responsibility for their mistakes even once they are pointed out (*black swan event!*). The prevalent view is that we can't possibly know everything, so all we can do is muddle along and hope things turn out for the best. There is a danger that in the end this Eeyore-ish culture will turn into defeatism and managers, worn down by their inexperience and persistent failure, will stop even trying.

The *ignorance of overconfidence* is found in companies where there are people with a lot of brains but not as yet much experience. These companies try to run before they can walk. They start off with a can-do culture, which is a good thing, but again repeated failure can lead to a collapse in morale and the original optimistic spirit turning into defeatism. Bullish optimism needs to be backed up by competence, skill and experience. Otherwise there is a risk that the company will execute the wrong strategy brilliantly.

The *ignorance of narrow-mindedness* can be seen in cultures that deliberately exclude knowledge and people that don't fit with preconceived notions of what is 'right'. These cultures are, by choice, inflexible and unwilling to accept anything new or different. They are very dangerous.

The *ignorance of the past* manifests itself in either restricted decision-making, or a blind desire for change at all cost. Both come from a culture where the past is no longer valued, and where only the future is seen as important. This comes from a faulty understanding of what we can learn from the past and the connections between past, present and future.

What connects all of these is if course ignorance itself, the lack of knowledge. In some cases knowledge has not yet been acquired; in others, it has been deliberately excluded in an act of wilful blindness. Either way the result is the same. The lack of knowledge hamstrings businesses; it leads to poor decision-making and poor execution, and once again, these kill companies – and people. It is essential that we eradicate cultures where lack of knowledge is acceptable, and transform them into cultures where knowledge of all kinds, from all sources, is valued.

Putting knowledge at the heart of everything

Teaching a company to learn, turning it into a *genuine* learning organization, is the only cure for cultures of ignorance. This is not a new idea.

Writers on organizational knowledge, such as Peter Senge in *The Fifth Discipline*, Arie de Geus in *The Living Company* and Ikujiro Nonaka and Hirotaka Takeuchi in *The Knowledge-Creating Company*, have argued for the creation of 'knowledge organizations' or 'learning organizations' dedicated to the creation of knowledge through learning, which de Geus famously claimed to be the only sustainable source of competitive advantage.[20]

What do these terms actually mean? The term knowledge organization confuses some, who think it is a special type of organization. Is there an opposite, a 'stupid organization', perhaps? Anyone familiar with my bank might well be forgiven for thinking there is, but that is not the point that de Geus and the others are making. Their manifesto is that organizations need to put the gathering and management of knowledge at the heart of their business model. A knowledge organization is not one that just collects a lot of facts and hoards them in its library. It also uses knowledge to innovate and create. It sifts knowledge from many different sources – not least from the minds of its employees, which are endless fertile and creative if we know how to engage with them – and puts it to work to create value. It doesn't just do the same old things over and over because that it all it knows how to do; it searches for new things to do, and new ways of doing the same things better. This is what Barwise and Meehan advise in *Beyond the Familiar*: make yourselves experts in the art of incremental innovation by constantly looking for little things that you can do better.

Barwise and Meehan cite a number of examples of modern companies that do this, including Apple and Procter & Gamble. But the absolute master of knowledge management was a largely forgotten figure, Edward Cadbury. In the late nineteenth and early twentieth centuries, the Cadbury family turned a small English chocolate company into the global leader in the confectionery market, a position it held for more than forty years. Cadbury Brothers is remembered for its philanthropic activities, but the real genius of Cadbury was its model of knowledge management.

Edward Cadbury saw his employees as a vast source of knowledge and ideas. He developed several methods for engaging with employees and getting their ideas. There were suggestion schemes – not those fig-leaf schemes that some companies have, where employee suggestions end up in the waste bin, but real schemes where ideas were genuinely taken up and employees were rewarded. There were works committees, where management and workers sat down around a table and discussed strategy and innovation on an equal basis. Cadbury also hired employees of proven intellect who would be capable of working with and engaging with management. The result was an almost unique company where everyone participated in innovation and, as one observer noted, 'Everybody thinks'.

The Tata Group also has schemes that recognize employee innovation and also one that I have not encountered anywhere else: an awards scheme called 'Dare to Fail'. Every year, three employees from across the group are singled out and rewarded for innovation efforts *that didn't actually work*, but were so audacious and ingenious that the Group wants them to keep trying. Tata has cracked the secret of how to learn from failure; and once you can do that, you really are managing knowledge.

Creating a culture where knowledge is at the heart of everything requires intelligent selection, leadership commitment and leading by example and organizational structures that support knowledge and learning. Both Peter Senge in *The Fifth Discipline* and Nonaka and Takeuchi in *The Knowledge-Creating Company* offer recipes for how to do so. Open communication and incentives for creating and sharing knowledge are among the key ingredients. Creating a knowledge organization is hard work (when was management ever easy?) but the rewards, as Cadbury and Tata and Apple have shown, are phenomenal. Manage knowledge well, and your company will reach its goals. Fail, and ignorance will eventually drag it down.

As for individual managers, they must learn, learn, learn. There is no excuse for not learning. Start with your own organization, and learn everything you can about it. Learn its roots, its blind spots, its warts, its weaknesses as well as its strengths, *and make that knowledge stick*. I am amazed by the number of executives who don't know enough about their companies, largely because they spend all their time in their offices or on Skype and never get out into the field and get their shoes dirty.

If, six months after taking employment, you do not know all the essential details about the company you work for and are not familiar with all its operations, then you should be fired. Your boss should also be fired, for not making sure that you got out there and learned about the business.

Six months not long enough? For really big companies, a year. No more, and preferably much less. In a year's time, your inexperience and lack of understanding could have killed the company.

---

1 Kenichi Ohmae, *The Mind of the Strategist*, New York: McGraw-Hill, 1982.

2 Lawrence Hrbeniak, *Making Strategy Work: Effective Execution and Change*, Engelwood Cliffs: Prentice-Hall, 2013.

3 Theodore Levitt, 'Marketing Myopia', *Harvard Business Review*, September–October 1975, pp. 1–14.

4 Nassim Nicholas Taleb, *The Black Swan*, London: Penguin, 2010.

5 Finkelstein, *Why Smart Executives Fail*, p. 138.

6 See Finkelstein and, for more detail, Pablo Triana, *Lecturing Birds on Flying: Can Mathematical Theories Destroy the Financial Markets?* Chichester: John Wiley, 2009.

7 Stewart Hamilton and Alicia Micklethwayt, *Greed and Corporate Failure: The Lessons from Recent Disasters*, Basingstoke: Palgrave Macmillan 2006.

8 Hamilton and Micklethwayt, *Greed and Corporate Failure*, p. 131.

9 Christoph Luenenburger, *A Culture of Purpose: How to Choose the Right People and Make the Right People Choose You*, San Francisco: Jossey-Bass, 2104.

10 W. Chan Kim and Renée Mauborgne, *Blue Ocean Strategy: How to Create Uncontested Market Space and Make the Competition Irrelevant*, Boston: Harvard Business Review Press, 2004.

11 Patrick Barwise and Seán Meehan, *Beyond the Familiar: Long-Term Growth through Customer Focus and Innovation*, Chichester: Wiley, 2011.

12 Suzanne Doyle Morris, *Beyond the Boys' Club: Strategies for Achieving Career Success as a Woman*, Milton Keynes: Wit and Wisdom Press, 2009.

13 http://bsr.london.edu/blog/post-126/index.html

14 Levitt, 'Marketing Myopia', p. 10.

15 Charles Baden-Fuller and John Stopford, *Rejuvenating the Mature Business*, London: Routledge, 1992.

16 Ernst Malmsten, Erik Portanger and Charles Drazin, *Boo Hoo: A Dotcom Story*, New York: Random House, 2006.

17 This passage is attributed to the Roman satirist Petronius, but was probably written by a disgruntled British soldier some time in the late 1940s.

[18] http://www.ft.com/cms/s/0/40f2047a-2de5-11e4-8346-00144feabdc0.html

[19] Furnham, *The Elephant in the Boardroom*, p. 199.

[20] Peter M. Senge, *The Fifth Discipline: The Art and Practice of the Learning Organization*, New York: Doubleday, 1990; Arie de Geus, *The Living Company: Habits for Survival in a Turbulent Environment*, London: Nicholas Brealey, 1997; Ikujiro Nonaka and Hirotaka Takeuchi, *The Knowledge-Creating Company: How Japanese Companies Create the Dynamics of Innovation*, Oxford: Oxford University Press, 1995. The comment about learning becoming a source of sustainable competitive advantage comes from de Geus, 'Planning as Learning', *Harvard Business Review*, March-April 1988, pp. 70-4.

Chapter 6

The unhealthy yearning for precision

In *The Republic*, Plato explains how people can become so frightened of the world around them that they turn away from the world and reject it. He describes a group of people living in a cave, who believe that the shadows they can see on the cave walls are the only reality. When they are taken into the outside world for the first time, they are shocked, startled, afraid. Rejecting what they see, they retreat into the cave and stay there, preferring the illusion of the shadows to the reality of daylight.

The metaphor of the cave shows the connection between ignorance and our third deadly sin, fear. If arrogance leads some managers and companies to over-reach themselves, fear causes others to hold back. Personal timidity is part of the problem, and we have seen many examples in recent years of directors sitting on their hands and not making a fuss, when instead they should have been challenging their CEOs and demanding explanations. 'Their behaviour and record suggest they rarely accepted their legally prescribed function as the guardian of shareholder interests', write Leonard Sayles and Cynthia Smith in *The Rise of the Rogue Executive*, and like many other commentators they suggest that a desire on the part of directors for an easy life and a wish not to rock the boat have been significant factors in many corporate downfalls.[1] Lower-level managers, with their own careers to think of, are equally anxious not to make waves.

Directors and managers of large companies are well paid and have prestigious positions. But often – too often – their fear of losing these things outweighs their sense of duty.

However, timidity on the part of individuals is only the tip of the iceberg. Cultures of fear are embedded in many organizations. There is a persistent belief among managers and companies that business today is more risky than ever before. Acronyms like VUCA – volatile, uncertain, complex and ambiguous – are routinely used to describe the business environment. Like black swan events, VUCA has become a convenient excuse for managers who are too confused or too frightened to face the challenges of management head-on. It is, say Nathan Bennett and James Lemoine, 'easy to use VUCA as a crutch, a way to throw off the hard work of strategy and planning – after all, you can't prepare for a VUCA world, right?'[2]

Fear of uncertainty and fear of the unknown are two of the most important shackles on management thinking today. Managers try to deal with them by reducing risk and seeking certainty. Of course, there is no such thing as certainty, and paradoxically our attempts to reduce risk may actually increase it. For example, fear leads companies to hold back from doing what they should do, from making key investments in technology or important markets, because they cannot be certain they will get the desired return, and this lack of investment can be detrimental to the company's long-term position. We talked in the previous chapter about overconfidence, but underconfidence can be just as damaging.

The term 'risk appetite' is sometimes used to describe a company's tolerance for risk and ability to handle it. Risk appetite is affected by a number of factors, including the nature of the business the company is in – some types of business are inherently more risky than others – and the nature of the risks it faces, but probably the most important factor is the company's own culture. Companies with a strong culture of risk management know almost instinctively what the right level of risk is; companies whose cultures are weak in their understanding of risk are more likely to take either too many risks or too few. Either can kill a company.

There is another aspect of fear which needs to be mentioned, and that is fear of what postmodernists call 'the other', that is, people not like ourselves. Fear of the other, or at the very least lack of understanding of the other, is one of the reasons why so many businesses do so badly when they first try their hand at marketing or operating overseas. As the sociologist Michel Foucault has shown, when we are frightened of people not like ourselves, we tend to either run and hide from them or attempt to control them. Either can be dangerous. A company unable to face the real world will remain frightened and confused, like the people in Plato's cave (Table 6.1).

Table 6.1 A Typology of Fear

Type	Manifestation
Fear of uncertainty	*We can't do that, it's too risky*
Fear of the unknown	*We can't do that, we don't have a plan for it*
Fear of the 'other'	*We can't work with these people, they're not like us*
Personal timidity	*Don't rock the boat*

What are the roots of fear? Plato thought it was ignorance, and that education could reduce people's fears. Some fears are probably innate in certain people; I don't know if geneticists have found a 'fear gene' yet, but it is certainly the case that some people have less tolerance for risk than others, even when they come from very similar backgrounds. Personal circumstance and past history also play a role. People who are further up the hierarchy of needs and have more to lose are often more risk-averse than those at the bottom of the pyramid, who must take risks in order to survive.

Much the same is true of companies. Entrepreneurs take more risks than established companies because they have to, and many writers have remarked on the conservatism that comes with size and success because the company now has more to lose. Rosabeth Moss Kanter's *When Giants Learn to Dance*, one of the best-selling guru books of the 1990s, remains an excellent examination of the phenomenon and what to do about it.[3] Companies that have gone through a particularly turbulent period can also become inherently more 'fearful' and less willing to take risks. All these companies try to manage or eliminate risk through more precise measurement and control, leading to *cultures of anxious precision*.

Much depends on personalities. An overly cautious CEO can infect the rest of the board, who in turn pass their caution on to the rest of the organization. Once managers and employees learn that they will not be rewarded for taking risks, and perhaps even punished for doing so, they themselves will adopt a more cautious approach.

The mirage of certainty

How many times have you sat around a table with a team and heard someone ask, 'Are we certain this is the right decision?' It is of course the wrong question, for in business as in most of life there is no such thing as certainty. Certainty implies an absence of doubt, and in human affairs there is always doubt. Yet paradoxically, most people do not like doubt; lack of certainty makes them anxious, unhappy and afraid. That is why we ask if we are *certain* this is the right decision, in the hope that one day, one time the answer might actually be 'yes'.

Accordingly, our *fear of uncertainty* manifests itself in a drive to find certainty. We want to know what is going to happen next, and when we realize we cannot find out, we retreat into the cave. Some of us put our faith in God, or gods, others cling to science in the belief that it can provide the answers. We want predictive tests that will tell us whether we are going to get cancer or dementia, we want weather forecasts that will tell us exactly what the weather will be tomorrow and we want models that will tell us how our businesses will perform and what will happen for *certain* in the business environment.

The latter in particular will never happen. According to Lawrence LeShan and Henry Margenau, it is theoretically possible to create models that will tell us what will happen in a closed environment, that is, one where all variables can be measured and accounted for. In an open environment, where other variables can enter at random from outside, this is impossible.[4] Businesses operate in open environments, and anyone who thinks they can account for every possible variable is deluding themselves. No mathematical model, no matter how big the supercomputer that produced it, can predict the future of a business with anything more than average confidence, and anyone who tells you otherwise is wrong.

Yet, we keep groping towards precision. Mathematical models for determining risk became popular in the 1980s, most famously in financial services where the Black-Scholes-Merton model for option pricing and then a whole raft of other models came into common use. As Pablo Triana describes in *Lecturing Birds on Flying*, by the year 2000 every financial services firm had a team of top-level mathematicians and physicists on staff whose sole job was to come up with ever more complex models. The trouble, says Triana, is that many of these did not work. The Black-Scholes-Merton model was flawed, and Triana assigns to a lead role in the financial crash of 1989. In the 2000s, a model for pricing collateralized debt obligations based on the Gaussian copula, which sounds like a species of small reptile but is in fact a complex mathematical formula, proved so misleading that people mistook high-risk securities for low-risk ones, and vice versa. Value at risk, another model to which financiers clung in the belief that it offered certainty, turned out to be full of holes too.[5]

Over and over in the book, Triana asks the question: why? 'Scientific prowess is not a requirement in order to be successful as a hedge fund, an asset manager or an investment bank', he says. 'Nothing in the products or markets dictates that you must have mastered econometrics or numerical methods prior to being allowed and able to play.... Elementary arithmetic and solid practical market knowledge remain the only true requirements'.[6] Triana is talking about financial markets, but he could equally be talking about *all* markets. For, despite the debacles of the 2000s, executives continue to put their trust in complex mathematical models and their use in many market sectors for predictive purposes is increasing.

 Absolute reliance on models, in the belief that these always tell the truth.

The answer to Triana's question 'why?' is, of course, fear of uncertainty. The idea of the VUCA world has taken hold in management thinking to such an extent that executives are now obsessed with uncertainty. The belief that change is happening at such a rate that no one can master it reduces some to frightened paralysis. They become deer caught in the headlights. Models appear to offer a defence against uncertainty. Their flaws and weaknesses are, or should be, well known; Triana, Nassim Nicholas Taleb, Espen Haug and others have pointed out these flaws many times. Yet executives continue to use them, almost desperately, in the hope that at the heart of the models they will find certainty. They are like thirsty travellers crawling towards an oasis in the desert that is in fact a mirage. Perhaps they even know it *is* a mirage, but they hope against hope that there might also be real water behind the illusion.

Not all models are bad, and I certainly don't mean to imply that we should never use models at all. Models can be a useful aid to strategic thinking; modelling operations systems and processes can help us spot potential flaws; modelling supply chains is a good way of finding out where weak points might lie, and so on. But there are definite limits to models, and in particular there are no reliable models for predicting human behaviour. An alternative trend developed over the past few decades is scenarios planning, in which planners try to determine not what *will* happen but what *might* happen.[7] Scenarios too have their risks and should not be relied on exclusively, but their use does tend to reduce linear thinking and lead to a broader approach to problem solving and risk management. Other companies have moved still further and adopted a 'positive risk management' approach which acknowledges that any situation can be potentially risky and tries to build risk management into all activities.[8]

Executives must get used to the idea that certainty is a mirage. The only certainty is that there is no certainty. If executives cannot get used to this idea and work their way through it, then maybe they are in the wrong job.

Obsessive-compulsive planning disorder

Closely related to fear of uncertainty is *fear of the unknown*. The two are of course closely related and overlap at many points, and can sometimes be indistinguishable from each other. For the purposes of this discussion, fear of the unknown means the fear that there are things out there that we need to know, but we don't yet know what they are; or in Rumsfeldian terms, unknown unknowns.

Some companies try to tackle this problem through massive and detailed research which attempts to account for every possible potential risk and threat. This is a largely pointless exercise for several reasons. First, it won't work; you will always miss something, and some threat will come out of an unexpected quarter. Science fiction writer Isaac Asimov satirized this approach to risk management brilliantly in the *Foundation* series of novels, in which a mathematical formula known as 'psychohistory' claims to have accounted for all possible variables and is thus able to predict the future. Of course it doesn't, and in the story everything goes badly wrong (to put it mildly). Second, the amount of time and effort and resource it takes to do this kind of research will almost certainly never yield a return on investment. And third, while the research is being carried out and plans prepared, the rest of the company sits and marks time instead of pressing ahead.

Despite this, many companies still cling to the model of detailed strategic planning as a way of trying to manage the unknown. Strategic planning is a comparatively new phenomenon, emerging in the 1960s and 1970s off the back of work by scholars such as Igor Ansoff and Kenneth Andrews.[9] It has been roundly criticized by Kenichi Ohmae and Henry Mintzberg (among others) and the flaws of strategic planning are now well known, but the practice persists.[10]

In a recent article in *Harvard Business Review*, Roger Martin links strategic planning directly to fear of the unknown. Many executives find strategy 'scary', he says, 'because it forces them to confront a future they can only guess at. Worse, actually choosing a strategy entails making decisions that explicitly cut off possibilities and options',[11] that is the beginning of path dependence.

The strategic planning process provides reassurance. It is a kind of security blanket. By the end of the planning process executives have convinced themselves that they have thought of everything, or at least most things, and now all they have to do is execute. Provided they stick to the plan as it is written down, nothing can go wrong; and just as importantly, if it does, no one can blame the managers, because they were only following orders.

So, the plan becomes a kind of household deity. All must bow down before the plan. Deviance from the plan will be punished; conformity to the plan will be rewarded. There is certainty in belief. And so planning becomes not so much a virtuous activity as a kind of obsessive-compulsive disorder, something that must be done to prevent all hell from breaking loose.

This, says Martin, 'is a truly terrible way to make strategy. It may be an excellent way to cope with fear of the unknown, but fear and discomfort are an essential part of strategy making. In fact, if you are entirely comfortable with your strategy, there is a strong chance it isn't very good'.[12] At the beginning of the second sentence, Martin hits the nail on the head; the *real* purpose of strategic planning isn't actually to make strategy, it is to help people cope with the unknown.

 Excessive and obsessive planning, which result in plans that no one can read or knows how to follow.

This isn't to say that you shouldn't plan at all. Some sort of guidance on strategy is usually necessary, and the act of planning does concentrate people's minds on the challenges and problems at hand. There are some like the late Jeremy Hope who argued against nearly all forms of planning, including budgeting, but that probably involves too great a degree of uncertainty and unknowing for most people to cope with.[13] Planning is fine, so long as you control the plan, rather than letting the plan control you.

Another way of coping with fear of the unknown is the belief, which again many executives cling to like shipwreck victims holding onto life rafts, that if they work hard enough and are diligent enough, they will succeed. There is no question of them being affected by luck; success, when it comes, is entirely due to their own efforts. Curiously, this view is supported by psychologist Adrian Furnham, who says that 'incompetent managers believe in luck, competent ones do not'.[14]

My view is exactly the opposite. Every manager is affected by luck at some stage in his or her career; competent managers are the ones who know this, and can take advantage of luck. Michael Wheeler, in a blog for *Harvard Business Review*, says much the same, arguing that Bill Gates had three immense strokes of luck during the formative years of Microsoft, each one of which changed the fortunes of the company. J. Paul Getty acknowledged the role luck had played in his own career; when asked the secrets of business success, he replied, 'Rise early, work hard, strike oil'.

'Luck is that which is beyond my control', says Ed Smith, international cricketer turned writer and commentator whose book *Luck* is one of the best modern works on the subject. 'Winning the lottery is luck. My genes are luck. My parents are a matter of luck. It is luck if an opponent drops a catch when I am batting.'[15] Injury and illness are often a matter of luck, and can strike even the best-prepared and most healthy people.

But the great majority of managers are not prepared to admit this. Several years ago, researching an article on luck for the *Financial Times*, I found it very hard to find anyone in a senior executive position in Europe or North America who was prepared to admit that luck played a major part in their career (an honourable exception was R. Gopalakrishnan of Tata Sons in Mumbai, who believes managerial luck is very important). Most of those I spoke to were in denial. They were convinced that their success was entirely due to their own efforts and those of their teams. I lost count of the number of people who quoted to me the adage sometimes attributed to the golfer Gary Player, that 'the harder I work, the luckier I get'.[16]

And yet, these are the very same people who are prepared – willing, even eager – to describe the unexpected as black swan events! It is the same old story: if I am successful, it's because I'm very clever and skilful and competent; but if something goes wrong, it's because something happened that was out of my control. But as Ed Smith says, when things happen that are beyond your control, that is luck.

Recognizing the role played by luck is one way of coming to terms with fear of the unknown. This emphatically does *not* mean leaving everything to chance (and as Smith points out, luck and chance are two different things). It means, as was pointed out much earlier by Niccolò Machiavelli, being alert to the possibility of luck, recognizing that sudden and unexpected events can occur and having the mental strength and flexibility to take advantage of them. One does not so much master luck, said Machiavelli, as observe and watch events unfold and then take advantage when one can.[17] Don't just watch the black swans, get out there and fly with them. But, that means living with uncertainty and the unknown. Not everyone can do that, it seems.

The widespread belief that the company is responsible for its own destiny, and luck plays no part in its success.

The danger of strangers

Xenophobia, the fear of strangers, takes a number of forms. In the media, xenophobia is usually taken to mean a fear of foreigners or outsiders, but as Michel Foucault has pointed out, it can also mean the fear of 'deviants' within our own society, people who behave in ways that are against the norms of behaviour that society has set for itself. Typically, says Foucault, society attempts to either expel these deviants or control them in some way; thus, for example, it was quite common to lock up mentally deficient or disturbed people in asylums away from the public gaze, confining them in places where their 'deviant' behaviour could be controlled.[18]

This *fear of the other* takes many forms. The disdain for women that we discussed in Chapter 5 has its roots at least in part in masculine fear of women. Freudian psychologists have a good deal to say on this subject, and in *On the Psychology of Military Incompetence* Norman Dixon comments on the hostility born of fear that women experience in a man's world. 'The real threat of women who do men's jobs is that in effiminizing the role they, by association, emasculate those who normally fulfil it', he says, or in simpler terms, men feel threatened by successful women.[19] In a fascinating recent article, Anne Karpf describes the long tradition of men trying to keep women silent and prevent them from speaking out and expressing their views, afraid that what women might say would undermine their own authority.[20]

Why should men be afraid of women in business? Caroline Turner thinks it might have to do with power. There are, she says, distinctly different masculine and feminine approaches to power. The masculine approach is to gather power to oneself and hold it close; the feminine approach is to share power and distribute it.[21] Fear of losing power may well be an important element, and that would explain why the tribe of middle-aged men is still so strongly entrenched in the boardroom and upper-level management; they are holding power to themselves. The same applies to ethnic minorities and foreigners, who as noted earlier are poorly represented on boards everywhere, not just in the West.

 All-white (or all Indian, or all Chinese), all-male boards and teams.

The fear of the other is also a real issue for companies working internationally, especially when they are just beginning the process of expansion. Any company that tries to expand overseas that does not have a cadre of senior managers with international experience is likely to run hard up against this issue. Some people are naturally suited to working in different environments and adapt readily to changes in their environment. Others struggle to adapt, and some never do. I have seen at first hand how some Europeans and Americans simply cannot cope with life in India, with the heat and the food and the extremes of wealth and poverty. Even worse, they cannot empathize with or understand Indians, or come to terms with the small but subtle differences in outlook and psychology, the 'software of the mind' of which Geert Hofstede speaks.[22]

One of the results of this fear of the other is instinctive suspicion and mistrust. The view persists in Western business that all Chinese and Indian business people are untrustworthy; the opposite view is that all Westerners are arrogant. Indian managers have told me that they also find it difficult to trust the Chinese, while Chinese executives say exactly the same about the Indians.

Fear and suspicion make negotiations difficult and can fatally hamper the trust that is so necessary to working with foreign partners. In the 1990s it was impossible to count the number of joint ventures between Chinese and Western firms that failed, not because the business model was not sound, but because the partners fell into an adversarial relationship. Of course, joint ventures between firms of the same nationality break down too, often, but the problem is compounded when two different cultures are involved. Around the same time, management consultants were recommending that Western companies not get involved in joint ventures at all, but insist on establishing wholly foreign-owned ventures. In that way, as in Foucault's asylums, they could discipline and control the 'other'.

The belief that the company can go into foreign countries and do things the same way it does them at home.

For much the same reason, some firms insist on importing procedures and management methods from their home country into overseas operations. American companies in Asia and Europe are particularly noted for their insistence on managing and leading American-style, but the problem is not confined to them alone; the first Japanese companies to expand into America had similar difficulties in imposing their own management methods on American business culture. Expatriate managers nearly always held all the key positions of power, and these lived odd, slightly surreal lives detached from the countries to which they were posted. I knew of a case of an American executive and his family in the 1990s who, having been posted overseas, took up residence in an exclusively American compound, shopped only at American stores, sent their children to American schools and, before leaving home, videotaped an entire year's worth of American television programmes so they would not have to watch foreign TV while living abroad. That would be just about understandable in Iraq, or Burma, or Tajikistan; but they were living in England! The use of expatriates has declined since, partly for reasons of cost, but there are still too many firms who insist that managing in foreign cultures is just the same as managing at home.

Fear of the other, both professionally and personally, dominates many lives and this too can infect entire cultures. It results in narrow thinking, and prevents the building of trust relationships with other groups. Breaking down cultural and other barriers and encouraging diversity is essential if progress is to be made.

Violent politeness

I have just encountered another example of luck. As I was writing the previous section an email from Thinkers50 arrived, with a link to a blog post from Gianpietro Petriglieri, an associate professor at INSEAD. He describes one of his favourite cartoons, showing an executive team

sitting around a boardroom table. The chairman asks, 'All in favour?'
All raise their hands in agreement, but above each head there is a
thought bubble with phrases such as 'You've got to be kidding', or
'Perish the thought.' 'I have a name for this cocktail of deference,
conformity and passive aggression', writes Professor Petriglieri. 'I call it
violent politeness.'[23]

Why does this happen? Why do people fail to speak out when they
know something is wrong? Why do they acquiesce in behaviours that
they know are wrong? The answer in the great majority of cases is
personal timidity, fear of consequences for themselves and perhaps
also their families and friends. This kind of fear is well known by
whistle-blowers. It takes courage to speak out, when you know that
you will immediately lose your very well-paid and prestigious job,
that you and your family will have to find a new means of subsist-
ence, and that you will very probably never work in this or any other
industry again.

Even in less serious cases, people are reluctant to speak up in cases
where there are repercussions for themselves. There develops what
some have called 'nodding dog' syndrome, in which members of teams
or boards simply nod in agreement every time the leader proposes a
new idea. This is highly dangerous, because, as Petriglieri says, not only
is there no criticism or dissent but also the team members become full
of pent-up frustration and anger; they can see the wrong things being
done but believe they have no power to prevent them. Few things in
work are more demotivating or demoralizing.

Petriglieri also observes that the same phenomenon happens at all
levels of the company. Junior executives do not speak up because they
are unsure of their position; senior people remain silent because they
are under more pressure (and, I would add, usually have more to lose).
'Time does not summon courage', he writes. 'It only morphs the fear
of speaking truth *to* power into the fear of speaking truth *in* power
[my italics]'.[24]

Anxiety and fear also lead to misplaced perceptions of risk and a lack
of risk appetite. Norman Dixon cites the example of the Royal Navy,
which has an automatic procedure of court-martialling any captain
who loses his ship. If the court-martial finds the captain was

blameless, then he is exonerated and free to resume his career. However, says Dixon, there is always the fear that whatever the circumstances, the captain might be found guilty, in which case his career would be ruined. As a result, some captains are reluctant to place their ships in risky positions, even though military necessity might require them to do so. Their avoidance of risk thus increases the real risk that they and their colleagues face; for example, if a captain refuses to take a risk with his own ship, his fleet might lose the battle.

As well as fear of authority, there is also the fear that derives from peer pressure. A culture of bullying emerges in some organizations. Sometimes, as in Enron, there is pressure to engage in or at least turn a blind eye to illegal behaviour; often this is done with a view to making as many people as possible complicit, so they will not dare to speak out or blow the whistle. In other cases, the culture of bullying allows the loudest and strongest and most ruthless to create power bases for themselves.

A culture of conformity, where questioning and dissent are discouraged or even punished.

Alfred P. Sloan, the legendary chairman of General Motors, had little time for nodding dog syndrome. 'I take it we are all in agreement on this issue?' he asked his board on one occasion, and every head nodded. 'Then, gentlemen', said Sloan, 'I suggest we defer this matter until our next meeting, and in the meantime go away and think of some good reasons to *dis*agree, so that we can have a proper discussion of the subject.' Encouraging people to speak out, in an atmosphere free of threat or danger, is the best way and probably the only way to dispel fear.

Cultures of anxious precision

I once knew a publishing industry executive who would not make any decision, large or small, without first consulting a spreadsheet. If the numbers added up, he would say yes; if not, then the answer was no. This included not just publishing decisions but some personal ones as well, such as where to send his children to school, and one wit at the office suggested that he also used the spreadsheet to regulate his bowel movements. Certainly it was never far from his hand, or his thoughts.

As with arrogance and ignorance, there are ways of dealing with fearful people. Often they lack confidence; sometimes they lack moral courage, the necessary quality which allows people to stand up and do what is right, regardless of consequences. Both can be instilled, given time, experience, encouragement and perhaps also coaching. The problem is compounded, however, when a culture of fear pervades the entire organization.

Companies that *fear uncertainty* tend to rely, like the spreadsheet-wielding executive above, on tools, metrics and models to, in effect, do their work for them. One of the reasons why managers get the big money is that they are paid to use their judgement, knowledge and experience. Abrogating responsibility to a computer programme questions why managers exist in the first place; why not just hand over control to a computer, turn out the lights and close the door? Computers don't fall ill, they don't want stock options or pension plans, and they never make sexist remarks about their female customers. What's not to like?

Companies that *fear the unknown* are, as I said earlier, very similar and there is often a lot of crossover between the two. Fear of the unknown often manifests itself in an obsession with planning, because planning creates the illusion of knowledge and offers the pretence that the future can be controlled. It rejects any role for luck or random events, and urges the vain hope that if we work hard enough we can control what is going on around us.

Fear of the other creates closed and inward-looking cultures where people tend to look, act and think very much alike. Conformity in these cultures becomes a defence mechanism, a way of holding back the strange and unfamiliar. Very often there is crossover between fear of the other and fear of the unknown. We fear those who are not like us because we don't know them. Companies with this kind of culture find it very difficult to operate in markets outside their own home turf.

Personal timidity is all these other fears writ small. Our fears make us anxious to protect what we have; we look at the risks of confronting the unknown, or the other, and decide it is safer to leave things as they are. This of course just increases the risk we already face, but most of us are capable of burying that knowledge and carrying on, hoping the status quo will hold out just a little bit longer. As I said earlier, this should not necessarily be accounted a vice and we should not look down on people affected by personal timidity as 'weak'. Most of us have probably had our timid moments at some time or another in our professional careers.

I call these *cultures of anxious precision* because in them, fear drives the need for certainty and conformity. There is a wholly irrational belief that if we can achieve certainty and conformity, we will have banished the source of our fears. That is why models and planning are such important security blankets; they allow us to pretend that we are in control. Some people and companies are aware that this is an illusion but carry on anyway; others never realize that the shadows on the cave wall are not real. It is hard to know which is more dangerous.

Only the paranoid survive

Accepting that the world is messy, confusing, imprecise, uncertain and full of strangeness is the key to dealing with fear. That, of course, is far easier said than done.

What is the solution? This is an area where groups working together, properly guided and mentored, can give themselves strength. The first prerequisite is to share fears and get them out in the open. Then, the fears themselves must be analysed and talked through. What is it that we really fear most? How can we confront that fear? How can we manage it? Not with models or planning or spreadsheets, but by learning to live with fear and uncertainty, by realizing that, as Sydney Finkelstein says, we live in a world of mistakes.

Having *some* fear in an organization culture is healthy, for lack of fear can easily lead to arrogance. A sensible level of fear is important when managing risk. Andrew Grove argued that every organization needs a level of paranoia. Some fears are irrational, but many others are quite justified and we are right to be afraid; just because you're paranoid doesn't mean that someone isn't out to get you. But to paraphrase what I said earlier, we need to control our fears, not let them control us.

Here are some of the coping tactics that might be considered:

Recognise that uncertainty brings opportunities, as well as challenges. Remember, everyone else is just as uncertain and afraid as you are, possibly more so. Try, as Machiavelli suggested, to see the world as being a place of possibilities, not just threats.

Accept that luck has a role to play in business. Learn how to take advantage of good fortune and manage the consequences of bad luck.

Scientific tools and methods of inquiry have a powerful role to play in business, but in and of themselves they are not sufficient. Peter Drucker always denied that management was a science, insisting that it was the last of the liberal arts. Experience and judgement are essential ingredients. This does not mean that I am arguing that managers should use their intuition; I am not wholly convinced that intuition exists, and I think that a lot of what we refer to as intuition or 'gut feeling' is very often a combination of common sense, experience and tacit knowledge. But not everything in management can be calculated or measured.

Use plans as a way of concentrating thinking, but do not rely on them. Be prepared to throw them away if circumstances change. Field Marshal Helmuth von Moltke advised his staff that 'no plan survives contact with the enemy'. I would amend this and say simply, 'No plan survives.' Every plan runs up against obstacles that force amendment or deviation. Sticking grimly to the plan when common sense tells us it should be abandoned is one of the worst things we can do.

Risk can be a powerful stimulant. Professional musicians know that when they go into a studio to record, they and their engineers and producers have control over all the variables. They are in a closed system, and they can produce pretty much whatever they want. Live performances, however, are quite different. There they are in an open system and there is no way of knowing what will happen, how the crowd will react. But this is what makes live performance so exciting; there is an edge of danger to which both performers and audience respond. That is why most musicians love performing live, and many of the best performances of all time are live performances.

Shortly after the Nazis occupied what was then Czechoslovakia in 1939, the Czech Philharmonic Orchestra played a live concert featuring *Ma Vlast*, the epic cycle of tone poems by the Czech composer Smetana that has become synonymous with Czech national pride. The power and passion with which the orchestra played were overwhelming. At the end, the audience went wild and then burst into an impromptu chorus of the national anthem. Everyone in the concert hall, performers and audience alike, knew that they were putting their lives at risk by playing, listening and singing; but they did it anyway.

More than seventy years later, listening to the recording of this performance makes the hair stand up on the back of my neck. That is greatness; greatness achieved in the shadow of fear.

It can be done. So, stop worrying and learn to love your fears.

---

[1] Leonard R. Sayles and Cynthia J. Smith, *The Rise of the Rogue Executive: How Good Companies Go Bad and How to Stop the Destruction*, Upper Saddle River: Prentice Hall, 2006.

[2] Nathan Bennett and G. James Lemoine, 'What VUCA Really Means for You', *Harvard Business Review*, January–February 2014, http://hbr.org/2014/01/what-vuca-really-means-for-you/ar/1

[3] Rosabeth Moss Kanter, *When Giants Learn to Dance: Mastering the Challenge of Management, Strategy and Careers in the 1990s*, New York: Simon & Schuster, 1989.

[4] Lawrence LeShan and Henry Margenau, *Einstein's Space and Van Gogh's Sky: Physical Reality and Beyond*, New York: Macmillan, 1982.

[5] Triana, *Lecturing Birds on Flying*.

[6] Triana, *Lecturing Birds on Flying*, p. 95.

[7] Pierre Wack, credited with introducing scenarios into business planning, has written eloquently of both the uses of scenarios and their dangers; see Wack, 'Scenarios: Uncharted Waters Ahead', *Harvard Business Review*, September–October 1995 and 'Scenarios: Shooting the Rapids', *Harvard Business Review*, November–December 1995.

[8] David Hillson and Ruth Murray-Webster, *Understanding and Managing Risk Attitude*, Aldershot: Gower 2012.

9 H. Igor Ansoff, *Corporate Strategy*, New York: McGraw-Hill, 1965; Kenneth R. Andrews, *The Concept of Corporate Strategy*, Homewood: Irwin, 1971.

10 Ohmae, *The Mind of the Strategist*; Henry Mintzberg, *The Rise and Fall of Strategic Planning*, New York: The Free Press, 1994.

11 Roger L. Martin, 'The Big Lie of Strategic Planning', *Harvard Business Review*, January–February 2014, p. 3.

12 Martin, 'The Big Lie of Strategic Planning', p. 4.

13 For example, in Jeremy Hope, *Reinventing the CFO: How Financial Managers Can Transform Their Roles and Add Greater Value*, Boston: Harvard Business Review Press, 2006.

14 Adrian Furnham, *The Incompetent Manager: The Causes, Consequences and Cures of Management Failures*, London: Whurr, 2003, p. 11.

15 Ed Smith, *Luck: A Fresh Look at Fortune*, London: Bloomsbury, 2012.

16 In fact the quote goes back to Thomas Jefferson, if not earlier: http://www.ft.com/cms/s/0/e70e9292-1127-11e2-a637-00144feabdc0.html#axzz3Cu8xmWOI

17 Niccolò Machiavelli, *The Prince*, Harmondsworth: Penguin, 1961.

18 Michel Foucault, *Discipline and Punish*, London: Allen Lane, 1977.

19 Dixon, *On the Psychology of Military Incompetence*, p. 209.

20 http://www.theguardian.com/tv-and-radio/2013/feb/01/fear-loathing-women-radio

21 http://www.forbes.com/sites/womensmedia/2012/08/27/do-women-fear-power-and-success/

22 Geert Hofstede, *Cultures and Organizations: Software of the Mind*, London: McGraw-Hill, 1991.

23 http://blogs.hbr.org/2014/03/why-work-is-lonely/

24 http://blogs.hbr.org/2014/03/why-work-is-lonely/

Chapter 7

The Creosote syndrome

One of the more memorable characters from *Monty Python's The Meaning of Life* is Mr Creosote, the gluttonous gourmand who eats everything in sight and then swells to such a monstrous size that he is unable to move. When restaurant staff tempt him with one last morsel, a 'wafer-thin mint', he knows he shouldn't eat it and refuses at first. Then his greed gets the better of him. He stuffs the mint into his mouth, swallows it, and explodes.

The Creosote syndrome, whereby companies gorge themselves on acquisitions until they explode – or implode – is well known in business. A famous example was Royal Ahold, the Dutch supermarket group that had been highly successful in its domestic market but had ambitions of becoming a world player. Over the course of eight years leading up to 2002, Royal Ahold spent more than €20 billion on acquisitions around the world, especially in the Americas. The company bought itself a major position in the US food retail sector and looked set to continue to expand, even though integration costs for the major acquisitions were far higher than forecast and currency devaluation in South America had cut deeply into profits there.

The wafer-thin mint for Royal Ahold was Argentina, where a relatively small acquisition went sour when a local partner defaulted on its debts. Thereafter, Royal Ahold unravelled with astonishing speed. Its American operations slid into loss; executives at one subsidiary tried to cover up their losses through a clumsy accounting fraud, which was discovered almost at once. Royal Ahold collapsed. Its CEO and CFO both lost their jobs and the company was investigated for criminal offences. It was one of the most spectacular falls from grace in modern business; and it could all have been avoided had Royal Ahold managed its growth strategy rather than simply gobbling up every opportunity that came along.

Greed on the part of individuals has led to some spectacular business failures, and we will look at this subject in more detail in the next chapter, on lust. Here, the focus is on corporate greed, or *cultures of conspicuous acquisition*, where growth, expansion, profit, market share and shareholder value become ends in their own right, goals to which the company is dedicated.

This is not to say that growth, expansion, profit, market share and shareholder value are not important. They are important, of course. Often these are the yardsticks by which a company is measured and, rightly or wrongly, that is a reality with which every business leader and manager has to live. But – and this again is a problem that often becomes more acute as businesses grow and mature – companies often develop a kind of corporate myopia about profit, growth and market share, choosing one of these things as all-important and ignoring everything else. Several years ago I ran across a book titled *Profit or Growth? Why You Don't Have to Choose.*[1] The first thing that went through my mind was, 'surely if you are having to choose, then you are doing something wrong'. That indeed is the point that the authors, Bala Chakravarthy and Peter Lorange, make in the book, but what worried me is that the point had to be made in the first place.

Puzzling over this, I finally worked out that the problem lies in how we perceive profit and growth: not as indicators of success, but as ends in their own right. Because corporate performance is so heavily driven by targets, there is a tendency to set big targets, ones that look impressive and show investors and the financial press how aggressive and thrusting we are. So we set big profit targets and then settle down to squeeze as much money as we can out of operations – and, of course, customers – so as to hit those targets. Alternatively, we set ambitious growth targets and set out to become the biggest in our sector/our regional market/the world.

This is where greed comes in. Each target we hit awakes in us the desire to go on and hit another, even bigger one. The success of our companies reflects on ourselves. The psychology is simple: my company is bigger/ more profitable/has a better share price than yours, therefore my company is superior to yours, and thus it follows without saying I am superior to you. Greed takes over from reason.

Greedy companies, then, are ones where the original goals of the business have been lost or forgotten and growth and profit take over as goal in their own right. When that happens, these companies are in danger of focusing on these pseudo-goals so completely that they lose sight of everything else. Their greed overwhelms them; they reach for more and more until they finally reach too far.

Table 7.1 A Typology of Greed

Type	Manifestation
Greed for growth	We want to be the biggest in the world
Greed for profit	The purpose of a business is to make money
Greed for market share	We want to dominate everyone
Greed for victory	We are the champions!

Creosote syndrome can manifest itself in several ways, as Table 7.1 shows. One common form of greed is the *greed for growth*, which triumphed over reason at Royal Ahold and led the company on its reckless strategy of growth which ended in collapse. Ford's greed for growth led it into reckless adventures such as Fordlandia, the disastrous attempt to set up a rubber production facility in Brazil in 1928 which ultimately cost the company more than $20 million (a lot of money in the 1920s).

The other major manifestation is *greed for profit*, the desire to make as much money as possible, as though he who has the biggest pile of cash wins. The belief in profit as a goal in its own right is surprisingly rare in business, but when it does occur it can be highly dangerous.

Less visible but more insidious and dangerous still is the *greed for market share*, which sometimes creeps into corporate culture without executives being aware of it. The myth that having the largest share of the market will lead to a position of competitive invulnerability is a very seductive one, particularly in industries where the market growth is relatively flat. Automotives and grocery retail are two sectors where greed for market share has led to some spectacularly bad decisions in the past, but no sector and no company is immune to this. Having a big share of the market is a good thing, of course, but dominating the market, far from being a recipe for success, can be a trap that leads to failure.

Simple greed alone is dangerous because, as above, it leads companies to overlook the really important things in business, but the danger factor is squared when greedy companies spend too long looking at their competitors. Greed is then compounded by envy. Our rival has a market share greater than our own; therefore, nothing will do but we must grow our market share until it is bigger than theirs. Companies that see their primary mission as being to out-compete and to 'win' over their rivals really are setting themselves up for a fall. Some forms of competition like price wars can, in the short term, be good for customers, but in the long run customers very often end up as collateral damage. Competition should be regarded as a necessary evil, *not* as a goal in its own right.

Growth and death

Royal Ahold is by no means the only company to have put greed for growth ahead of experience, wisdom and common sense. Other recent examples include Lehman Brothers, Swissair and Marconi, which we encountered earlier in this book, and Nortel. If anything, Nortel's rise and fall were even more meteoric than those of Royal Ahold. Nortel went from being an obscure Canadian telecom company to a global giant with revenues of more than $30 billion and a share price of nearly $125; and then it crashed, its share price falling to less than 50 cents, all in the space of four years.

'Binge' is the word commentators usually use to describe Nortel's growth strategy. There is little evidence of planning. Some highly expensive acquisitions duplicated things that Nortel was already doing quite efficiently in-house. The huge growth was achieved at the expense of profits by taking on a massive debt; and when the dotcom bubble burst in 2001 and tore the bottom out of the telecoms market, Nortel's debt carried it down. The company ceased trading in 2002, throwing more than 60,000 people out of work.

 A series of rapid acquisitions funded by debt, especially when those acquisitions do not seem to relate to each other.

Greed for growth has always been with us. In the later Middle Ages, Florence emerged as the centre of the European banking industry, and in the fourteenth century the largest and most prestigious bank in Florence was the Society of the Bardi. The Bardi lent money to business magnates, nobles, kings and popes, but their problem was that they didn't know when to say no. More and bigger loans were embarked upon, including a massive series of loans to King Edward III of England to help him finance the opening stages of the Hundred Years War. The inevitable happened; Edward could not afford to pay back his debts, and the Society of the Bardi crashed.[2] The banks who invested heavily in high-risk securities before 2008 were guilty of much the same greed for growth.

Again, growth in and of itself is not a bad thing, but it is important to make a distinction between *healthy growth* and *greedy growth*. A measure of growth is good for companies; so long as it is controlled and managed and in line with the company's strategy and goals, growth is a positive force. Greedy growth, on the other hand, is growth for its own sake, mindless growth in the belief that all growth is good and that the aim of every business is to get to be as big as possible. Size matters; big is better, and bigger is better still. That way of thinking leads to mindless acquisitions, and eventual disaster.

But even controlled growth has its dangers. As companies get bigger, they become harder to manage. The CEO can no longer see the big picture. Royal Ahold's management team in the Netherlands had no idea what was going on in the North American and Latin American subsidiaries, not until it was too late. Unless physical growth is accompanied by an equal growth in management systems, there is a strong risk that parts of the company, at least, will spin out of control. GlaxoSmithKline's failure to control its managers in China have cost the company $300 million in fines and seen the prosecution of some of its executives, as well as damage to its reputation worldwide.[3]

Alfred Mond, known to the British press as 'the Great Conglomerator', was another who believed in growth for its own sake. Starting out in the 1920s with a small family-owned chemical company, Brunner Mond, Alfred Mond expanded in all directions, building a huge conglomerate known as Imperial Chemical Industries (ICI) with interests in chemicals, agricultural fertilisers, explosives, paints, plastic products, pharmaceuticals and motorcycles.[4] Mond's insatiable desire for acquisitions seemed to have no bounds, and in the novel *Brave New World*, Aldous

Huxley satirized him as 'Mustafa Mond', the world dictator. But Mond at least knew how to integrate his businesses, and ICI prospered – at first. After Mond's death in 1930, the acquisition spree continued, but his successors did not have his acumen and the group began to struggle to maintain cohesion. By the 1950s, it was a lumbering conglomerate of over a hundred businesses with no central ideology or mission. It took a massive and very expensive restructuring programme to get ICI fit once more.

 A lack of central ideology or belief that unites the various elements of the company.

Growth is risky if it gets out of control, and even controlled growth creates businesses that are increasingly difficult to manage. Why, then, do companies succumb to greed for growth? The usual answer is that shareholders demand growth in order to boost the value of their own assets, but there are two problems with this. First, uncontrolled growth does not lead to shareholder value; in the cases of Royal Ahold, Marconi and Nortel, the case was quite the opposite. Second, greed for growth affects not just publicly quoted companies but also state-owned and privately owned ones. Shareholder pressure for growth did play a role at Nortel – shareholders too can be afflicted by greed for growth – but at Royal Ahold it seems clear that the shareholders played little part in influencing the strategy of rapid growth; the impetus for this came from the boardroom.

Another argument is that scale gives companies more protection against fluctuations in markets and the economy, and this is true up to a point. Bigger companies have more resources to draw upon to help them ride out economic downturns; they have more money to spend on innovation and more people to participate in innovation efforts. But again, there are limits to the value of scale. Once companies grow past a certain point, they become less flexible and less able to adapt to changes. This actually increases the risks they face rather than decreasing them. IBM in the late 1970s was by a distance the largest computer maker in the world, but its smaller rivals were running rings around it; as a result, despite its size, IBM came perilously close to complete collapse in the 1980s.

The real pressures for growth are twofold: peer pressure and human nature. Very few people go into a career in management because they want a nice easy job with a good pension at the end of it. Most managers go into management in the first place because they want to do things. They find it very difficult to do nothing, even when nothing is in fact the right thing to do. When the market is rising and other companies are growing, we are naturally inclined to want to grow our own company too; if possible, at a faster rate than the guys across the street. Our competitive instincts come to the fore. My company is bigger than yours; I am better than you.

Once again, these instincts are not necessarily bad things. The trick is to channel them in such a way that the urge to do, to create, to grow is given an outlet that is also beneficial for the long-term health of the business. Innovation is in fact a terrific way of letting the restless spirits in a company blow off some steam; and it can also yield results that are good for the company. Strategic divestments are a good way of resizing the company and perhaps giving its strategic direction a tweak. Setting up a new company gives the more adventurous managers something to do, and stops the rest from becoming too complacent. There are plenty of things a company can do, apart from growing recklessly, to satisfy its urge to be active.

But growth for growth's sake has now become institutionalized in management culture. Growth is good. Students are taught this mantra in case studies, and solemnly warned that the only options are to 'grow or die'. Analysts and brokers look at growth rates as a key metric. And of course, as noted earlier, managers are also rewarded for achievement; there are no bonuses for sitting still. Business culture actively pushes companies and managers towards greed for growth, and as long as it continues to do so, there will be business failures.

The deluded obsession with profit

The idea that the primary purpose of a business is to make a profit is relatively new. It is usually attributed to free-market economists, especially those of the Chicago School who took their cue from the late Milton Friedman (whose view was, rather, that the first duty of a business is to return value to shareholders). This slightly spurious academic credential allows companies with cultures of greed to pursue profit while at the same time claiming to be high-minded and pure of intent. It is not an edifying spectacle.

So that there should be no misunderstanding, let me make it clear that I am all in favour of profit. I run a business myself, and profit features fairly largely in my thinking. Businesses need to make profits; a business that does not make profits will not survive. I also agree with that rather surprising authority on the subject, St Thomas Aquinas, who argued in the mid-thirteenth century that not only were business people entitled to make profits, but also that their profits should increase according to the level of risks they ran. Aquinas disapproved of the notion of inherent value; a good, he said, was worth whatever people were willing to pay for it at a given time and place, and if they were willing to pay a high price, then the businesses that sold those goods were entitled to what they could get.[5]

Problems begin when companies see profit, like growth, as an end in itself and set their goals and targets accordingly. If you believe that your only purpose is to make profit, and reward your staff solely on the basis of the profits they earn for the business, then you are setting yourself up for some very unpleasant unintended consequences. The first and most obvious of these is a desire to cut corners so as to make or exceed profit targets. That desire will increase if managerial bonuses are tied to hitting those targets, for then the company is in effect incentivizing corruption. The collapse of Royal Ahold was triggered in part by the revelation that one subsidiary had been cooking the books in order to avoid exposing a profit shortfall. At time of writing, British supermarket group Tesco is under investigation for overstating profits at a time when corporate profits have been falling.[6]

 A heavy emphasis on profit targets, especially when those targets are linked to rewards and bonuses.

More serious, and with potentially graver long-term consequences, is the change in corporate mindset that a focus on profit can lead to. The focus switches away from stakeholders and onto the company itself; its needs are all that matters. Customers are there to be milked of as much money as possible; suppliers are to be squeezed into providing goods or components at lower and lower prices; employee wages are to be held down and staff benefits reduced (although senior management wages and perks are usually the last things to be cut), all so that the company can make more profit.

Stakeholders are not stupid; they know when their own interests are being sacrificed so that the company can meet its profit targets, and if they have any choice at all, they will switch their business and their labour elsewhere. Those who don't have a choice will stay with the company, but they will be resentful and looking to get their own back. An atmosphere of antagonism between a company and its customers, suppliers and employees is not conducive to good prospects for long-term growth. A short-term profit gain will have to be paid for somewhere down the line.

Of course, profit is not and never has been the primary aim of any well-run business. I am reminded again of R. Gopalakrishnan's comment that 'profit is a by-product of what we do'. If a company fulfils its real objective – the provision of goods and services that people want and need – in an efficient and effective way, then it will make a profit and no sensible person will begrudge that profit. But profit comes from the mission, not vice versa.

The even more deluded obsession with market share

Like greed for profit, companies that indulge in greed for market share are able to claim that their greed has intellectual grounding. In this case they can call upon a highly influential piece of business research, the Profit Impact of Market Strategies (PIMS) project of the early 1970s.[7] Researchers observed a correlation between market share and profitability, and suggested that an increase – or decrease – of 10 per cent in market share would be accompanied by a 5 per cent increase or decrease in return on investment. Several generations of managers and business leaders have now grown up with the idea that market share directly equates to profitability.

Several words of caution are in order. First, the rise in profitability that accompanies an increase in market share has never been entirely explained, but is probably due to the economies of scale that come with increased market share. But economies of scale are a two-edged sword. Big companies can produce physical goods more cheaply – there is some doubt about services – and thus increase their margin of profit, but only up to a point; eventually, the law of diminishing returns takes over. What is more, the economists tell us, economies of scale can usually only be achieved at the expense of flexibility.

Two sectors where big companies dominate, and where market share is a very significant factor in strategy making, are automotives and grocery retailing. Investment costs in both sectors are high and there are substantial barriers to entry, meaning that both are dominated by long-term incumbents. It is notable that in both sectors market share and profitability have little long-term relation to each other. Through most of the first decade of this century, General Motors had the largest share of the worldwide car market, but in 2009 it filed for bankruptcy with debts of $170 billion. Tesco, the British supermarket chain with the highest market share for over a decade, is also the one in the most financial trouble. The most profitable companies in both sectors are not the ones with the largest market share; they are the ones that got their strategy right in the first place. What is more, given the size of these companies, they are unable to adapt quickly when they run into trouble. It took years to sort out General Motors and get it back on track, and unless its new CEO is a miracle worker, it will take years to do the same with Tesco.

 Any strategy based on market share as the end game.

Of course economies of scale do help, especially in research-intensive industries like pharmaceuticals where it can take $1 billion to bring a new drug to market. My point is not that economies of scale are not useful; rather, it is that they have their limitations, and any strategy based solely on achieving economies of scale by conquering and occupying market share also has its limitations. Making strategy on this basis introduces another form of myopia.

The first problem with the PIMS research, and the market share school of thought more generally, is that it works well only in a purely static market where there is a finite pool of customers. But markets are rarely static. Usually they are either expanding, with more customers spending more money, in which case it is perfectly possible to be highly profitable no matter what your market share is, or they are contracting, in which case smaller nimbler companies will stand a better chance of adjusting to changing market conditions than the behemoths that rely on economies of scale.

The second problem relates to the discussion above: should market share in any case be the primary goal? If a company serves its customers well, meets their needs, keeps them happy and coming back for more while all the time making a profit, then it doesn't need to worry about market share. It can diversify its product offering to its existing customers, it can innovate, it can enter new markets – all of which have the potential to bring about long-term growth.

Some investors won't like that. They will want to apply the PIMS model and will insist on rising market share, profit and growth. In that case, management should have the courage of its convictions and suggest they take their investment elsewhere. If they want quick returns, or even quicker losses, there are plenty of risky tech stocks out there, or they can go to the nearest racecourse and pay a call on the bookmakers. Smart investors who understand the business – and there are some – will invest where they can see a future. That brings us of course to the question of what kind of investors you really want and whether going public really is the best thing for a business, which is another story and probably another book entirely.

 Allowing investors to call the shots on strategy. Most investors aren't interested in strategy. Most investors can't spell strategy.

The myth of competition

Greed for market share leads us inevitably to the issue of competition, and the notion that market share is only gained by taking it away from rivals. The idea that companies exist only to compete with each other is nearly as pernicious and misleading as the idea that companies exist only to make profits. The intellectual justification here is Darwin, or rather that crude offshoot of Darwin's theories known as 'social Darwinism', which applied part of Darwinian theory to society and economics. I've lost count of the number of times I have heard managers explain earnestly to me how it is right that, in business, the weak should perish and the strong survive because that is what Darwin said.

In fact, as Geoffrey Hodgson and Thorbjørn Knudsen wrote in their excellent book *Darwin's Conjecture*, Darwin said no such thing.[8] What he *said* was that it is not the strongest that survive, or the most intelligent, but those that are best able to adapt and evolve. Sometimes this means competition, but Darwin also discussed concepts such as mutual aid, sympathy and cooperation, whereby species collaborate and work together to ensure the survival of each other. Hodgson and Knudsen went on to point out that economies and markets work on much the same principles, and that cooperation and mutual interest are at least as important as head-to-head competition, if not more so.

And, of course, deep down we already know this, and probably if left to our own devices we would collaborate more freely; there would be more give and take between companies, there would be more partnerships between supposed rivals with the aim of serving customers more effectively. But we are beaten over the head by free-market economists, who insist that competition is necessary in order to ensure efficient markets, and strategy gurus, who tell us that competition is what keeps companies lean, hungry and fit, for if there is no competition we will sink into sloth, idleness and complacency.

As if. Running a business on its own is hard enough; why should we go out and pick fights with random strangers in order to make it harder? Do artists engage in fistfights with other artists in order to sharpen their painting technique? Do poets attack the publishers of rival poets in order to stop their work from being printed? Do scientists defame other scientists so that people will stop reading the work of their colleagues and read their own work instead?[*] Why then should managers go out and attack other managers, instead of saving their energy to do what they are supposed to do, which is serve customers?

But they do, and so we are deluged with books with titles like *Marketing Warfare, The Basics of Business Warfare* and *Financial Market Warfare* (and as I write this sentence, a press release pops up on my email announcing the publication of *Building a Culture to Win: Unveiling 'Top Gun' Strategies for Successful Organizations*). We are encouraged to think about strategy in military terms, and the more enthusiastic of us even read the works of Clausewitz and biographies of Napoleon and Alexander the Great in hopes of learning the secrets of competitive success. There was a fashion in the 1970s and 1980s in the West for *The Book of Five Rings*, the memoir of the famous Japanese swordfighter Miyamoto Musashi, in which he describes the secrets of success that led him to victory in more than sixty duels. (Did readers fully understand that these were duels to the death? I wonder, if Miyamoto had described in graphic detail what a human body looks like after it has been slashed across with twenty-four inches of steel, whether the book would have been so popular.)

More popular still these days are sporting metaphors. Business is full of slang and jargon derived from football, baseball, cricket and other sports. We talk about 'winning teams', we have 'cheerleaders' who promote ideas and new initiatives, we even have 'coaches' who help us to get the best out of ourselves. In American business a pilot project from which nothing much is expected might be called a 'Hail Mary'; in Britain, borrowing from snooker, it might be called a 'shot to nothing'. Top sportsmen and women are brought into firms as motivational speakers, the view apparently being that a little of their stardust will rub off on us and make us into winners too.

Sporting metaphors abound in *Playing to Win* by A.G. Lafley, the much admired chairman and CEO of Procter & Gamble.[9] Chapter titles include 'What is Winning', 'Where to Play', 'How to Win' and 'The Endless Pursuit of Winning'. Winning is getting harder all the time, declares Lafley, because we (wait for it) live in a VUCA world. Here are some of the questions he suggests you ask yourself:

- Have you defined winning?
- Have you decided where you can play to win?
- Have you determined how, specifically, you will win?[10]

---

[*] A scientist friend informs me that sometimes they do exactly that, which rather undermines my argument.

Win? Win *what*, for God's sake? Is there a contest? Do we get prizes at the end, or trophies? Does A.G. imagine himself standing on a podium at the end of the reporting year, holding a bouquet while someone hangs a gold medal around his neck and a band plays the P&G company song? The only trophy that matters, the only prize worth having in business, is satisfied customers. The game of competition is just that, a game, played by managers in order to boost their own egos. They pretend that in managing a business they are doing something really butch and heroic, and they can feel superior to other people; especially the people in the companies we have 'defeated'. My company beat your company; I am better than you.

This is sheer nonsense. If companies spent half as much time thinking about their customers as they do about their rivals, they would probably make a lot more money. I will make a statement here and now that will probably offend most readers, but I will make it anyway: the word 'winning' has no place in the world of business. We are not here to 'win'. We are here to create value, to give satisfaction to other people and, in the process of doing these things, earn a profit. *That* is what matters.

Of course there is competition in business, for resources, for talent, for the attention of customers trying to make the best choice in a crowded and busy marketplace. We do compete for these resources when we must; but we compete more often than we should. The so-called 'war for talent', for example, could be ended at a stroke if businesses would agree to make proper collaborative investment in education and development of future generations of managers rather than sloughing off responsibility to the business schools and then complaining about the quality and quantity of graduates they produce.

The myth of competition is that competition is an end in itself. Greed for victory is a dangerous distraction from the real purpose of business. Forget about winning; once again, it is not about you. Concentrate on the people who matter, the other stakeholders and above all, the customers.

 An excessive focus on competition.

Greed and corruption

Greed of any kind leads almost inevitably to corruption, and whenever people and institutions compete with each other – especially when the prize is money – there is temptation to step outside the rules. Some people are philosophical about this and regard corruption as a kind of transaction cost, an inevitable part of the workings of a free competitive market. 'If you open the door', said former Chinese leader Deng Xiaoping, when warned that introducing free markets and competition in China could lead to a rise in corruption, 'it is inevitable that a few flies will get in.' That is a dangerous attitude to take. It is a short step from condoning and tolerating corruption to engaging in it oneself.

Unrestrained greed leads to cultures where greed is considered acceptable and even a good thing. Not everyone disagreed with Wall Street trader Ivan Boesky when he said that 'Greed is good.' A certain amount of greed, we are told, is a useful stimulus; it spurs people on to make greater efforts, makes them work harder and be more creative because they know they will be rewarded for their efforts.

Possibly, although much the same argument was used in favour of flogging in the Royal Navy; a touch of the lash now and then makes the sailors more disciplined and better fighters. (If that was actually true, then why did the Navy abolish flogging?) But greed also creates cultures like that of the South Sea Bubble from 1711 to 1720 when the London establishment and financial community took collective leave of its senses and plunged in pursuit of wealth for its own sake. Charles White Mackay, in *Extraordinary Popular Delusions and the Madness of Crowds*, chronicles this era of mass insanity in some detail, and offers this example of how far things went:

> *The most absurd and preposterous of all, and which shewed, more completely than any other, the utter madness of the people, was one started by an unknown adventurer, entitled,* A company for carrying on an undertaking of great advantage, but nobody to know what it is. *Were not the fact stated by credible witnesses, it would be impossible to believe that any person could be duped by such a project. The man of genius who essayed this*

bold and successful inroad upon public credibility, merely stated in his prospectus that the required capital was half a million [pounds sterling], in five thousand shares of £100 each, deposit £2 per share.... Next morning, at nine o'clock, this great man opened an office in Cornhill. Crowds of people beset his door, and when he shut up at three o'clock, no less than one thousand shares had been subscribed for and the deposits paid. He was thus in five hours the winner of £2000. He was philosopher enough to be contented with his venture, and set off the same evening for the Continent. He was never heard of again.[11]

Yes, this man was a con artist; but he could not have flourished except in an environment where greed was considered good. American health care company HealthSouth falsified its accounts, inflating income by as much as 4,000 per cent per annum for some seven years before the bubble burst and the company collapsed. Why did it get away with it? Because some of its senior executives were so excited by the company's performance that they did not ask questions. How were Barclay's traders able to rig the LIBOR rates so as to boost their own bonuses? Because they worked in a culture where bonuses represented not just money, but status as well. Greed is good.

Greed distorts judgement in many ways. It takes our minds off the real goals of the business, but it also warps our sense of right and wrong. Greed tells us that the ends justify the means, that the only thing that matters is that we meet our targets for profit, growth and market share, and any means we use to reach those targets is justified. Greed creates a moral vacuum in business cultures, a vacuum that sucks in the careers of managers and destroys them; and sometimes destroys companies too.

Cultures of conspicuous acquisition

Individual greed is often driven by a number of separate factors, two of the most prominent of which are fear and testosterone. We dealt with fear in the previous chapter, and lust is the subject of the next one. But how does the greed of a few individuals end up infecting entire companies to create cultures of conspicuous acquisition?

The source of the infection can usually be traced to a few dominant people, often the people at the top of the organization. These people set the tone for the rest of the organization through their personal example, but they also have a powerful lever of influence in the form of rewards systems, especially performance-related bonuses. If bonus schemes are based primarily or solely on hitting targets for growth, profit or market share, this will encourage a culture of collective greed.

Few companies are as blatant as the software giant Oracle, which in the 1990s offered to pay its sales staff bonuses in the form of gold bars.[12] Now, on one level it doesn't matter whether bonuses are paid in the form of hundred dollar bills or gold bars, or cowrie shells or dried squirrel's heads (all of which have been legal tender at some point in the past), but the symbolism was powerful. Oracle's salespeople were being rewarded in gold, the precious metal that has been one of the most potent symbols of greed down through history from King Midas to *The Desolation of Smaug*. On this occasion there was a public outcry and Oracle discontinued the practice; but there are plenty of other more subtle ways of reinforcing cultures of greed.

Nor does the impetus always come from the top. Any influential small group within a company can set the tone and change the culture. *Inside Arthur Andersen*, one of several books to chart the downfall of this once-proud firm, describes how the locus of power shifted from the accounting side of Arthur Andersen, famous for its probity and its high ethical standards, to the consulting arm, smaller but more profitable and more greed-driven. A few key figures in the consulting side began putting pressure on the accountants to be more flexible in their standards. Lacking the power to resist, the accountants complied. The result was Enron, with Arthur Andersen being dragged down in its wake.[13]

These and other examples cited above show, I hope, how easy it is for cultures of greed to get established in an organization. Often the initial motive is a good one. Growth, profit, market share, all are important, and there is plenty of academic research and intellectual justification for their pursuit. At risk of repeating myself, the problems begin when the metrics and targets for growth, profit and market share take over from the original goals of the business. That is why I refer to these as cultures of conspicuous acquisition: because growth and expansion become the things that the company is most proud of, that it boasts about, that it flags in its annual reports. Its real achievements are glossed over or lost entirely – or, sometimes as in the case of HealthSouth, never existed at all.

Greed for growth is a particularly easy trap to fall into because growth is so important. The problem is that we often mistake what growth is. We equate growth with physical growth, expansion, the setting up of new business units, new subsidiaries, the acquisition of new customers, and sometimes overlook the fact that there are other kinds of growth too: growth in intellectual capital, growth in business relationships, growth in terms of improved effectiveness and efficiency and better management systems. Outward growth is too often privileged over inward growth, probably because the latter is easier to measure and value. Despite what shareholders might say, that is not a good enough reason.

Scale is of course important, and a business has to be robust enough to survive. But continuous, unrestricted, unplanned, blind growth is actually one of the surest ways of killing a business. Good growth, not greedy growth, must be the way forward.

Greed for profit, as I have said, is surprisingly rare; I have worked with very few businesses over the last twenty years where profit was the dominant motive, and I tried not to be involved with these for very long. But when greed for profit does occur, it is dangerous. Greed for profit encourages the downplaying of the needs of other stakeholders in favour of our own, and it encourages us to cut corners, including ethical corners.

Greed for market share is a dangerous trap. Despite the PIMS research, there are plenty of examples of industries where the company with the largest market share is also the one in the deepest trouble. Building strong relationships with the customers you have is usually better – and almost certainly cheaper – than trying to steal customers from another company. The greed for market share also leads us into the dangerous fallacy that competition is the end game. I'll say it again, just to annoy you still further: the word 'winning' has no place in business.

Perhaps surprisingly, it turns out money isn't everything

There have been various attempts over recent years to come up with new definitions of terms such as 'profit' and 'growth' which might reflect a company's achievements more broadly. The work that has been done on valuing human capital has been particularly interesting, even if it is not yet widely accepted.[14] These efforts are laudable, but the solution to the problem of greed goes deeper. We need to stop thinking of businesses as machines for making money, and start thinking of them as what they really are: institutions that serve the people.

The idea that businesses exist to make money is well established in both business culture and urban folklore more generally. It is, however, a misconception. Making money and earning profits is a by-product of the wider exercise of producing goods and services that customers want and need. If a company does *not* produce goods and services that customers want and need, then pure and simple, it will not make a profit. The only way to stay alive then is to enter the bubble world of acquisitions, stacking up acquired companies to fill the balance sheet; but sooner or later, the price for these acquisitions has to be paid, and the only way to pay it is to create customers and generate revenue. Otherwise the bubble will burst, as is it did for Nortel, Royal Ahold and many others.

Ford, in its early days, understood exactly the relationship between customers and business. Henry Ford had an almost instinctive connection with the American public; he knew how people thought, what they wanted and what their dreams were. In the end, Ford did not sell cars. He sold *mobility*, the opportunity to get behind the wheel and move on to a different town or a different state in pursuit of opportunity. Personal mobility gave people a chance not just to fulfil their own dreams but also to become part of the larger American Dream. Lehman Brothers, too, understood in its early days that running a bank was about much more than making money; it was about providing a vital service that a hungry, growing economy needed. Banking was not just business, it was a social mission. Only much later did the bank lose sight of that mission and succumb to the greed for profits and growth, just as Ford did.

'All markets cater to the needs of the people', wrote the fourteenth-century polymath Ibn Khaldun, and nothing has happened in the intervening centuries to prove him wrong.[15] History, past and present experience all show that the businesses that make money over the long term are those that develop close relationships with customers; and do so by delivering quality consistently over time. In *Beyond the Familiar*, Patrick Barwise and Seán Meehan give a profile of Aggreko, a company that specializes in providing temporary power supply and temperature control systems, both on long-term contracts for cities and corporations and for one-off occasions such as major sporting events and also the inauguration of US presidents. Aggreko's brand promise is 'exceptional service and total reliability, period'. Barwise and Meehan describe how the company prepared for the inauguration of President Barack Obama in 2009:

> *Everything has been planned to the last detail. There is no margin for error. All contractors are best in class and deemed totally reliable – not 95%, 99% or even 99.9% reliable, absolutely totally reliable.[16]*

Aggreko's number one priority is its customers. Are they happy? Are they receiving good service? Where are the faults that need to be fixed? Aggreko is one of the very few companies that measures not only customer satisfaction, but customer *dis*satisfaction as well. Customer satisfaction surveys, Aggreko managers feel, very often ask the wrong questions. People will tell you why they are happy, without necessarily telling you why or even if they are also unhappy. So Aggreko makes its customers its number one priority; and in doing so, it makes a lot of money.

Aggreko is not a greedy company; a greedy company would squeeze its contractors on price rather than worrying about quality, and would focus on grabbing the biggest possible market share rather than delivering the best possible service. Instead, Aggreko concentrates on service, and the profits flow in naturally; £246 million of profit in 2013, on revenues of about £1.5 billion.

Getting rid of greed means establishing a culture where, again, the focus is on stakeholders, not on the company itself. Building relationships and establishing a position in the market and a reputation for excellence, coupled with efficient and effective operating and management systems, is the primary recipe for management success; but in all that recipe, the most important ingredient is customers. Money isn't everything. Customers are.

Ah, some of you will be saying at this point, if only it were that easy. There is more to running a successful business than just customer focus.

To which I reply: have you tried it?

[1] Bala Chakravarthy and Peter Lorange, *Profit or Growth? Why You Don't Have to Choose*, Harlow: FT Press, 2012.

[2] Marilyn Livingstone, 'Plus ça Change: Why Banks in Trouble Are Nothing New', *Corporate Finance Review*, (March–April 2008), pp. 24–9.

[3] http://www.ft.com/cms/s/0/ef7f7e1a-ed35-11e2-ad6e-00144feabdc0.html#axzz3Et79BVIg

[4] Hector Bolitho, *Alfred Mond, First Lord Melchett*, London: Martin Secker, 1932.

[5] For more detail see Raymond de Roover, 'The Concept of Just Price Theory and Economic Policy', *Journal of Economic History* 18 (1958), pp. 418–34; repr. in Mark Blaug (ed.), *St Thomas Aquinas*, Aldershot: Edward Elgar, 1991, pp. 97–113.

[6] http://uk.reuters.com/article/2014/10/01/uk-tesco-probe-idUKKCN0HQ33L20141001

[7] Robert D. Buzzell, Bradley T. Gale and Ralph G.M. Sultan, 'Market Share: A Key to Profitability', *Harvard Business Review*, January 1975; Buzzell and Gale, *The PIMS Principle: Linking Strategy to Performance*, New York: The Free Press, 1987.

[8] Geoffrey M. Hodgson and Thorbjørn Knudsen, *Darwin's Conjecture: The Search for General Principles of Social and Scientific Evolution*, Chicago: University of Chicago Press, 2010.

[9] A.G. Lafley and Roger Martin, *Playing to Win: How Strategy Really Works*, Boston: Harvard Business Review Press, 2013.

[10] Lafley and Martin, *Playing to Win*, p. 212.

[11] Charles White Mackay, *Extraordinary Popular Delusions and the Madness of Crowds*, London: Richard Bentley, 1841, pp. 55–6.

[12] Mike Wilson, *The Difference Between God and Larry Ellison*, New York: HarperBusiness, 2003.

[13] Susan E. Squires, Cynthia J. Smith, Lorna McDougall and William R. Yeack, *Inside Arthur Andersen: Shifting Values, Unexpected Consequences*, Engelwood Cliffs: FT Prentice Hall, 2003.

[14] See for example Alan Burston-Jones and J.C. Spender (eds), *The Oxford Handbook of Human Capital*, Oxford: Oxford University Press, 2011, and also Michael Reddy and Ann Graham (eds), *The Human Capital Handbook*, http://www.humancapitalhandbook.co.uk

[15] Ibn Khaldun, *The Muqaddimah*, trans. Franz Rosenthal, London: Routledge, 1986, vol. 2, p. 276.

[16] Barwise and Meehan, *Beyond the Familiar*, p. 42.

Chapter 8

Lust in action

The word 'lust' is usually equated with sex, and sexual desire does play a role in some management failures. But lust, according to the *Oxford English Dictionary*, can also mean 'strong or excessive desires' more generally. Early Christian theologians equated lust with sensual gratification, but its roots are deeper than that.

Ultimately, lust is about control. Greedy people want more of everything; lustful ones want to control what is already there. Of course, there is a good deal of overlap between the two, and the greed that leads us to pursue growth, profit and market share is very often accompanied by the lust for control and domination. I have split the two concepts, however, because their manifestations and consequences can be very different. Here, I will concentrate on those aspects of lust – broadly defined – that do not overlap with the elements of greed that we discussed in the previous chapter.

At the heart of the lust for control and domination is aggression. For alpha males, or those who see themselves in that role – and this can include women – lustful behaviour is a channel for establishing dominance over others. Freudian psychologists would probably say that sexual desire lies at the heart of the lust for power; that is as may be, but much of the damaging behaviour caused by lust has, overtly at least, little to do with sex and much more to do with power. The amount of dominance and control one can establish is a critical factor in personal self-esteem. I have power over you; therefore, I am better than you.

Power is of course an interesting concept in its own right. Why people feel the need to have power over others is a subject that has occupied many psychology textbooks, and as many texts on organization behaviour. There is of course a positive side to power, as Rosabeth Moss Kanter explains:

> When managers are in powerful situations, it is easier for them to accomplish more. Because the tools are there, they are likely to be highly motivated and, in

turn, to be able to motivate subordinates... They gain the respect and coopera-
tion that attributed power brings. Subordinates' talents are resources rather
than threats.[1]

Kanter's view assumes that power is wielded for benevolent means. But, as a famous article by Seth Rosenthal and Todd Pittinsky, 'Narcissistic Leadership', points out, this is not always the case. Some leaders 'are principally motivated by their own egomaniacal needs and beliefs, superseding the needs and interests of the constituents they lead'.[2] Rosenthal and Pittinsky draw a line between *charismatic leadership*, which seeks to motivate people, and *narcissistic leadership*, which seeks to exploit people in order to gather more power for oneself, be it the referent power that comes with reputation, or actual mental and physical control over other people – or both.

Manfred Kets de Vries talks about the extremes of such behaviour and the lengths to which the lust for power can take people in his study of despots and tyrants, and while he talks primarily about political leaders, there is no doubt that similar behaviour can be found in the world of business too.[3] Harold Geneen, the tyrannical head of American conglomerate ITT, rode roughshod over his managers and employees and drove the group down the road to ever greater expansion, gathering ever more power to himself as he did so. Like Henry Ford before him, Geneen enjoyed the media attention his success brought him, and grew ever more arrogant in his pursuit of power; and ever more willing to take risks. 'If risk is a bucking bronco, a conglomerate is the best way to enjoy the ride', he wrote.[4]

But Geneen's lust for power proved his undoing. His 'wafer-thin mint' came when it emerged that in the 1970s he had offered the US Central Intelligence Agency $1 million if it would help prevent the left-wing government of Chile from nationalizing ITT's holdings there. Soon after, with CIA help, the Chilean government was overthrown by a military coup. The lengths that Geneen would go to get and keep power scandalized the world, and ITT's offices were picketed and even bombed. Financial performance began to suffer, and the company's share price slid from $60 to $12. In 1978 Geneen was fired by his own board, and never held a senior management position again (Table 8.1).

Table 8.1 A Typology of Lust

Type	Manifestation
Sexual lust	I want pleasure and don't care how I get it
Lust for domination	I want to dominate other people
Lust for recognition	I want everyone to know how good I am (FIGJAM)
Bureaucratic lust	I want to build an empire with me as its leader

As in previous chapters, our interest here is not in the behaviour of individuals, save as that behaviour affects and impacts on the rest of the organization, as on the culture that permits and even encourages such behaviour. Harold Geneen was a brilliant and charismatic individual, but no one person has enough power to force an entire organization to do its will. Henry Ford was able to dominate and control Ford Motors, thanks to the acquiescence of pliant subordinates like Charles Sorenson, and Richard Fuld's ambitions could have been reined in had his board of directors been more proactive. The point, as Manfred Kets de Vries makes very clearly, is that *no one person* is responsible for failures. Leaders rely on a coterie of people around them who share a common culture and worldview, which means that they condone or even encourage what the leader does.

Sex, lies and the Internet

William Whiteley was a brilliant businessman. A self-made man, he left school in 1845 at the age of fourteen and apprenticed in the retail trade. A visit to the Great Exhibition of 1851 gave him the inspiration for building a large retail outlet selling a variety of goods under one roof, a kind of Crystal Palace of retailing. He visited Paris where he saw the first experiments in department store design carried out by Aristide and Marguerite Boucicaut at Au Bon Marché. In 1872 he established Britain's first department store, Whiteley's in London. Whiteley's caught the public imagination, and was an immediate success. Whiteley himself became known as the 'the Universal Provider', and it was said that he could supply anything from pins to elephants. Queen Victoria was among his customers.

In the late 1870s Whiteley took a mistress, Louisa Turner, whom he kept in a flat in Brighton on the south coast of England, visiting her at intervals. In 1879 she gave birth to a son, Horace. The Universal Provider refused to acknowledge the child as his own, and had no contact with the boy. In 1907, Horace decided he had had enough and forced his way into Whiteley's office, demanding that Whiteley acknowledge him as his son. When Whiteley refused, Horace drew a revolver and shot him dead.[5]

Few managers and leaders suffer the consequences of sexual desire quite so fatally as Whiteley, but it has certainly wrecked a good many careers down through the years, and continues to do so. The worst problems are often ones of double standards. Whiteley, while keeping a mistress of his own, insisted on segregating his male and female staff and fired any staff who engaged in relations with each other. Henry Ford kept a mistress too, but banned women from the site of the rubber plant at Fordlandia on the grounds that their presence would be bad for the moral fibre of the workers. Billy Butlin, pioneer of holiday camps in Britain, insisted on 'wholesome behaviour' and strict decorum among staff and guests alike while living with his first wife's sister as his mistress. All these things cause resentment amongst employees, though few go as far as Whiteley's staff who on several occasions tried to burn down the department store.

Whiteley's business never fully recovered from his death, and the store failed to keep pace with new rivals such as Harrod's, John Lewis and Selfridges. Generally, though, it is fairly rare for the sexual misdemeanours of a single person to have an impact on a business.[6] More dangerous is the emergence of cultures that appear to condone inappropriate sexual behaviour. Such a culture was exposed in the late 1950s by journalist Edward R. Murrow, who revealed the widespread practice of American companies providing prostitutes to favoured customers or potential customers as a kind of sweetener to encourage them to do more business. Murrow estimated that in New York alone more than 30,000 women made their living in this way, some actually being listed on the payrolls of companies.[7] A similar scandal erupted at Volkswagen in the early 2000s, and reports of similar practices have emerged in Hong Kong and Japan.[8] While no companies suffered major damage from these scandals, there is no doubt that for a time, at least, their reputations were tarnished. And individual careers can be affected; the revelation that US Secret Service agents were using prostitutes while on duty in Columbia was among the factors that cost the director of the service his job.

Sexual harassment continues to be an issue in many organizations. As well as being morally unacceptable, sexual harassment causes disturbances in the workplace and often affects people who are not themselves direct targets; it is not just the human rights of the victim that need to be considered, but also the overall harmony of the business. A serial sex pest can do as much harm to group morale, if not more, as a workplace bully. The Tailhook affair, where American navy officers were alleged to have sexually assaulted eighty-three women and seven men over the course of a four-day conference in Las Vegas in 1991 was a major scandal in its own right, but what really shook the naval establishment was the revelation that senior officers present at the conference were aware of the assaults and took no steps to prevent them. Again, the US Navy survived as institution, but many careers were damaged or destroyed: not just those of the assaulters, but of the victims too. Good managers will be alert to the signs of sexual harassment and will crack down hard on it.

The problem is compounded further when the manager himself or herself is the harasser. A Canadian company was forced to part with its CEO a few years ago when he mistook a gift from a female colleague as being an invitation to make sexual advances to her. He proved to be one of those men who are incapable of understanding the meaning of the word 'no'. Formal complaints were made, and even worse, the matter became public and was reported in the media around the world.

Air India has suffered a series of claims of sexual harassment over the years, most notably in 2009 when a pilot and a male member of cabin crew exchanged punches while their plane was in mid-flight, over allegations that the pilot had harassed a female flight attendant.[9] That incident – which was also reported worldwide – caused immense reputational damage to Air India. The event was of course investigated and the crew members involved grounded; but the problem persists. Air India has many problems at the moment, and this sort of behaviour on the part of staff and managers, and the company's failure to crack down on it, is not helping either its reputation or staff morale.

 A culture where sexual harassment is winked at, or excused along the lines of 'boys will be boys'.

This is not to say that we should go back to the days of Ford and Whiteley and ban all social and sexual contact between members of staff. Indeed, there is research which suggests that 'hot' workplaces where staff are encouraged to socialize together and where relationships are commonplace have higher morale and are more productive and innovative than 'cold' workplaces where relationships are frowned upon or banned. The danger signal is when sexual relationships that are non-consensual and unequal begin to become acceptable.

A high incidence of divorces and extramarital affairs can also be a sign that not all is well in the corporate culture. One has to be careful here not to intrude on private matters, of course, and sadly many relationships do break down. The time to worry is when you look around a social gathering and see large numbers of 'trophy wives' (or, less commonly, trophy husbands). In the past it was almost de rigueur in some company cultures for men, on reaching a certain managerial eminence, to put away their first wife and marry another, much younger and more glamorous one.

I have lost count of the number of cases I have found where senior managers divorced their wives and remarried ballerinas. Why ballerinas? I have a theory, as yet unproven and probably unprovable, that when some men look at ballet dancers gliding across the stage they see their ideal woman: beautiful, graceful, sexually alluring; and silent.

The obvious question at this point is, why does this matter? Why should high divorce rates and trophy wives be a danger signal? The answer is that these things are often symptoms of deeper problems. High divorce rates might be a signal that managers are under too much pressure and are failing to manage their own work–life balance. In that case, they are probably underperforming as managers too. Alternatively, we could be looking at a 'macho' culture where men put their own interests first and undervalue women. Most of the men who married ballerinas were not huge fans of ballet (to those that are, and who married for love, I apologize, but you are in a minority). They married women they thought they could control; and where they wish to control their wives, they may wish to control other things and other people as well.

 High divorce rates among senior managers and board members.

All of these things – sexual hypocrisy, sexual harassment, sex for control and cultures of sexual exploitation – matter much more now than they did a hundred years ago, or fifty, or thirty, thanks to the power of the Internet. In past times, it was easier for companies to stifle news of bad behaviour, or at least keep it within bounded circles. Today, email and social media mean that each individual indiscretion is known about worldwide in seconds. Even harmless affairs can become the stuff of Facebook legend.

The Internet loves sex, and if you are in any kind of position of responsibility or power, there will be someone out there waiting to plaster descriptions of your sexual activities all over the World Wide Web. The three things to remember about having a love life in the Internet Age are: discretion, discretion, discretion. Do nothing you would be ashamed of were it to form the basis of headline in tomorrow's newspapers (because there is an excellent chance that it will).

And generally speaking, when your company is making headlines because of the sexual activities of its managers rather than its corporate performance, you have a problem. If your managers are spending more time thinking about their groins than thinking about their customers, then their attention is in the wrong place. In and of itself, sexual misdemeanours are not company killers (whether or not they should be is a matter for a separate debate). The real problem lies in the culture that permits such things to happen.

The urge to dominate

From the urge to dominate sexually we move on to the urge to dominate more generally, the lust for control. Here we see particularly strongly the overlap referred to above, between greed for growth, profits and market share and lust for control. Having dealt with issues external to the company in the last chapter, I want to focus now on internal matters, how the lust for control affects organizations from the inside and prevents them from running smoothly.

The lust for control and dominion over others is stronger in some individuals than in others. Quite often this manifests itself in a fairly benign form as ambition or drive. One of the further paradoxes of management and leadership is that a measure of ambition is necessary in order to succeed – again, as has often been pointed out often over the years, people become managers because they want to get things done[10] – but at the same time ambition is a trap which can bring people low.

It has even been questioned whether those who *want* to rise to senior positions are really the best people to lead us; does their desire to lead mean they are more focused on themselves than on their followers or their customers? The British politician Eric Pickles once commented that any teenager who sets out with the serious ambition of becoming prime minister or president when they grow up probably needs psychiatric help. Certainly, there have been successful self-effacing leaders who channelled their ambitions into their companies rather than their own careers; William McKnight of 3M was one, Li Ka-shing of Hutchinson Whampoa and Ratan Tata of the Tata Group are two others.

However, there are also many others who see senior positions as a route to personal power. Like arrogant managers, these can be identified and either controlled or pushed out of the organization. Most businesses would probably agree that there is no place in their midst for people who seek personal gain rather than success for the organization as a whole. Nonetheless, cultures do emerge – again, often without anyone realizing it – where the lust for control becomes an established part of that culture and competition for personal gain dominates or even eclipses the goals of the business.

 A culture where the formation of personal power blocs and 'fiefdoms' is seen as normal, and where there is a strong cult of personality.

In *Management and Machiavelli*, Anthony Jay describes cultures which are based almost entirely on personal power.[11] He uses the metaphor of 'baronial warfare' to describe how power is used. The 'barons' are powerful managers who control a part of the organization and seek to expand their own power base at the expense of their rivals. In effect, they see the organization as zero-sum entity, where each can only expand by taking power from someone else. The idea that growth could come through collaboratively growing the entire organization does not occur.

Among the examples Jay cites is the American firm General Dynamics, which was made up of nine virtually independent business units all at feud with each other. Frank Pace, who took over as chief executive in 1957 'found himself virtually a prisoner of his feudal barons'.[12] Between 1960 and 1962 General Dynamics lost $425 million, then a world record for corporate losses.

Jay believes the problem at General Dynamics and other companies affected by baronial warfare could be solved by the imposition of strong leadership from the centre, a king (or queen) who brings the warring barons to heel. That itself, as the history of actual baronial warfare shows, is far from easy and far from bloodless; it took the leaders of Japan under the Meiji emperor nine years to quell the last of the barons and bring Japan under control.[13] Restructuring and reorganizing companies to bring about more central control requires a degree of ruthlessness which few managers possess to the required degree. Much more common, as we saw earlier, is a botched restructuring which leaves the company in worse shape than it was before.

Further, some corporate cultures actually think baronial warfare is a good thing. In a kind of bizarre corporate version of *Game of Thrones*, in the late 1970s Coca-Cola supremo Robert Woodruff (known universally as 'the Boss' thanks to his majority shareholding in the company, though he held no senior position) decided to replace his CEO, Paul Austin, and offered the position to whichever of his senior managers could take it. There followed a scramble for power, a three-cornered fight between Roberto Goizueta, Ian Wilson and Donald Keough. Goizueta and Keough eventually formed an alliance to force out Wilson, each agreeing to appoint the other as his deputy if the other should win the top post. Most of the board preferred Keough, but Goizueta countered by winning support among Coca-Cola's bottling companies, promising the stronger ones that they could take over some of the smaller divisions, and also courted some of the other leading shareholders. In 1981 Goizueta took over as chairman and chief executive, but did honour his agreement by making Keough his number two.

Was this a good thing? Had this resulted in the right choice? Four years later, facing increasing competition from Pepsi, Goizueta led Coca-Cola into its greatest public failure, the disastrous scrapping of its iconic Coke brand in favour of 'New Coke'. Many tens of millions were invested in this project, but less than two years later as sales plummeted, Goizueta was forced to bring back the old brand; New Coke faded discreetly from the scene. It seems clear that Goizueta himself rammed this project through, actually concealing it from 'the Boss', Robert Woodruff.[14] Of course, a word of caution is in order: Keough or Wilson, had they been successful, might well have made the same mistake. The point is not who was in charge; the point is that an adversarial culture based on personal control had clouded people's judgement, both about the company and its products and about who should be its leaders. Coca-Cola lost focus, and though never in any danger of collapse, paid a heavy price.

Column inches

Some companies also develop narcissistic cultures where lust for recognition becomes a dominant feature. Again, there are strong overlaps with the lust for control, in that recognition and control often go hand in hand; the more power you have, the more admired and flattered you are. Ida Tarbell, in her great early twentieth-century polemic against the Standard Oil Company, wrote despairingly of a generation of young people in America and around the world who admired almost to the point of reverence business leaders such as John D. Rockefeller who had climbed to dominance by devious, immoral and illegal means.[15] None of that apparently mattered; all that mattered was that they succeeded, and the ends thus justified the means.

Rockefeller, to be fair, did not seek public recognition; indeed, he actively avoided it. But plenty of other business people love the limelight. They desire fame, and the more famous they become, the more they court fame. For some, being on television matters more than running the business. For others it is not so much the fleeting fame of the media, Andy Warhol's 'fifteen minutes' that matters as much as immortality in the form of the businesses they run. 'Becoming CEO of Ahold was only the first step', write Stewart Hamilton and Alicia Micklethwayt of Ahold's former leader, Cees van der Hoeven. 'He had to stamp his own impression on the company.'[16] Scent-marking by incoming CEOs is not uncommon, and often takes the firm of reorganizing or restructuring, the new man or woman seeking to mould the company in his or her own image. As we saw earlier, these restructurings generally cause widespread unhappiness, leaving most people wondering what was wrong with the old way of doing things; the only people who are happy are the CEO, who believes he/she has now cemented his/her place in history, and the consultants who earn substantial fees when they come in to pick up the pieces.

Entrepreneurs also like to stamp their own personality on the companies they create, again in the (usually mistaken) belief that this will bring them immortality. It did, in a way, for Henry Ford and also for Bernie Ebbers at Tyco, two narcissistic leaders in the classic mould who deliberately courted attention. Ebbers's announcement that he was divinely favoured was a fairly blunt assertion of narcissism; Ford was more subtle, dispensing Olympian wisdom about business, politics, society and the world at large through his books and speeches and inviting the world to tell him how clever he was.

 Celebrity CEOs.

Leaders like van der Hoeven, Ford and Ebbers don't just lead in a narcissistic manner, they create cultures where everyone else is expected to behave narcissistically as well. People are rewarded and publicly recognized for their personal achievements rather than their contributions to the company. This brings us back to bonuses, and of course, nowhere is the culture of lust for recognition more prominent today than in financial services where large bonuses – despite numerous efforts to cap them in recent years – remain the order of the day. Bonuses have been linked to the development of a culture of greed in the financial services community, but the culture of recognition lust they spawned is far more powerful and much harder to eradicate. It is not just money that bankers and traders seek when they chase bonuses; it is recognition. There is a pecking order in many companies, with those with the biggest bonuses at the top of it. My bonus is bigger than yours; therefore, I am better than you.

Again, this wouldn't matter except that the pursuit of personal recognition impairs judgement and distracts people from the real purpose of their business. Nick Leeson loved the adulation he received as a top trader in the Singapore stock market, and it was the reputation he enjoyed as much as the money he earned that set him off on the road to ruin. You could say that he knew the risks he was running, but the problem is that he also took the bank that employed, Baring's, down with him.

Yet, as I remarked in the opening chapter of this book, Baring's senior managers were not blameless. They helped create the culture that encouraged traders to seek recognition and become famous for their daring and skill. They cannot hide from their own responsibility in the Leeson affair; as subsequent inquiries showed, their failure to institute adequate controls over Leeson was in large part responsible for the failure.[17] Similarly, Barclay's senior staff should not have escaped censure over the LIBOR scandal when traders conspired to rig inter-bank lending rates in order to boots their own bonuses. They created that culture; they sowed the wind.

 The prevalent belief that personal bonuses are more important than the company's goals.

The lust for recognition is, like the lust for control, okay in small doses. It does no harm to encourage people to seek recognition for their genuine achievements. It is when the recognition becomes more important than the achievement that we run into problems. If staff and managers are working primarily or solely towards a goal of recognition, then their own personal agendas will start to take over and the goals of the company will be shunted to one side.

The bureaucratic glutton

To those familiar with the old definition of lust, bureaucratic lust sounds like a contradiction in terms. The very word, with its connotations of dullness and conformity, is a veritable passion killer; our hearts do not beat louder when we hear 'bureaucracy' whispered – however sensuously – in our ears. No one, apart perhaps from the occasional tax inspector, has ever employed the word 'bureaucracy' in a proposal of marriage.

But bureaucratic lust, the lust for ever-expanding dominion and empire, is a very real force in business. That great analyst of bureaucracies, C. Northcote Parkinson, observed that the purpose of bureaucracies is 'to multiply subordinates, not rivals'.[18] Bureaucracies don't like fights; they prefer peaceful expansion by diplomatic means, but their lust for domination is no less potent for that. Greedy managers go out and conquer; bureaucratic ones colonize the host body of the organization from within, and in doing so they establish dominion.

Not all bureaucracies are bad. Some small, lean bureaucracies are incredibly efficient. The possession of a small but very effective governing bureaucracy is one of the key factors that allowed the tiny nation of England to punch above its weight in European politics for several centuries. And there will be times and places when some element of bureaucratic structure and control is necessary. Completely anarchic organizations *are* possible, but they only flourish in rare circumstances. Most people, it seems, do need and want an element of control in their lives.

The problem comes when the bureaucracy gets out of control and, as Parkinson describes, sees its own perpetuation as the only goal that matters. *Enabling bureaucracies* are those that help other people to achieve their goals, and help the company as a whole to pursue its mission. *Toxic bureaucracies* hinder the company's mission and crush the aspirations and hopes of individuals, usually for no other reason that these endanger the bureaucracy's own power and expansion. Nothing matters now but the bureaucracy. George Orwell described the triumph of political toxic bureaucracy in his novel *1984*, but plenty of us have experienced life in toxic bureaucratic businesses, the chief difference being that Room 101 is full, not of rats, but of procedures manuals.

 Bureaucracies that control power and information without sharing them.

Toxic bureaucracies can take hold almost anywhere in an organization, but they are most likely to flourish where there is a large number of (necessary or unnecessary) rules, where there is relatively little direct customer contact and, most importantly, the local department already has a certain amount of power over other parts of the organization. Compliance offices, health and safety departments, quality control managers and others are prime candidates for bureaucratic infection, but by far and away the preferred host for the bureaucratic virus is the finance department, where all three conditions obtain. Finance managers, once sucked into the bureaucracy, begin to think first and foremost of how they can expand the power they already possess at the expense of those around them. I control your budget; therefore, I am better than you.

Ripping down the walls around the finance department and breaking down its bureaucracy is a major task, but it has to be done. In *Reinventing the CFO*, Jeremy Hope argued cogently that in many organizations the finance department acts effectively as a brake on investment, innovation, pretty much everything.[19] De-bureaucratizing, he believed, could make the finance department an engine of growth, not a harness of restraint.

Toxic bureaucracies are oriented first and foremost towards their own expansion and survival, and they are willing to use any means to ensure that survival. And once we reach a point where the ends justify the means, we are of course opening the door to potential corruption. To some people, the term 'bureaucracy' has become almost synonymous with corruption. This is ironic, when we consider that bureaucracies were first developed as a means of ensuring reporting, control and accountability and were therefore a defence *against* corruption.

What has happened to bureaucracies? Purely and simply, they have become vehicles for the lust for domination over others. When the wrong people get control of bureaucracies, they have to hand the perfect tool for establishing control. Halting their progress and levering them out is, as Jeremy Hope says, very difficult, time-consuming and expensive. It is far better and far less expensive to prevent toxic bureaucracies from forming in the first place.

Cultures of selfish domination

The question of balance between the needs of the individual and the needs of the organization has preoccupied management writers for decades. Some are in no doubt; Luther Gulick firmly put the needs of the organization first and argued that individuals should sublimate themselves to the greater good of the business, even being prepared to sacrifice their own jobs if necessary.[20] Charles Handy was not so sure, and argued for a balance between the needs of the two; after all, organizations full of unhappy people tend to be a lot less effective than organizations full of happy ones.[21] It has also been observed that the more 'collectivist' nature of Asian cultures makes people there more group-oriented and therefore staff and managers work to serve the business first and themselves second, while in the more individualistic West it is often the other way around.

We have to beware of generalizations, of course, and there is plenty of toxic bureaucracy in east Asia; also, there is some anecdotal evidence that in China and Japan, young people are becoming more individualistic and less willing to stand in a row every morning and sing the company song. Similarly, in the West there are companies where people do identify strongly with the mission and goals of the business and are willing to make sacrifices to reach those goals. Much depends on the culture of the company itself. Is it an enabling culture which draws people together willingly, where leaders see their main task as serving their followers? Or is it a *culture of selfish domination*, where the gratification of a few individuals takes precedence over the needs of the business – and the rest of the members of the organization?

We have already seen some of the ways that lust affects businesses and hampers their quest to fulfil their mission. *Sexual lust*, the kind most people think about, if it is allowed to run out of control leads to problems such as sexual harassment and public affairs that form the basis for unfavourable publicity. But further, a lack of sexual self-control can also be a symptom of deeper problems of excessive aggression, misogyny and the narrow-minded thinking that we also saw when we discussed arrogance and fear. (Sexual lust, arrogance and fear: spot the connection.)

The *lust for domination* leads to cultures where personal power is esteemed and encouraged. Barons set up their own power blocs and fight each other for control; the one with the most supporters or who can control the largest part of the organization is deemed the winner. This is doubtless very entertaining for the barons themselves and allows them to be swash-buckling and aggressive, but it doesn't usually serve the interests of the business. Customers and employees tend to be the chief collateral damage of these conflicts, along with the reputation of the business itself.

The *lust for recognition* manifests itself in cultures where people are encouraged to gratify their personal narcissism. Bonuses and other forms of recognition are linked to personal status and self-esteem, and managers who hit their targets are praised and exalted above others. We all like to be recognized for our achievements, of course, but there is a line between recognition for achievements and recognition for its own sake that must not be crossed.

Bureaucratic lust is similar to control lust in some ways, but relies more on subtle conquest than outright aggression. Bureaucracies often start in one part of a business and then spread out to control much or all of it. It is rare to find rival bureaucracies competing for control within the same business, at least for long; sooner or later they will come to accommodation and team up to divide power between them. Bureaucratic lust once again draws the company's attention away from its real goals, as everyone concentrates instead on ensuring the perpetuation of the bureaucracy itself.

'The expense of spirit in a waste of shame is lust in action', wrote William Shakespeare.[22] Lust saps the energy of companies; it turns them in directions that diverge from their true goals. The last thing I want to sound like is a puritan, but allowing these cultures of selfish domination to develop is both dangerous and costly. Cultures like the ones described above add nothing positive to the balance sheet. They are, rather, a cost; they waste time, they waste resources, they waste reputation and above all they waste people.

Three reasons why self-control is a really good idea

Cultures of selfish domination are just that: selfish. They privilege the desires of the individual over the needs of the business, and in doing so they impair the ability of the business to perform; which means in turn that customers receive a lower quality of service. Lustful managers gratify their desires not only at the expense of the company, but of society as well.

Oh, very well, some might say, but so what? *I'm* what matters, and so long as I get what I want, who cares about the rest of you? It would be nice to think that people with this outlook on life never get hired into positions where they have authority over other people, but then it would also be nice to think that pigs could, with a proper runway and a good tailwind, become airborne of their own volition.

So, two points have to be made. First, if you take the position that your own interests are all that matters, and you work in an organization where everyone else takes the same view, then you won't be employed by that organization for very long because, even if no one sensible comes along and fires you, eventually your attitude will disgust your customers and your employees so much that they will leave, and the company will collapse. Second, if you spot people with these attitudes in your organization, then it is important to get them out, as quickly as possible, before they do damage.

There are three reasons why lust is a bad idea, and why self-control and shifting the focus to other people is a good thing. Here they are:

First, self-control means you and your company don't make headlines for the wrong reason. Contrary to received wisdom, there is indeed such a thing as bad publicity; ask Air India, or Harold Geneen. Reputation, or goodwill, is one of a company's most valuable assets, and contributes hugely towards such things as the value of the corporate brand. Unacceptable behaviour by staff and management, especially on an ongoing basis, can corrode reputation very quickly. As Benjamin Franklin said, it takes ten years to build a reputation and ten minutes to lose it. A single indiscretion can not only damage a brand, it can destroy careers.

Second, self-control keeps everyone focused on the things that actually matter, the aims and mission of the company and, above all, its customers. Lust, as we said, drags attention away from these. Self-control helps us to remember that other people matter too; perhaps more than we do, or at least just as much.

Third, self-control allows us to bring internal harmony to organizations. No matter how you see organizations, as machines or biological organisms or political systems or active minds, or any other of Gareth Morgan's eight metaphors, it is still necessary for the parts to work in harmony with each other.[23] As long as lust dominates, harmony will never prevail; the clash of personal interests will generate too much friction. Even toxic bureaucracies, designed to reduce conflict and sublimate all to a central will, do not create harmony because the consensus they create is forced and imposed, not voluntarily entered into.

In order to create harmony, we have to be prepared to negotiate, sublimate our lusts for whatever we lust for and be willing to give something away to our colleagues, subordinates and leaders. We have to be willing to surrender partial control over ourselves; knowing that at the same time, we are gaining partial control over others. Our responsibility is twofold; to use our own control wisely, and to submit to the control of others politely and with dignity.

Sounds simple, when put like that, doesn't it? Then why is real harmony so rare?

---

[1] Rosabeth Moss Kanter, 'Power Failures in Management Circuits', in Derek S. Pugh (ed.), *Organization Theory*, London: Penguin, 1997, p. 322.

[2] Seth A. Rosenthal and Todd L. Pittinsky, 'Narcissistic Leadership', *The Leadership Quarterly* 17 (2006), pp. 629.

3 Manfred F.R. Kets de Vries, 'The Spirit of Despotism: Understanding the Tyrant Within', INSEAD working paper, http://www.insead.edu/facultyresearch/research/details_papers.cfm?id=13452

4 Harold S. Geneen, *The Synergy Myth, and Other Ailments of Business Today*, New York: St Martin's Press, 1997; for an appraisal of Geneen's management style and attitudes see Anthony Sampson, *The Sovereign State of ITT*, Greenwich: Fawcett Publications, 1974.

5 R.S. Lambert, *The Universal Provider: A Study of William Whiteley and the Rise of the London Department Store*, London: George Harrap, 1938.

6 Although as journalist Daniel G. Jennings point out, there has been very little research in this area; Jennings asks, and we are entitled to ask with him, why this is so, http://www.moneyexaminers.com/sex-scandals-kill-stock-prices/

7 http://www.bloombergview.com/articles/2013-02-21/the-strange-history-of-corporate-sex-scandals

8 http://www.theguardian.com/world/2008/jan/13/germany.automotive

9 http://news.bbc.co.uk/1/hi/world/south_asia/8289313.stm

10 See for example http://www.forbes.com/sites/karlmoore/2014/10/02/millennials-work-for-purpose-not-paycheck/

11 Anthony Jay, *Management and Machiavelli*, London: Hodder & Stoughton, 1967.

12 Jay, *Management and Machiavelli*, p. 44.

13 From the accession of the Meiji Emperor to the final quelling of the Satsuma revolt in 1877.

14 Frederick Allen, *Secret Formula: How Brilliant Marketing and Relentless Salesmanship Made Coda-Cola the Best-Known Product in the World*, New York: HarperBusiness, 1994.

15 Ida M. Tarbell, *The History of the Standard Oil Company*, New York: McClure's, 1904, 2 vols.

16 Hamilton and Micklethwayt, *Greed and Corporate Failure*, p. 149.

17 The Bank of England concluded that 'those with direct executive responsibility for establishing effective controls must bear much of the blame'; *Report of the Board of Banking Supervision Inquiry into the Circumstances of the Collapse of Barings, 18 July 1995*, http://www.numa.com/ref/barings/bar00.htm; see also Helga Drummond, 'Living in a Fool's Paradise: The Collapse of Baring's Bank', *Management Decision* 40(3) (2002), pp. 232–8.

18 C. Northcote Parkinson, *Parkinson's Law*, London: John Murray, 1957.

19 Jeremy Holt, *Reinventing the CFO*, Boston: Harvard Business School Press, 1996.

20 Luther H. Gulick, *Administrative Reflections from World War II*, University: University of Alabama Press, 1948.

21 Charles Handy, *Understanding Organisations*, London: Penguin, 1976.

22 Sonnet 129.

23 Gareth Morgan, *Images of Organization*, Newbury Park: Sage, 1986.

Chapter 9

The curse of Descartes

If you drive the backroads through eastern Alsace, along the western edge of the Rhine valley, you will from time to time see strange protuberances rising from the ground, lumps of concrete and rusting steel, all facing east towards Germany. These are the remains of the Maginot Line, the strongest system of fortifications ever built, dwarfing even the Great Wall of China in their sheer complexity.

The Maginot Line was a vast improvement on the trenches of the First World War, which were protected only by barbed wire and sandbags. Here, the casemates were made of reinforced concrete proof against even the heaviest artillery shell. Stronger still were the miniature fortresses, or *ouvrages*, stuffed full of artillery and machines guns, that protected potential weak spots in the line. The French soldiers who defended the line did not live in muddy dugouts; they had comfortable underground living quarters with air conditioning. Underground railways brought in fresh supplies and ammunition, enabling the garrisons to hold out for months. The engineers who designed the Maginot Line thought, and military experts around the world agreed, that the line was impregnable against direct attack.

Work on the line began in 1930 and proceeded through the years of economic depression that followed, at a cost that nearly bankrupted France. The finishing touches were still being added when the Second World War broke out in 1939. The following spring, Hitler turned his armies against France. The German generals took one look at the Maginot Line and did not even try to attack it. Instead, they drove their tanks around the *end* of the line through Luxembourg and Belgium, carved through the French reserve troops waiting behind the Line, and in six weeks knocked France out of the war.[1]

Why was the Line built? Because the French military planners and strategists were unable to think outside of a tightly defined world of imagination where linear rather than lateral thinking predominated. The First World War, at least on the Western Front, had been a war of static defence. It followed, in their minds, that the next war would be exactly the same. In a classic example of wilful blindness, they ignored other developments in military technology, especially improvements in tanks and aircraft, and concentrated on building the perfect defensive system. (They succeeded, too; the Maginot Line probably *was* impregnable, if anyone had been stupid enough to attack it directly.) They failed to notice that the world had moved on, and the old assumptions no longer held good.

Maginot Line thinking is one by-product of linear thinking, the view that things happen as a series of logical steps. If we can decode the sequence of steps, the series goes, then all we need to do is follow each step in turn and we will get to the desired end. How many times have you sat in a meeting and watched a manager or consultant show a PowerPoint presentation which gave a series of five, or six, or seven, or however many steps that had to be followed in order to carry out a programme? Bring the right people and the right resources together and follow the right sequences of steps, and we will succeed. Bring the right amount of concrete and steel together, plan the system carefully and follow the plan, and we will have the perfect defensive system.

Businesses engage in Maginot Line thinking all the time. Strategic planning is full of examples of companies thinking that the world has not changed and the old realities still hold true. Sometimes they invest heavily in out-of-date technology; sometimes they cling to management systems and organizational structures that no longer work; sometimes they assume that customers will continue to want what they have wanted in the past; and sometimes they assume that their employees love the company and want to work for it, when that is no longer true.

It is not just business where this happens, it is all of life. Put 'steps to success' into the search field at Amazon.com books, and see how many results you get. I did just now and found over 20,000, with titles relating to business, sport, gardening, art (!), childcare (!!!) and virtually every other aspect of human endeavour. Anything you can think of doing, there is someone out there waiting to show you the linear process to do it, the path to success.

We think in linear fashion, in the West at least, because that is how we are taught. The person who probably more than any other influenced us towards this way of thinking was the French philosopher and mathematician René Descartes, who in the seventeenth century expounded a philosophical concept known as Cartesian dualism (the ideas actually go back to Aristotle and Plato, but Descartes expanded them and gave them their modern form).[2] Put *very* simply, Descartes postulated that the mind and body are two related but separate entities, not a united whole. This might seem both perfectly logical and relatively innocuous, but it opened the door to a new way of thinking about causation as a step-by-step process. Descartes himself believed that all natural phenomena, including human behaviour, could be explained by step-by-step causation.

In one famous example, he describes what happens when a child puts its foot too close to a fire. The heat of the fire plays on the skin, which moves and activates a nerve beneath, which in turn activates the muscle in the leg so that the child pulls its foot back without conscious thought. Everything that happens, happens in a logical order that can be easily explained once we know the science behind it.

Cartesian dualism was one of the building blocks of the Enlightenment, a time when people stopped accepting established explanations for things and went out and tried to discover the real causes of natural phenomena and human behaviour for themselves. Huge advances were made in the sciences, including physics, chemistry, medicine and psychology, and our perception of the world changed forever; mostly for the better. But Cartesian dualism also gave us linear thinking, and the *cultures of linear logic* that we see around us in management today.

Linear thinking lies at the core of the first modern theory of management, the scientific management developed by Frederick Winslow Taylor and his colleagues around the beginning of the twentieth century. Taylor started from the position that the working practices in most companies are inefficient. Again simplifying greatly, he took a Cartesian perspective and looked at the processes of causation in work: why do we do things the way we do them? Breaking down work into its component tasks, Taylor identified sources of inefficiency and eliminated them, redesigning work to make it optimally efficient.[3]

Again, there is nothing particularly wrong with this and scientific management's time-and-motion study techniques are still used today.

Where Taylor and his friends went wrong was in trying to turn this quite good management tool into an entire philosophy of management. They came to believe, in the words of Taylor's colleague Frank Gilbreth, that there was 'one best way' to manage. In other words, not only could management problems be solved by linear, step-by-step processes of analysis and change, but also that there would always be one 'best' process, one way of doing things that was superior to all the others, and that it was this way that should be sought.

It is hard to think of any single idea in management that has done more damage or destroyed more value.

If it were true that there was one best way, and *if* it was possible to identify what that way was, then this idea might have merit. But there is almost never a single, most effective 'best' way. Usually there is a variety of ways, a plethora of ways, and some will be right for some companies and some will be right for others, depending on the time and place. What is 'best' also changes with time, technology and people.

There are many ways to solve problems, and not all of them are linear in nature. Companies and managers need to find the right solution for *them*, not the right solution copied out of a recipe book or consultancy report.

But the lure of the one best way is very strong, especially in the West. (Many commentators have argued that Eastern cultures are more naturally attuned to lateral thinking, in part because of the philosophical influences of Confucianism and Daoism, and therefore Chinese and Japanese companies in particular are less likely to be locked into linear thinking.[4]) Every decade or so there comes along a guru – Tom Peters with radical reorganization in the 1980s, Michael Hammer and business process re-engineering in the 1990s, the various prophets of e-commerce in the 2000s – who offers us a seductive vision of a peaceful and prosperous future if only we accept their prescription for the one best way and follow their step-by-step guides to success. And companies and managers fall for the seductive message, in their thousands and their tens of thousands, and start down the road towards certainty that the one best way pretends to offer (Table 9.1).

Table 9.1 A Typology of Linear Thinking

Type	Manifestation
Path dependent routines	*This is how we've always done it*
Reliance on targets	*You can't manage what you can't measure*
Exclusive short-termism	*The next quarter is all that matters*
Inflexible tools for thinking	*Only if the spreadsheet says so*

In fact, as we saw earlier with attempts to eliminate risk, this certainty is actually a mirage. Reliance on linear thinking increases risk, because it increases wilful blindness and closes down possibilities. We *know* there are other ways of looking at the world, but we refuse to accept them because they are not 'right'.

We don't like instinct or intuition because they are fuzzy, uncontrollable and unmeasurable; not realizing that what we perceive as instinct and intuition are in fact based in tacit knowledge and personal experience and are thus real and meaningful. We don't like luck because we can't control it, and when we can't control something we get nervous.

We don't really do holistic thinking; the minute we see a whole, our first reaction is to break it down into its parts in order to see how it works, like children disassembling a watch hoping to find time inside. We are uncomfortable with concepts like culture and human relationships and even knowledge because it is hard to quantify them, so we either come up with spurious and unhelpful methods of measuring them, or reject them as unimportant and retreat towards the illusive certainty of hard financial numbers, data and spreadsheets. The cave is safer than the real world; let's stick to what we know and, as Levitt said, keep the plant running at full blast.

That is why I count reliance on linear thinking as a sin, because it locks our minds into predetermined grooves and won't let us think about the world in any other way. Once more, I am not dismissing linear thinking entirely, and lateral thinking too has its problems. But we need to be able to do both, to come at the world and its problems from multiple perspectives. Failure to do so leads instead to the search for the chimera of the one best way, and that in turn leads to path-dependent thinking, blinkered understanding and, sometimes, ruin.

We've always done it this way (part 2)

During a recording session, the cellist Mstislav Rostropovich became so angry that he laid down his instrument and walked out of the recording studio. The studio manager asked what was wrong, at which the cellist reeled off a list of his complaints. 'But I've had thirty years experience of running a studio', argued the manager. 'No', said Rostropovich. 'You have had one year's experience, repeated thirty times over.'

In Chapter 4 we saw how arrogance can lure companies into the trap of path dependence. Their confidence in their own abilities and their own products is so great that they fail to look out for threats and weaknesses. But path dependence has another source too: a reliance on linear thinking and a belief, like the builders of the Maginot Line, that events follow one another in a predictable and logical order. The French engineers believed that the next war would be just like the last one; Rostropovich's studio manager believed that running a studio consisted of doing the same things over and over again without change. The recipe was successful once; all we need to do is keep doing the same things, over and over, and success is bound to come again.

A stubborn reliance on what has always worked in the past is the last and greatest of Sydney Finkelstein's 'seven habits of spectacularly unsuccessful managers'.[5] Finkelstein goes on to give a long list of examples of companies and managers where this way of thinking had contributed to failure. We've seen a number of examples already in this book: Henry Ford sticking with the Model T despite increasing evidence that customers were switching to more sophisticated cars such as the Chevrolet Model D and later the Standard Six; Lehman Brothers continuing its high-risk investment strategy despite increasing signs that the world was about to change; Motorola continuing to pour money into analogue mobile phones while Nokia and others were riding the wave of the digital revolution; Harold Geneen's clinging to the conglomerate model at ITT long after it was past its sell-by date, and so on.

Very often, the 'we've always done it this way' mindset takes hold because people can no longer remember or imagine another way of doing things. Their education and training conditions them to think about problems in narrow ways; and corporate cultures reinforce this conditioning by encouraging people to follow routines. Now, routines in and of themselves are great. They give us signposts and reminders of what we need to do, they offer excellent opportunities for monitoring and controlling so that senior management can check whether what should be done is being done, and they are particularly useful for new staff and managers who need to learn their new roles in a hurry. Routines *should* be like the lines actors learn before doing a play; they help us understand and give structure to our roles.

 Excessive insistence on conformity to routine.

Once again, though, danger comes when the routines take over from the mission of the business. Then, fulfilling the routine becomes a purpose in and of itself. Compliance with routines brings rewards, failure to fully comply brings punishment. The main goal of every manager is conformity. If you do things the right way, you will succeed. And if success does not come? Well, it's not your fault: you carried out the routine.

I recall vividly asking the marketing director of a publishing company why a particular project had sold far less than we expected. 'I can't understand it', she said frowning. 'We ticked all the boxes on the marketing plan.' The failure was not her responsibility; her department had done everything it usually did to sell books. My next question – whether there was anything they could do that was not in the marketing plan – met with blank incomprehension.

In what other walk of life would this attitude be acceptable? Imagine going to a restaurant and being served a meal that was essentially inedible, and upon complaining to the waitress, being told that it was not the chef's fault as he had followed the recipe to the letter; or seeing your favourite sports team suffer a heavy defeat and then being told by the coach that nothing was really wrong, they used the same game plan they had in every other match and it had always worked before; or going to a concert and listening to a terrible cacophony but being assured that it wasn't the fault of the musicians, they were just playing the notes on the pages. Any chef or coach or conductor who tried to deploy such an excuse would be laughed out of the house.

But the idea that if you can tick all the boxes you will succeed, and even worse, that if you don't succeed it is not your fault because you did what the procedures manual says you were supposed to do, is widely pervasive in business. It is fairly rare to find businesses where the culture encourages people to break out of the straitjacket of previously set routines and procedures and do things their own way. The idea that staff might be wandering around on the shop floor using their own initiative and doing things they were not told to do fills many managers with fear.

So, the thinking continues, at all costs we must keep control of what people do; even if it turns out in the end that they are doing the wrong things. If we have tested and proven routines that worked in the past, then we must stick with these; and then when things start to go wrong we cling to our established routines all the more firmly, like drowning people clinging to the flotsam of a wreck, because the routines are the only certainty we have.

Kodak dominated the film camera market for over a century, and indeed played a major role in creating that market in the first place. In some countries, Kodak became synonymous with photographic film. When digital photography arrived on the scene, Kodak's response was to apply linear thinking to the problem. It developed its expertise in digital and developed cameras very like the ones it had been developing before, but with a digital memory rather than film. One result was the Kodak Easyshare DX6490, perhaps the best camera Kodak ever made. Professional photographers praised the combination of high-quality optical lens and digital storage.

The DX6490 was Kodak's Maginot Line. It was the perfect camera for yesterday. Kodak failed completely to realize how the digital revolution had changed not just cameras, but also how photographs are taken and used. The entire concept of a camera as a separate piece of technology is being fast eroded by mobile phones with built-in cameras as people now take photographs in quite different ways than they did a generation ago. Doing what the company had always done, making and selling cameras, was no longer relevant.

In 2012, Kodak declared bankruptcy.

The reluctance or refusal to accept new ideas.

You can't manage what you can't measure

The phrase 'you can't manage what you can't measure' is often wrongly ascribed to quality guru W. Edwards Deming. So far as I can tell, it actually originated with Robert Kaplan and David Norton in *The Balanced Scorecard*.[6] Certainly, Kaplan and Norton quote this mantra with approval, and it forms part of the core ideology of the balanced scorecard, another of those generational guru concepts that popped up in the 1990s and, if the websites of consultants and coaches on the Internet are anything to go by, still lingers today. Its intellectual roots go back to Taylor, and before him to the scientist Lord Kelvin who declared that 'science begins with measurement'. And since we continue with the pretence that management is a science, it therefore follows that management requires measurement.

And to an extent, it does. There are plenty of things in management that can and should be measured, often. Measurement shows us where we are and how far we have progressed, just as the milometer or GPS system of a car shows how far it has travelled on its journey and thus how far there is to go. However, contrary to Kaplan and Norton, and Taylor, not everything in a business can be measured. There are no reliable metrics for measuring culture, for example; indeed, if you were to try to measure culture, what would you measure? It is impossible to measure human relationships in a meaningful way, mostly because they change constantly in kaleidoscopic manner. And while various attempts have been made to value knowledge capital, it is pretty well impossible to measure knowledge itself; much of the knowledge held within a business is tacit knowledge, and because no one truly knows what the company knows, it is impossible to measure it.

The problem begins when, as consultant Paul Glen says, 'you can't manage what you can't measure' is transformed into 'if you can't measure it, it doesn't matter'. 'We not only ignore hard-to-measure aspects of work such as relationships', he says, 'but also self-righteously see that approach as a virtue.' He lists a number of ways in which that attitude impacts on work. 'Project leaders become obsessed with process-prescribed approvals while ignoring the mutual trust required to get them ... Developers adhere to the precise content of a requirements document – as if ticking off 100% of the require-ments is more important than making sure the product makes sense'.[7] But in some cultures of linear logic, that is exactly the case. The target is not to deliver a usable product; the target is to comply with the specification.

Writing for Forbes.com, Liz Ryan has a different complaint. 'Measurement requires stopping the action, getting outside of it and holding it up against a yardstick, exactly the opposite of the activity that would create products or ship them, make our customers happy or move our business forward in any way', she says.[8] The same complaint was registered against Taylor's time-and-motion studies; the process of measurement interfered with the workflow and was itself costly in terms of time and resources, and there were doubts as to whether the costs could be recouped through increased productivity. This is an argument which is rarely heard when the introduction of metrics is discussed, but it should be: will measurement add value, or will it turn into a cost?

The refusal to accept that things which cannot be measured or valued are important.
The introduction of metrics which add cost but do not add value.

Ryan also believes that most metrics are imposed unwillingly on a largely resentful workforce, who don't see the need for them and find them an irritating distraction. 'Most of the time in the business world, goals come down from on high', she says, 'and the appropriate measur-ing devices, rubrics and protocols come with them'.[9] This too is part of a long tradition. Writing in the early 1930s, W.F. Watson described how workers in steel mills, knowing they were being observed for a time-and-motion study, would deliberately speed up or slow down their work rates in order to render the studies inaccurate; or, growing bored with this, they would beat up the time-and-motion man and steal his stopwatch.[10]

The other negative aspect of measurement is the cult of targets. Targets, like measurement, are very useful things to have. It can sometimes be hard to keep focused on the long-term goal, especially when that goal is something that might take years to achieve. Targets, like metrics, help to break strategies up into bite-sized chunks and allow us to gauge progress as we go along. Targets *can* also be good for morale; achieving a target is a tangible mark of progress and will help to boost team spirits.

But in cultures of linear logic, however, targets like metrics take on a new importance. Indeed, they can become all-important; whether a team or an individual hits their target can determine whether they will receive bonuses or promotion. Hitting targets in some companies is a fast way to promotion, while missing them can be a form of career suicide, regardless of the quality of one's work or any other achievements. From there it is a short step to a culture where the only thing that matters is the target, and the mission and purpose of the business take a back seat, or are forgotten altogether. We saw in Chapter 3 how this happened at Lehman Brothers, with ultimately fatal consequences for the business.

The most extreme form of target-setting and penalties I have encountered comes not from the free-market West but from the command economy of the old Soviet Union. In the late 1930s there arose a management philosophy known as Stakhanovism, named after a coal mining team leader named Aleksey Stakhanov. One day in 1935, Stakhanov's team produced 102 tons of coal in a six-hour shift, fourteen times the average team output. The Soviet authorities rewarded the team and promoted Stakhanov who went on to become a kind of roving consultant, touring around coal mines and other industries giving motivational speeches and advice on how to increase output. Meanwhile, the authorities then raised the output targets demanded of other teams to the levels achieved by Stakhanov; if he can do it, they said, so can you. Some miners met their targets and worked themselves to death. Others failed and were sent with their families to labour camps, never to return. Quite how many died as result of Stakhanovtsi target setting has never been determined, but the number is likely to be in the tens of thousands. (Decades later, it was discovered that Stakhanov had cheated, adding the output of several other teams to his own.[11])

These days, managers aren't sent to labour camps for missing targets, but one's career can still end up metaphorically in Siberia. Few financial services traders who miss targets last for long; there are plenty of others lusting after their jobs, and those who can't meet the targets are swiftly swept aside. Cees van der Hoeven of Royal Ahold is an example of an executive whose staff were required to concentrate on targets to the exclusion of nearly everything else. According to Stewart Hamilton and Alicia Micklethwayt, van der Hoeven operated a strict policy of 'no surprises in the boardroom'; board meetings usually contained a recital of which targets had been met, and woe betide any manager who failed. Accordingly, managerial attention was concentrated on hitting targets, not on the wider needs of the business.

How targets are set is also a matter of some importance. There is sometimes an assumption that any target is better than none at all; without targets, staff will not know what is expected of them. This is quite wrong. First, if management is doing its job properly and communicating the company's mission and purpose, then most staff will already know what is expected of them without the need for targets. Second, setting the wrong target and then working diligently towards it is immeasurably worse than having no target at all; it is the short term of equivalent of the problem of brilliantly executing the wrong strategy that we discussed in Chapter 4.

 Too many targets, and/or targets which are badly defined and set.

Targets should be used sparingly, and *only* as guides or marker points along the way to the company's ultimate goal. Beware, too, of the all too common practice of shooting an arrow, hitting something at random and then painting a target around it and pretending that was what you meant to do all along. If you do this, sometimes you will get lucky and end up going in the right direction, but more often not.

Even more invidious is the key performance indicator (KPI). Like targets (with which they are often confused), KPIs can be very useful in tracking progress towards a goal. Arnold Weinstock, who built up GEC to be Britain's leading electronics firm in the 1970s, had a system of six KPIs for each business unit in the firm, which he monitored on a daily basis. This simple dashboard allowed him to understand what was happening within the firm at a given moment, which parts were doing well and could be left to get on with it and which needed attention. Weinstock would never have made the mistake of confusing the KPIs with the goal of the business, but lesser managers and leaders frequently do. KPIs in some companies are now the weapon of choice for managers who want to bash their subordinates. Failing to deliver on a KPI can once again mean a ticket to career Siberia.

I mentioned earlier that all this nonsense is sometimes blamed on W. Edwards Deming, the quality guru. How appalled he would have been to hear it. Actually, not many people knew more about measurement than Deming. He was part of the pioneering movement in statistics in the 1930s and worked with founders of the movement such as Walter Shewhart, Ronald Fisher, Joseph Juran, Arnold Feigenbaum and C.V. Rao, as well as the Japanese quality engineers Taiichi Ohno and Shingo Shigeo. This experience taught him that targets are in fact futile. One of Deming's 'fourteen points' of good management was 'eliminate work standards, quotas, management by objectives and management by numbers'.[12] Deming believed that quotas and targets actually acted *against* quality and harmony in the workplace. They encouraged staff to think about themselves, not about the company and its customers. Real quality is a journey, not a destination and it is essential, when embarking on that journey, for the organization to work together as a harmonious whole.

Another of Deming's fourteen points was simply: 'Drive out fear.' Now *that* is an interesting idea. I wonder if anyone has tried it?

The ditch and the stars

Cults of linear logic also have a bias towards short-termism, which the *Financial Times Lexicon* defines as 'an excessive focus on short-term results at the expense of long-term interests'.[13] The *Lexicon* goes on to cite research which suggests that short-term strategies 'are often based on accounting-driven metrics and profit maximization that fail to fully reflect not only the complexities of corporate management and investment, but also the significant opportunities and risks associated with these strategies', or to put it a little less ponderously, go for quick wins without taking account of the long-term consequences.

The causes and consequences of short-termism have been widely discussed and debated. Dominic Barton, managing director of McKinsey, has weighed into the discussion several times, referring to the 'tyranny of short-termism' and in 2014 laying into major share owners such as pension funds, insurance companies and sovereign wealth funds who he sees as the major culprits. 'Too many of these major players are not taking a long-term approach in public markets', he says. 'They are failing to engage with corporate leaders to shape the company's long-range course. They are using short-term investment strategies ... and letting their investment consultants pick external asset managers who focus mostly on short-term returns. To put it bluntly, they are not acting like owners'.[14]

Roger Martin, on the other hand, argues that the problem is deeper, and that the focus on short-term or long-term shareholder value misses the point. Asked whether companies should concentrate on producing shareholder value in the short term, Martin replied that they shouldn't bother worrying about shareholder value at all: 'The best way to serve shareholders is to have a great company.'[15] Martin believes that the whole concept of shareholder value is fundamentally misguided because, once again, it takes management attention away from managing the company for the best interests of all its stakeholders and concentrates on just one, the shareholders. This, in effect, distorts management. It creates a myopic view in which part of the purpose of management is sloughed off and neglected in favour of other parts.

Barton and Martin are both right, of course. Asset owners are behaving like idiots. Milking companies for shareholder value will, undoubtedly, kill the geese that are laying their golden eggs. Companies can only be squeezed for so long until the juice runs dry. Martin's point that creating excellent companies is the only way to create shareholder value is true too. And that cannot be done by looking only at the short term and concentrating on the next quarterly target.

A word of caution is in order here, though. It is axiomatic today that companies *should* (but don't) focus on long-term growth and development. But too much focus on the long term has its risks too. The story is told of Thales, the early Greek philosopher, who was so busy concentrating on the stars and trying to work out their positions and orbits that he did not see the ditch under his feet and fell into it. The long term is important, vitally so, but the short term matters too. It is no good having a brilliant long-term vision if you trip over some little short-term problem that could have been avoided.

One of the many paradoxes of management is that we need to look at both the short term *and* the long term, one eye on each, at the same time. The stars are important; but so too is the ditch.

Excessive focus on either the short term or the long term, rather than a balanced view of both.

Only if the spreadsheet says so

I mentioned in Chapter 6 the publishing executive who was unable to make a decision without first consulting a spreadsheet. Over the course of the past two decades, spreadsheets have become - for some - indispensable decision-making tools.

No, wait, that's not quite correct. They have - for some - become the decision-makers. Having a spreadsheet means you don't have to make a decision; you feed the data into the spreadsheet and it makes it for you. That way if someone questions the result, you can - as this executive frequently did - shrug your shoulders and say, 'I know, it seems odd, doesn't it? But that's what the spreadsheet says, so there it is. We don't have a choice, really.'

This attitude is particularly shocking given that the reliability problems of spreadsheets are widely known. One study reckons that a staggering *94 per cent* of spreadsheets in use have some sort of built-in error. Another suggests that only a small number of companies realize that there are reliability risks associated with spreadsheets, and even fewer know what to do about this.[16] The majority plough blissfully on, believing that their spreadsheets tell them the truth, the whole truth and nothing but the truth. (But, the next time someone tells you that numbers never lie, check their spreadsheet.)

There is a deeper problem with tools like spreadsheets, however. Because they can only process a limited range of data, they effectively shut out those data, information and knowledge that cannot be processed within their parameters. Just as metrics encourage us to downplay or dismiss factors which cannot be easily measured, so spreadsheets encourage us to ignore things which will not fit easily into a cell. Is there a spreadsheet yet designed that has a cell or series of cells for wisdom? If so, I have not seen it.

 Reliance on spreadsheets to make decisions, rather than personal judgement.

Spreadsheets encourage us towards linear thinking because they are themselves linear. We see data go in and results come out, and take it on trust that there is a process of cause and effect at work. And, just as with other forms of linear thinking, spreadsheet-derived thinking induces wilful blindness. Anything that doesn't fit the model gets left out. This impoverishes thinking and weakens management.

When I was younger I knew a man who, when confronted with a choice of two options, would toss a coin. 'Do you really make decisions based on whether a coin comes up heads or tails?' he was asked. 'Of course not', came the reply. 'I toss the coin and wait to see which choice comes up. I then have to confront the notion of taking that option. If I am happy, I know I am doing the right thing. If I feel uncomfortable I know I am doing the wrong thing. Then I put the coin away and choose the other option.' The coin toss did not make the decision; it merely helped him sharpen and focus his thinking and then make the decision he had unconsciously known all along was the right one.

Spreadsheets can do the same. Put the data in and look at what comes out; and then, if your experience and tacit knowledge tell you this is wrong, throw the spreadsheet away and do what you know to be right. That's how spreadsheets should be used to make decisions.

PowerPoint makes us stupid

'PowerPoint makes us stupid' was the blunt view of General James Matthis of the US Marine Corps, quoted in the *New York Times* in 2010.[17] General Matthis was expressing a view that is becoming more prevalent in the US armed forces, at least, that the overwhelming use of PowerPoint is now a serious problem. As well as the huge amount of time that officers now have to spend preparing PowerPoint presentations – platoon commanders on the front line brief their soldiers with PowerPoint presentations before going out on patrol – there is a fear that PowerPoint, like spreadsheets, is narrowing focus and leading to myopia. The only information that gets presented and passed on is that which will fit easily on a PowerPoint slide.

PowerPoint is dangerous, said another general, H.R. McMaster, because 'it can create the illusion of understanding and the illusion of control'.[18] Modern PowerPoint has many wonderful presentation features including the ability to use graphics and video, and it is quite easy to blind an audience with dazzling presentations and make them think that what they are seeing is the whole truth. As Marshall McLuhan said, the medium becomes the message; the content of the slides, such as it is, can be easily hidden behind the presentation.

It can also be used to daze audiences and stun them into passive acceptance, the famous 'death by PowerPoint'. The US Army admits that it uses this technique deliberately in press conferences, producing PowerPoint presentations of such crashing tedium that by the end few if any of the assembled reporters are still awake. This is known as 'hypnotizing chickens'.[19]

Two other problems with PowerPoint should be mentioned. The first is that hardly anyone who presents PowerPoint presentations knows how to do so. 'Death by PowerPoint' becomes a slow agonizing torture as we wait to see which will happen first: the presenter gets hopelessly tangled up in his/her slides and runs out of time, or our central cortex collapses and our brains dissolve into grey sludge. Speaking personally, I will run screaming from the room if I hear one more person read their own PowerPoint slides aloud. It's been twenty years, and I have had enough. No more.

Much more serious is the problem of linear thinking, which PowerPoint embodies to the full. Concepts are presented one after another, in sequence, and there must be no deviation from that sequence. How many of you have sat through some version of this scene?

PRESENTER: And so in this slide, we see how changing demographics mean there is now a higher proportion of 18–25 year-old consumers in this geography. These clearly represent a potential future customer segment.

AUDIENCE MEMBER (lifting hand): Do we know what sort of spending power these 19–25 year-olds have? Anything on their propensity to consume?

PRESENTER: Er... yes, but that information is on slide 97, and we're still only on slide 23. Do you mind if I deal with that point when we come to it, later in the presentation?

By the time we reach slide 97, of course, the audience member will (a) have forgotten the question, (b) have fallen asleep or (c) both. PowerPoint's linear format discourages questions, discourages discussion, discourages creative thinking. Audiences are expected to sit still, in silence, and receive the message.

I don't like PowerPoint very much (what gave it away?) and rarely use it in my own teaching and presenting because it stifles free thinking. For very formal presentations I will use a few pictures or quotes, but on the whole I prefer to do without it. I find this allows me to work *with* an audience rather than lecturing *to* them (or *at* them), and they can freely contribute their own thoughts, ideas and experiences, which are usually much more profound and relevant than my own. Both I and my students find that the learning is much richer, broader and deeper as a result. Companies that ban PowerPoint or at least restrict it report the same. You get much more original thinking and ideas out of a group of people sit around a table talking, perhaps with a facilitator, than you do out of the same group sitting half-asleep in front of a PowerPoint presentation.

 People reading their own PowerPoint slides during presentations.

This said, I have seen some brilliant PowerPoint presentations which were stimulating and lively, but only because the presenters really knew what they were doing. Companies should either train their managers to use PowerPoint well, or dispense with it. Otherwise, it simply becomes one more tool reinforcing linear thinking.

Cultures of linear logic

All the foregoing may have induced readers to think that I have no time for linear logic. That is of course untrue; I respect logical thinking in others, and try to employ it myself. Once again, though, we have to realize that not every problem or very issue can be understood logically. That is the main shortcoming of cultures of linear logic; they fail to see that there is a world beyond linear thinking, or to take account of such things as tacit knowledge and experience and wisdom.

Some companies develop *path-dependent routines* because they cannot think what else to do. Some of this, as we saw in Chapter 6, is a matter of fear; people like to cling to certainty. But sometimes too there develops an ingrained belief in routines as a good thing in their own right. The belief that if we follow set procedures a step at a time we will always get the result we desire dies very hard, and not even bitter experience seems to shake it (a prolonged spell of putting together flat-pack furniture using nothing but the diagrams that come with the product might do the trick, perhaps).

Other businesses become *reliant on targets* to the point where the targets become more important than the mission and purpose of the business. The view that 'you can't manage what you can't measure' stresses metrics and hard data over soft knowledge and things that can't be reliably measured, resulting in incomplete and partial pictures of the business and its environment.

Related to this is *exclusive short-termism*, which sees the next quarter or the next month as all that matters; so long as the goals for that period are met, the rest of the future can take care of itself. This again results in a squeeze on thinking and ideas and an ultimately myopic view of the company and its customers. While it is always necessary to take the short term into account, a balanced view of short term and long term are necessary.

Finally, the reliance on *inflexible tools for thinking*, including but not limited to spreadsheets and PowerPoint, narrows thinking still further. Much of the problem with both centres on their misuse by managers who don't fully understand them, but at the heart of both is the same concept of linear logic, of a step-by-step approach to thinking and problem solving that, in both cases, had the unintended consequence of stifling creativity and relegating tacit knowledge and wisdom to a back seat. PowerPoint doesn't exactly make us stupid, but it certainly encourages us to think in a very limited fashion.

Like PowerPoint and spreadsheets, linear logic should be regarded as a tool, a very important one but a tool nonetheless. It helps us to understand and solve problems, but the key word is 'helps'. It is necessary for problem solving, but it is not always sufficient. Other kinds of knowledge and thinking need to enter the mix too. By relying on linear logic, we are in severe danger of confusing the tool with the task.

Does it weigh the same as a duck?

The curse of Descartes is that we see problems in terms of linear cause and effect, rather than seeing them holistically. We attempt to unravel the Gordian knot, rather than simply cutting through it as Alexander did.

Holistic thinking as an art is in danger of dying out, thanks in part to how we are educated. From a fairly young age our minds are trained to dissect problems, to separate out concepts and establish their logical order. I have for some years used the concept of organizational metaphors developed by Gareth Morgan in *Images of Organisation*: organizations as machines, organizations as biological organisms, organizations as psychic prisons and so on.[20] Every year an earnest discussion breaks out; which of Morgan's eight metaphors is most important? Which comes closest to describing the reality of organizations? I then make the point that Morgan himself does not prioritize them. None of the eight metaphors offers a full picture, he says; each is only one perspective. If we want to truly understand organizations, we need to consider all eight perspectives simultaneously.

Some students grasp this at once. Others struggle, and continue (almost) instinctively to search for the one best metaphor. This is not a reflection in any way on their intelligence or ability; rather, it says something interesting about the training and experience they have received in the past.

A colleague recently put a question to me. He was working with an organization that wanted to know if there was any way of measuring its values system. All I could think of in reply was: does it weigh the same as a duck?

For anyone not familiar with the film *Monty Python and the Holy Grail*, a word of explanation is in order. A group of peasants are trying to determine whether someone is a witch. As it was common to burn witches, they assumed witches must be made of wood. Wood, they knew, floats on water. Next, to determine if she was made of wood, they resolved to weigh her in a pair of scales next to something else that floats on water, namely, a duck. If she weighed the same as a duck then she would be made of wood and, therefore, a witch.[21]

The peasants started with two false assumptions: (1) that because witches burn, they are made of wood, and (2) that anything that floats on water has the same weight as any other thing that floats. Attempting to measure a system of values starts from two similar false assumptions: (1) that all values systems have identifiable components and raw materials that can be analysed, and (2) because of this, values systems can be compared and measured against each other on a scale.

But values systems are unique. I don't mean the things that companies publish in their 'values statements', which very often have nothing to do with the actual values of the organization; I mean those real values that people genuinely hold. If you want to understand an organization, find out what it believes in. And that, I am afraid, is not something that can be measured.

With this thought in mind, here are my two recommendations for breaking out of cultures of linear logic. Like all culture-breaking exercises, this will take time and will cause pain, but it must be done if the company is to find and exploit all the knowledge it needs in order to survive and prosper. In keeping with the spirit of this chapter, I emphasize that these two suggestions are offered in no particular order, and that both should be implemented together, not one after the other.

First, encourage people to think of the company as being a unique entity. Stress its nature, its heritage, what it does differently from other companies, what makes it special. Break down the idea that textbook or cookie-cutter solutions can be applied. Encourage people to sit around tables or stand around the water cooler and talk about new ideas that apply to this company here and now. A hundred years ago exactly, the economist Robert Hoxie wrote a swingeing critique of scientific management's apparent wish to reduce all businesses to a single set of common denominators, and concluded:

> We speak of modern industry as though it were all of one piece. But in fact, there is no single necessary or logical line of industrial development; no perfectly uniform set of conditions and problems in different industries or even in differ-ent shops with the same general productive output. There can, then, be no single system of organization of methods equally applicable to all industries and to all shop conditions. Adequate management as applied to any shop is not a ready-made garment to which it can be made easily to conform, but must be worked out but the slow and painful process of cut and try.[22]

Broaden out Hoxie's words to include modern service and technology businesses as well as old-fashioned 'industry', and you will find those words are as true today as they were a hundred years ago. Yes, firms should learn from the example of other firms and hunt out examples of best practice; but they should do this magpie-fashion, picking out the things they really want and will be helpful to them and adapting those things for use, rather than adopting other models wholesale. The right solution for the right business at the right time should be the goal; and to achieve that, firms must be capable of learning from a broad range of sources, not a narrowly defined band of linear logic.

The second point takes us back to the discussion of values systems mentioned earlier. You don't have to measure values in order to understand them, just as you don't have to measure culture or human relationships or trust. But you can deploy these things to strengthen a company. Take Deming's advice; abolish targets and quotas, drive out fear and instead remind your managers and staff *why* the business exists, *why* it is doing what it is doing, *why* that matters. Use metrics as tools to aid understanding; use spreadsheets to nudge your thinking along; use PowerPoint if you absolutely must, but ultimately *you* make the decisions, not the tools. You take responsibility. You lead the way.

And if you absolutely insist on measuring values, here is my advice. Write down the organization's values on a piece of paper (which is of course made from wood fibre) and put it onto a scale. Then take it away and put a duck onto the same scale. If the paper and the duck weigh the same, then you're good to go.

---

[1] J.E Kaufman and H.W. Kaufman, *Fortress France: The Maginot Line and French Defences in World War II*, Mechanicsburg: Stackpole Press, 2011.

[2] Richard L. Amoroso, *Complementarity of Mind and Body: Realizing the Dream of Descartes, Einstein and Eccles*, Hauppauge: Nova Science Publishers, 2012; see also LeShan and Margenau, *Einstein's Space and Van Gogh's Sky*.

[3] Frederick Winslow Taylor, *The Principles of Scientific Management*, New York: Harper & Bros, 1911; Robert Kanigel, *The One Best Way: Frederick Taylor and the Enigma of Efficiency*, New York: Viking Penguin, 1997; Chapter 5 of Morgen Witzel, *A History of Management Thought*, London: Routledge, 2012.

[4] This too could be the subject for a separate book, but as a starting point I recommend Hofstede, *Culture's Consequences*, and Michael Harris Bond et al., *The Psychology of the Chinese People*, Hong Kong: The Chinese University Press, 2008.

[5] Finkelstein, *Why Smart Executives Fail*, pp. 235–7.

[6] Robert S. Kaplan and David P. Norton, *The Balanced Scorecard: Translating Strategy into Action*, Boston: Harvard Business Review Press, 1996.

[7] Paul Glen, 'Even if You Can't Measure It, You Still Must Manage It', http://www.computerworld.com/article/2494697/it-management/paul-glen-even-if-you-can-t-measure-it-you-still-must-manage-it.html

[8] http://www.forbes.com/sites/lizryan/2014/02/10/if-you-cant-measure-it-you-cant-manage-it-is-bs/

[9] http://www.forbes.com/sites/lizryan/2014/02/10/if-you-cant-measure-it-you-cant-manage-it-is-bs/

[10] W.F. Watson, 'Scientific Management and Industrial Psychology', *English Review* 52 (1931), pp. 444–55.

[11] Morgen Witzel, 'Stakhanov, Aleksei Grigor'evich', in Morgen Witzel (ed.), *Biographical Dictionary of Management*, Bristol: Thoemmes Press, 2002, vol. 2, pp. 946–7.

[12] W. Edwards Deming, *Out of the Crisis*, Cambridge, MA: Center for Advanced Engineering Study.

[13] http://lexicon.ft.com/Term?term=short_termism

[14] Dominic Barton and Mark Wiseman, 'Focusing Capital on the Long Term', *Harvard Business Review*, January–February 2014, http://hbr.org/2014/01/focusing-capital-on-the-long-term/ar/1

[15] Cited in Steve Dennison, 'Why Can't We End Short-Termism?', Forbes.com, http://www.forbes.com/sites/stevedenning/2014/07/22/why-cant-we-solve-the-problem-of-short-termism/

[16] Kenneth R. Baker, Lynn Foster-Johnson, Barry Lawson and Stephen G. Powell, 'Spreadsheet Risk, Awareness and Control', Spreadsheet Engineering Research Project (SERP) working paper, Tuck School of Business, Dartmouth College, n.d.

[17] 'We Have Met the Enemy and He Is PowerPoint', *New York Times*, 26 April 2010, http://www.nytimes.com/2010/04/27/world/27powerpoint.html?_r=0

[18] 'We Have Met the Enemy and He is PowerPoint', *New York Times*, 26 April 2010, http://www.nytimes.com/2010/04/27/world/27powerpoint.html?_r=0

[19] 'We Have Met the Enemy and He is PowerPoint', *New York Times*, 26 April 2010, http://www.nytimes.com/2010/04/27/world/27powerpoint.html?_r=0 If you have not read this article, you really should.

[20] Morgan, *Images of Organization*.

[21] https://www.youtube.com/watch?v=yp_l5ntikaU

[22] Robert F. Hoxie, *Scientific Management and Labor*, New York: D. Appleton & Co., 1915, pp. 113–14.

Chapter 10

Nobody cares

The last sin and the worst in our list of seven is lack of purpose. Managers forget why they are managing, leaders no longer lead and the company drifts. Customer focus is forgotten; staff and employees see the company as something that owes them a living rather than an entity with a purpose and the company's sense of identity is lost; and once that goes, brand and reputation swiftly follow.

Sydney Finkelstein refers to some companies as 'zombie companies', companies that have systematically lost touch with reality.[1] The question is, why does this happen? Why do companies lose their grip? If you look closely at these zombie companies you will often find that they have *cultures of emptiness*. Their moral core has been hollowed out, and the space filled instead by self-interest, laziness, disinterest, cynicism and, in some cases, corruption. With their purpose gone, they have no reason to exist, and sooner or later they will either be snapped up by a predator or will collapse of their own accord. Both Ford and Lehman Brothers lost their sense of purpose, the former sometime in the 1920s and the latter in the late 1960s. Ford did ultimately rediscover its purpose and stage a revival under Henry Ford's grandson; for Lehman Brothers, there was no road home.

By 'purpose', of course, I mean the reason why the business exists in the first place. Every business has a purpose, at least when it starts out. Over time in some companies, this purpose gets lost and forgotten. Without a purpose to guide them, these companies become hollow. They become zombies.

Sydney Finkelstein gives a long list of zombie companies, including Schwinn, the American bicycle maker. Founded in 1895 Schwinn, like Ford, was in the business of providing affordable transport. Although the bicycle market declined as cars became more popular and available, Schwinn tracked the changes in the industry and evolved, producing bicycles for sport and recreation as well as transport. By the end of the 1960s, Schwinn was selling a million bicycles a year around the world.

But the old story played itself out once more: Schwinn's executives grew arrogant and complacent. They forgot their purpose. Innovation in new models dwindled and the customers began switching to rival brands. Employee relations declined and there was a strike at the company's main US plant. Rather than fixing the problem, executives decided to outsource production to Japan and then Taiwan. The relationship with the Taiwanese partner, Giant Bicycles, worked well at first but then Schwinn tried to do a separate deal with Giant's rival, China Bicycle Company. Giant, which had all of Schwinn's technology, retaliated by launching its own brand in competition with Schwinn, and China Bicycle soon followed suit.

You can guess the rest. Schwinn went bankrupt in 1992, while Giant lived up to its name and became a leading global manufacturer of bicycles. Schwinn forgot its purpose, and paid the price.

Another once-famous name that lost its purpose was the chocolate maker Cadbury. As recounted in Chapter 5, this small family firm rose to dominate the global confectionery market, a position it held for more than forty years. But in the late twentieth century – especially once the Cadbury family ceased to play a major role in setting strategic direction – Cadbury lost the ethos that had sustained it and became 'just another business'. Executives and staff alike no longer seemed to care much about why Cadbury existed or what it did, so long as it made money. Gradually the company lost its way. By 2007 it was only a matter of time before it was taken over, and in 2010 the company was purchased by Kraft. The Cadbury brand still survives on confectionery wrappers, but it no longer means much. All that really remains is Cadbury World, a chocolate-oriented theme park on the outskirts of Birmingham where the company was founded.

These are just two examples; most people will be able to think of others without much difficulty. Unlike previous chapters, where I sketched out a rough typology of different aspects of 'sin', here I want to concentrate on the manifestations, the signs of loss of purpose that allow it to be spotted; hopefully in the early stages, before it has a chance to take hold (Table 10.1).

Table 10.1 Symptoms of Loss of Purpose

Type	Manifestation
Over/underpromotion	The wrong people in the wrong jobs
Poor communications	Meaningless or empty statements in communication, especially with employees
Refusal to take responsibility	A common attitude of 'not my problem', or 'above my pay grade'
Blame and denial	Whatever goes wrong is someone else's fault
Apathy	Social loafing; nodding dogs; failure to keep promises; laziness
Cynicism and detachment	Lack of identification with the company; lack of belief in its purpose
Ethical collapse	Unethical and immoral behaviour across a wide spectrum

In cultures of emptiness, managers are no longer doing what they should do, which is to guide the company and harness the efforts of all its staff and employees towards its purpose. Let's face it; managers have only one real function, and that is to ensure that things get done. But in cultures of emptiness, managers stop caring about getting anything done. The only important things now are the ones that perpetuate them in their position or help them gain promotion; everything else can go hang. When that happens, managers are no longer creating value. Instead, they act as a drag on the company and hold it back.

If you are ever in a company where staff are seriously asking questions such as, 'what is it that our managers actually do?', watch out. If staff don't know what managers do, then either the managers are incredibly bad at communicating, or they aren't doing what they should be doing.

What happens to companies that they lose their purpose and their way? Why do managers forget why they are there? Weak or incompetent leadership is usually blamed for the loss of purpose and moral core, and certainly leaders have to take responsibility for letting this happen on their watch. But leaders don't lead alone, and leadership is exercised by many throughout the organization, or should be; the growing separation of leadership and management means that managers are increasingly refusing to take on leadership responsibility on the grounds that 'that's not part of the manager's job'. (I'll have more to say about this later in the chapter.) Also, the drift into a culture of emptiness is often a slow one, and takes place over the tenure of two or three CEOs.

Margaret Heffernan, Sydney Finkelstein, Adrian Furnham and most of the other authorities I have cited in this book agree that a systematic refusal to confront reality, an unwillingness to deal with facts that don't fit with one's preconceived point of view, is a root cause of many corporate collapses and downfalls. But why should managers and executives reach the point where they no longer *want* to know what they *need* to know? Some become complacent, others become frightened, still others become greedy or selfish or too wedded to a single way of thinking, but all stop *caring*.

In an ordinary company, a manager who stops caring about his or her job would be identified and weeded out. But in companies where the culture of emptiness has taken root, everyone stops caring. There is no one with sufficient power and voice to remind the rest of the organization why they exist. Those few who do still care become progressively more disillusioned. Then they stop caring as well.

Disappointments, defeats, failure to achieve what everyone hoped for can all contribute to general disillusionment, but I believe the most common cause of cultures of emptiness is simply drift. People stop caring because there is no impetus for them to care; no one reminds them of why they are in business, no one pushes them towards that central purpose. They become cosy and comfortable and wedded to the status quo. Then, to fill the emptiness, the sins begin, greed and arrogance and lust; or else fear, because managers see the emptiness and don't know how to fill it.

Once the culture of emptiness takes hold, it is incredibly difficult to root out. It took wholesale changes at Ford, including a near corporate death experience and a complete change of senior management, to recall the company to its purpose. Many companies never recover. As I said in Chapter 1, prevention is far cheaper, easier and less painful than cure. Here then are some of the signs of a culture of emptiness which, if spotted in time, can help companies to change, recover and move on.

The wrong people in the wrong jobs

The best and most talented managers in the world will fail if they are hired into the wrong jobs. Good companies know this, and spend a great deal of time and money hiring people with the right 'fit' between their own values and skills and the company's needs, who will make a positive contribution towards the company's purpose. Others miss the point and hire the wrong people for the wrong reasons.

Some managers are incompetent from the beginning. They are either 'cognitively challenged', or were born lacking courage or judgement or ability or communications skills. They are not good managers, no amount of training will ever make them into good managers, and they should never, ever be promoted into management positions. Doubtless, they are good people and have other strengths; find out what those are and employ them in that capacity, or not at all. This, however, is not the primary problem.

Much worse is promoting people for the wrong reasons. Canadian psychologist Laurence Peter famously identified the Peter Principle, which briefly stated is that 'in a hierarchy, employees rise to the level of their own incompetence'.[2] Too often, says Peter, people are promoted on the basis of past performance, either as a reward for doing well, or in the belief that if someone did well in their last job, they will do equally well in their next. Certainly there remains a widespread belief that the skills of management are transferrable, and that someone who is an inherently good manager will do well in any managerial role.

This view persists despite widespread evidence to the contrary. Two examples will have to suffice. First there is Sir Clive Woodward, coach of the World Cup-winning England rugby team, who was hired to be performance director of football team Southampton in the belief that managing one sports team was very like managing another. His experience at Southampton was far from an unqualified success and he departed less than two years later. The other is John Sculley, world-beating CEO of PepsiCo who managed the seemingly impossible feat of taking over as world market share leader from Coca-Cola (they really care about these things in soft drinks, you see) and was then hired to replace Steve Jobs at Apple. Apart from the resentment he faced from Jobs loyalists, Sculley was out of his depth at Apple and made a series of bad decisions. Apple prospered during Sculley's time at the helm, but whether it did so because of Sculley's efforts or in spite of them remains a moot point, and he was ultimately forced out.

Norman Dixon in *On the Psychology of Military Incompetence* notes that the Peter Principle is very much prevalent in the military, and gives a number of hair-raising examples of perfectly good company commanders turning into disastrous generals. To go back to Peter, the point is that all of us are good at something, but very few of us are good at everything. Promotion should be decided on the basis, not of what the person has done, but what they are capable of doing and whether they can handle the increased responsibilities and pressures of their new job.

 Promoting people on the basis of past performance is common practice.

The appearance of the Peter Principle should sound a warning because, however well-intentioned, this is a sign that focus is beginning to drift away from the company's purpose. Of course, people who do well should be rewarded; but there are other methods of reward that can be equally appropriate. There will always be difficult cases where people desperately want to be promoted, either for the increased salary or the increased status or both; but if they are not suitable for the job, then they should not be given the post. The best way of heading off these problems is to set expectations beforehand and make it clear that success is not a guarantee of promotion. Hold out other rewards instead.

A more overt warning sign is the hiring or promotion of 'people like us'. Sometimes this stems from fear and a desire to keep out the 'other', but sometimes it is because management has descended into a cosy boys' club where members look out for each others' interests. Both have the same effect of reducing challenge and stretch and encouraging group-think, but when a 'jobs for the boys' mentality sets in we also know that people in management have stopped thinking about the company and its customers and are now thinking mostly about themselves.

A variant of this is to make sure that the safe jobs where failure is unlikely are given to members of the club while outsiders are placed in more risky posts. Writing in 2005, Michelle Ryan and Alex Haslam identified the phenomenon of the 'glass cliff' whereby women receive promotion to posts with a high chance of failure, on the grounds that if they do fail they are expendable; the less risky jobs, as noted, go to men.[3] The careers of Ina Drew at Morgan Chase, Mary Barra at General

Motors and Kim Campbell and Julia Gillard as prime ministers of Canada and Australia, respectively, have been cited as examples of glass cliff promotions, and the appointment of Marissa Mayer as CEO of Yahoo! was believed to be a glass cliff promotion though so far she has confounded expectations.

 Promoting or hiring people for reasons other than competence. Under-promotion, or the failure to promote people to a level where they can fully exercise their talents.

Over-promotion is widely discussed; less well known is the under-promotion that results when promotions are made on the basis of personal relationships rather than merit. 'Jobs for the boys' promotions also block the road to promotion for those junior managers who do have the right stuff for senior management and would exercise a positive influence and create value if given senior posts. This also denies companies access to the talent they badly need. Once again, promotion and hiring must be in line with the company's needs. If they are not, then selfishness has begun to creep in and the purpose is starting to fade.

Corporate bullshit-itis

A very senior and respected management guru, whom I shall not embarrass by naming, used this phrase in an interview I did with him more than twenty years ago, and it has stuck in my mind ever since. Norman Dixon also includes an entire chapter on 'bullshit' in *On the Psychology of Military Incompetence* and sees it as an important force in hampering organizational effectiveness.

We are talking, of course, not about the common agricultural by-product of the same name, but about the rituals, traditions and procedures that accrue in any organization, their origins often forgotten. Most companies have traditions and rituals; they form part of the company culture and can be a strong reinforcement to that culture. Several recent research studies have reported on how rituals in business can make people happier, more aware of the rest of the organization and even lower blood pressure and reduce stress.[4]

This is fine so long as the culture is a positive one. But in cultures of emptiness, the rituals *become* the culture. Preserving the rituals becomes all-important. In business, rituals often take very trivial forms, such as lengthy and incomprehensible paperwork and reporting procedures, the practice of regular meetings for the sake of having meetings, not because there is anything in particular that needs to be discussed, and of course the use and overuse of our old friends the spreadsheet and PowerPoint, making and communicating decisions through these channels alone. Pecking orders such as who gets what offices or which level of company car and, of course, bonus and reward schemes are also forms of ritual which can take on so much significance that they influence personal goals.

Rituals for their own sake, says Dixon, are 'a natural product of authoritarian, hierarchical organizations...they have three common denominators. The first is constraint; the second, deception; and the third, substitution for thought'.[5] Rituals *constrain* by reminding people who they are, what their position is in the pecking order and who is really in charge. This has the further effect of shutting down debate or dissent. Once, during a meeting with a team of American consultants, I disagreed with a statement made by the head of the team. He said nothing, but after the meeting, one of the junior consultants took me to task. I should never, he said, challenge the boss. Why not? I asked. 'Because he's the boss', came the reply. My tactless response – 'In that case, all the more reason to challenge him' – did not endear me, and I was never really forgiven.

Rituals *deceive* because they fool us into thinking that so long as we repeat the rituals we are doing the right things and the organization will be successful. And finally, they are *substitution for thought*, thanks to the numbing effect of repeated performance. Now, this too is not necessarily a bad thing in and of itself; some forms of yoga, for example, rely on repeated mantras to suppress conscious thought and allow meditation, and I referred earlier to the physically calming effect that some business rituals are observed to have.

That is one thing, but the *deliberate* substitution of thought by rituals – like the 'hypnotizing chickens' PowerPoint presentations used by the US Army on journalists – is exactly the opposite of what businesses need. And of course we come full circle, for one of the main purposes of substitution of thought is to constrain and suppress dissent. Hence, propaganda – sorry, corporate communications – forms another important ritual which can be used for control. A steady stream of Big Brotherish messages to staff can be a good way of preventing them from knowing what is really going on.

 Rituals that must be strictly adhered too, but contribute nothing of value to the business.

Diversity is the natural order of things, says Norman Dixon, but 'bullshit' is the enemy of diversity and sucks organizations into a tight spiral of conformity in which only 'people like us' are tolerated.[6] Some rituals encourage diversity and enable people to do their jobs better. But when a culture of emptiness takes over, rituals lose their rationale and become meaningless pantomimes that everyone must dance to, then in the words of the Chinese sage Laozi, 'ceremony is the merest husk of faith and loyalty; it is the beginning of all confusion and disorder'.[7]

Above my pay grade

Refusal to take responsibility is an increasingly common problem in management. Earlier in the book I mentioned an article for *The Conversation* in which I suggested Malaysian Airlines should have moved more swiftly after the disappearance of flight MH370 to assist and comfort relatives of the passengers. Readers criticized my position, claiming that Malaysian Airlines was not responsible for the hijacking and disappearance of its aircraft and, therefore, it had no responsibility towards its passengers and their families. I remain staggered by the sheer inhumanity of his point of view, but the fact that people are uttering it also suggests a problem of hollowing out. If you are able to take the view that you have no responsibility to your customers, then you are in grave danger of forgetting the primary purpose of the business: which is, of course, to serve customers.

Two problems lead to this state of affairs. One is what a consultant friend refers to as 'a culture of entitlement' among businesses, the view that customers should give them their money without the business itself having to do much about it; customers are there to serve the company, not the other way around. This in turn stems from the drift and complacency that I referred to above. Customers are, after all, difficult and complicated people to deal with, sometimes eccentric and sometimes unreasonable; it is simpler to ignore them and just get on with doing the easy things, like running the plant at full blast.

The second is the deliberate separation of leaders and managers, which positively discourages managers from taking responsibility and stepping up in times of crisis. This separation, which stems from academia and is fuelled by coaches and consultants, has been growing steadily for the past twenty years. The role of leaders is to create vision, give guidance, set direction, make strategy and generally do all the really big stuff, while managers are there to carry out the orders of leaders, check and monitor progress, ensure compliance and do all the boring things that leaders can't be bothered with.

Leaders are leaders and managers are managers, it is said, and never the twain shall meet. Leaders should never descend to the level of management and take on day-to-day management tasks, and heaven forbid that any manager should poach on the preserve of the leaders by stepping up and taking responsibility; that is what the leaders are there for.

'I've always been told to think of myself as either a leader or a manager, but never as both', a student said to me several years ago. I don't think I have ever heard anything more horrifying in a classroom; but of course, he was not alone. That there is a difference between leaders and managers is now orthodox thinking. And so, as I wrote in the *Financial Times* (in part in response to this conversation), we have leaders who cannot manage and managers who will not lead, giving us a lethal cocktail of ignorance and incompetence at the head and heart of our businesses.[8]

Earlier I made plain my views on leaders who cannot or will not manage, but managers who cannot lead are even more dangerous; first, because there will *always* be times when managers must accept responsibility for others, and second, because they run a much greater risk of being disconnected from the purpose of the company. If mission, vision and strategy are imposed on them from above, together with a list of tasks they must complete, their commitment will be much less than if they are actually involved in formulating these things all along. And, as Nonaka and Takeuchi pointed out in *The Knowledge-Creating Company*, managers have a great deal of knowledge and wisdom of their own. They should be encouraged to become part of the leadership process, not remain divorced from it.

But so long as managers are told not to think of themselves as leaders, so long as they are assigned the drudge work that leaders think is beneath them, they will lose interest and start thinking more about themselves than the company; and the hollowing out will begin.

 Managers who refuse to take responsibility or accept the burdens of leadership.

Blame and denial

Closely following the refusal to take responsibility come cultures of blame and denial, where everything is always someone else's fault. There seems little doubt that, in the Western half of the world, the increasingly litigious nature of society as a whole has contributed to this state of affairs, and people and companies are reluctant to admit responsibility on the grounds that they will be sued into oblivion if they do so.

The distinction between blame and responsibility is also disappearing. Many people no longer recognize any difference between the two concepts; if something goes wrong and you have a responsibility, then it must also be your fault. But in fact there is a considerable difference. If you and I pass each other in the street and you slip and fall, then of course I have a responsibility to you; common decency and humanity suggests I should stop and help you. I am responsible for checking to see whether you are injured and for summoning help if needed, and if I shirk that responsibility and walk away, leaving you lying bleeding on the ground, then there is something gravely wrong with me. But I am not at fault; I am not to blame for your accident. I was not responsible for you falling over, but I am responsible for helping you back on your feet again.

The Malaysian Airlines case illustrates this perfectly. In no way could the airline be said to be at fault or be blamed for the disappearance of MH370. No sensible person would sue the airline for the loss of the aircraft. But the airline still had a responsibility to the relatives of passengers and crew. Turning its back on them would have been immoral. Yet, companies continue to behave as if they admit to responsibility for anything bad that happens, they might then be blamed.

 A general inability to distinguish between blame and responsibility.

This is short-term thinking. By protecting their reputation in the immediate future, companies are sacrificing the long-term trust of their stakeholders, and demonstrating that their culture has become hollow; the company itself is all that matters, not the customers or shareholders. A culture of purpose, on the other hand, would take responsibility even for things which were not its fault, and would shoulder the burden on behalf of customers and shareholders.

Sounds impossible? In 2002, the Indian banking house Tata Finance was revealed to have a black hole in its finances, debts of unknown size created by accounting error and possible fraud. The bank's chief executive and several other senior managers were arrested. Tata Sons, which owned a controlling interest in Tata Finance, had a choice. It could throw the chief executive to the wolves, blaming him and his managers and side-stepping any responsibility; or it could intervene, take responsibility and ensure that customers were looked after. It chose to do the latter. Even before the total amount of the losses – some $400 million – was known, chairman Ratan Tata announced that the rest of the Tata Group would cover the debt; every rupee would be paid back to investors in Tata Finance.

Why? Ratan Tata later told me that the group's reputation was involved; if he had not stepped in, people would have felt they could no longer trust the Tata name.[9] Of course that was important, but that attitude would not have been taken unless Tata already had a strong sense of its own purpose and why it was in business in the first place.

Social loafing and nodding dogs

The concept of social loafing was discovered in 1913 by the French engineer Max Ringelmann who observed that when a group of men pulled on a rope, each pulled less hard individually than they did when pulling alone, without the support of the group. Later experiments found that when asked to clap hands, a person will clap more loudly on their own than they will when part of a larger group. 'Social loafing', then, is the view that when we are in a group with others, we can ease off a little and not try quite so hard; the others will do the extra work and cover for us.

It is not clear how much social loafing is deliberate and how much is unconscious, nor does it really matter very much; the consequences are the same. We set people to work in groups in the belief that synergies will be created between group members and their combined effort will be greater than the sum of their individual efforts. Social loafing says the opposite; we would be better off separating group members and putting them into cubicles to work alone, as their individual output would be greater.

Of course, all sorts of conditions have to be applied to this finding, and there is no doubt that in some environments, at least, groups do produce more than just the sum of their individual efforts. (It is always worth checking that this is actually happening, however. Too many people, too often, take the efficacy of group working on trust, and the notion that we work better in groups becomes an act of faith unsupported by evidence.) This happens when groups are motivated and have a clear purpose in mind. But when purpose is obscured or lacking, group members will begin to question whether their own efforts are really necessary, and begin slacking off.

 Signs of social loafing, people not pulling their weight when working in groups or teams.

Social loafing is an important sign that a culture of emptiness may be setting in. Another is the phenomenon of nodding dogs, referred to earlier in the book; people who sit in meetings and say little or nothing but simply nod their assent to whatever measures are put before them. Some people don't speak up because of fear, but others stay silent simply because they can't be bothered, they don't care enough to make their opinions known. If groups have the wrong dynamic, it can sometimes take a while to realize that this is happening. If, for example, a group is dominated by two or three noisy extroverts, one can be forgiven for assuming that other group members are simply quiet by contrast. Over time, though, if some group members do not contribute anything useful and never question or challenge a decision, it is worth looking again to see if they are simply nodding dogs.

Nodding dog managers, who never voice an opinion of their own but agree with whatever is put in front of them.

Detachment and cynicism

Another sign of a culture of emptiness is employees leaving in large numbers because they have become detached from the company and wish to go somewhere else where they can find more purpose and meaning. Writing for Forbes.com, Lynda Shaw refers to a company with an 'employee bell curve', where 'the largest proportion of staff with average to good skills … was the group that left more frequently, in other words the core of employees. Those that tapered away to the left of the bell were people who were not that good, but were retained due to unstable head count. At the other end of the distribution curve was a small group of people who were excellent at their job, but were in danger of being demotivated by unrest'.[10]

High staff and management turnover.

There are a number of possible reasons for high staff turnover: the company may be paying lower than normal wages, or there may be strong competition for talented staff, or the company may be in a sector where staff tend to be young and restless and want to give themselves other opportunities (hospitality and publishing are two examples). But if staff turnover rates start to exceed the average for the sector, and especially if those good staff who are the core of the business start departing in large numbers, then there is clearly a problem.

As Shaw suggests, in many cases the problem is that staff are simply not engaged with the company and its purpose. They don't understand why they are doing what they are doing. Either managers have failed to communicate properly, or else managers themselves are no longer sure of their purpose. The former can be fixed easily by improving communications channels and helping managers acquire better communications skills; the latter suggests a culture of emptiness may be developing, in which case more drastic measures are needed.

From detachment from and disinterest in the company, it is a short journey to cynicism about it and its purpose, and indeed to a more general cynicism about everything to do with business. Managers begin to question whether the business really has a purpose that is worthwhile; from there, they go on to question the whole idea of purpose. It is quite true that many companies' mission statements are laughable, but the idea of a mission is very serious and important indeed. When you hear managers scoffing at the very idea of a 'mission', take note; those managers are no longer very much interested in what they do, and a culture of emptiness is taking hold. These managers need to either rediscover their purpose, or get out of management, because if they remain in their present posts then sooner or later they will become liabilities.

Cynicism in one of its most extreme forms comes in an article by entrepreneur and *Financial Times* columnist Luke Johnson, who claims that 'only the cynical survive'. 'Lying is endemic in business', declares Johnson, before going on to state that salesmen always lie to sell goods ('which salesmen ever pointed out the defects in their wares?') and that in the cosmetics and beauty trade, 'customers implicitly conspire with the purveyors of such products: they *want* to believe that make-up will give them the appearance of being more glamorous and desirable'.[11]

Johnson is of course quite wrong. Even if lying is endemic in business, which I doubt, the examples he has chosen give him, er, the lie. Good salespeople *do* tell customers about the limitations of products and don't push them to buy products which are not suited to their needs, because they know that unhappy customers will never be seen again while good ones will come back for more; and it is much, much cheaper and easier to serve existing customers than to convert new ones. Nor do women (or men) who buy cosmetics necessarily buy them because they want to look 'glamorous and desirable'; quite often, they buy them for reasons connected with confidence, self-esteem or just for the sheer fun of it. No lies are involved.

I cite this article not just to criticize it (though I enjoyed reading the online feedback, where another reader described the article as 'contemptible'), but because this is a symptom of a culture of emptiness. If you hear people talking casually about lying to customers, or employees, or shareholders, then you know that a moral vacuum is starting to open up inside the company.

And from there, it is only a matter of time until the end. If lying has become part of the company's culture, then you know that managers truly no longer care. They are no longer helping the company towards its purpose; they are now just parasites. This company is now a zombie company, one of the walking dead. You would think that in these situations managers would be so disillusioned that they would leave, go and do something else that would give them some self-respect. Some, the ones who are not too far gone, will do so. The others will remain, carrion birds feasting off the rotting corpse of the business, still drawing their pay cheques and collecting their bonuses as customers desert, employees are laid off and the share price heads through the floor. What was the word? Contemptible. Yes, that was it.

Ethical collapse

And so we come to the ultimate stage in the process of decay, which Marianne Jennings describes as 'ethical collapse'. There are, she says, seven warning signs of ethical collapse:[12]

- Pressure to maintain numbers
- Fear and silence

- Young and inexperienced executives combined with a larger than life CEO who dominates his or her management team
- A weak board of directors
- Conflicts of interest which are overlooked or unaddressed
- Innovation like no other (or in other words, the belief that the company is so good that it doesn't have to follow the rules)
- The belief that goodness in some areas atones for evil in others, or that doing good things for some people makes up for doing bad things to others.

'When companies stand up and go on about their ethics and social responsibility, I start digging, because the more they say, the more I worry about what's really going on', Jennings later said.[13] I've worked with Marianne for the past fifteen years, and I know she is not exaggerating. Her case file of morally bankrupt businesses must fill several rooms.

The presence of any of these seven signs suggests trouble ahead, and the presence of all seven is a fairly sure recipe for disaster. Companies which start to exhibit these signs are no longer focused on their mission, or on their customers. They are now more interested in themselves. The next stage is that they lose sight of the distinction between right and wrong. Their managers and executives take what they can for themselves, and see no harm in doing so; indeed, the culture of the organization now encourages this behaviour. That in some ways is the worst of it; there is no longer any sense of guilt or wrongdoing, only a vague sense of entitlement and superiority. I'm the Master of the Universe. I deserve this because I am better than you. FIGJAM.

From there, it is usually only a matter of time. Nemesis can take many forms – regulators, auditors, bankers, angry shareholders, disappointed customers, employees who vote with their feet – but whatever form it chooses to take, it will come.

What is a business for?

The only sure way to deal with cultures of emptiness is to re-evoke the sense of purpose that the business once had; or to give it a new purpose.

Businesses do not exist just to make money for their owners and managers. They are established to provide goods and services that society deems desirable and necessary. As the American historian John Davis pointed out forcefully in his history of corporations, society creates businesses because it believes that they are the best way of fulfilling social needs.[14] The entrepreneurs who found successful businesses do so because they can see a need that is not being met. Ford saw a way of satisfying the desire for inexpensive cars; the Lehman brothers offered a brokerage service that cash-poor Alabama farmers badly needed. Whatever the need, if it can be filled effectively and efficiently, then two things will happen: (1) customers will be happy and (2) the company will make a profit.

Companies also can – and sometimes must – change their purpose as they grow and evolve, or as the market changes around them. In *Rejuvenating the Mature Business*, Charles Baden-Fuller and John Stopford consider how this can be done. One key task is to re-awaken an entrepreneurial spirit within the firm. Challenge its members, set them tasks that will shake them out of their standard routines, confront their fears, challenge them to look beyond their own wants and needs and consider the wants and needs of others, and how to meet them. Baden-Fuller and Stopford also argue that businesses need to look outside their own narrow little worlds, to learn from what is happening in other sectors and even outside of business entirely.[15]

Eighty years earlier, the American engineer Harrington Emerson made the same argument, urging business leaders and managers to draw lessons from science, art and music. He claimed the three most important influences on his own management thinking were a breeder of champion racehorses, a geological surveyor and a conductor of classical music.[16] Emerson too believed that every business has a purpose, a goal in society to fulfil.

Whether the company stays true to its roots like Tata or Apple or reinvents itself periodically like Nokia, there must always be a purpose of some kind. The purpose is the firm's sheet anchor; it keeps people focused and draws them together. It is the campfire around which people can gather and sing, the communal rice bowl where people meet to eat and talk; whatever your culture, choose your metaphor. Without purpose, firms drift into selfishness, egoism and corruption.

To give a firm purpose, I suggest four things need to be done. Once again, this is not a step by step guide; these four things overlap, and often need to be done simultaneously.

Define the purpose clearly. What does the firm do? What value do customers want and need from it? Remember that the real value often goes far beyond the product or service itself. Ford was not selling cars so much as personal mobility. Banks, when functioning as they should, enable our financial system and help companies do business; look at the state of the American economy before banks became established institutions, or that of India before independence when the banking system was tightly regulated and controlled by the British. Cosmetics firms don't sell lipstick and make-up; they sell pleasure and self-esteem. Think about these things, what the firm does and why it does it.

Nor should this be exclusively the task of the leaders. As we saw earlier, staff tend to resent things being imposed on them from above. Get everyone involved in the definition of purpose, find out what others think the purpose is. The results could surprise you.

Share the purpose with everyone, clearly and honestly. The process of defining and creating purpose can also be used to share the purpose around the organization. This is vitally important. There is much cynicism about mission statements, values days and other methods of sharing purpose, and it has to be said that quite a few companies get these wrong. It is not good enough to say, 'here is our mission, these are our values, now get on with it'. Staff, starting with senior executives, should be prepared to live those values. Their behaviour must show that the values matter. Also, communication must be clear. Avoid vague statements or clichés when setting out the company's purpose, tell it like it is. And, above all else, don't lie.

Remember that the purpose is a journey, not a destination. Some organizations – charities set up to deal with the consequences of a specific disaster, research organizations with a remit to solve a particular problem – have a finite goal in mind and once that goal is reached, they put themselves out of business. Most of the time that doesn't happen. Even if products and markets change, needs remain the same. People take photographs for different reasons and in different ways than they did before the digital age, but they still take photographs as memorials of people and places and events. And needs do not go away.

So, rather than getting caught up in the fallacy of targets, concentrate instead on delivering what customers need, day in and day out, week in and week out, year in and year out, short term and long term. Everyone in the company should recognize this, and be willing to make that endless journey.

Quietly urge those who do not share the purpose to seek employment elsewhere. They will be happier, so will you, and so will your customers.

---

[1] Finkelstein, *Why Smart Executives Fail*, pp. 167–8.

[2] Laurence J. Peter, *The Peter Principle*, London: Pan, 1969.

[3] Michelle K. Ryan and S. Alexander Haslam, 'The Glass Cliff: Evidence that Women Are overrepresented in Precarious Leadership Positions', *British Journal of Management* 16(2) (2005), pp. 81–90.

[4] Heidi Grant Halvorson, 'New Research: Rituals Make Us Value Things More', *Harvard Business Review*, http://blogs.hbr.org/2013/12/new-research-rituals-make-us-value-things-more/; 'Harvard Academics Find Rituals Can Be the Rite Stuff for Businesses', *Financial Times*, http://www.ft.com/cms/s/2/4c306c96-dfda-11e2-bf9d-00144feab7de.html#axzz3FH4CKRWx.

[5] Dixon, *On the Psychology of Military Incompetence*, p. 179.

[6] Dixon, *On the Psychology of Military Incompetence*, p. 185.

[7] Laozi (Lao Tzu), *Daodejing*, trans. John C.H. Wu, London: Shambhala, 1900, p. 45.

[8] http://www.ft.com/cms/s/2/0f0eeee0-9891-11e2-867f-00144feabdc0.html#axzz3FH4CKRWx

[9] Witzel, *Tata: The Evolution of a Corporate Brand*.

[10] http://www.forbes.com/sites/lyndashaw/2014/09/30/employee-engagement-doesnt-seem-to-be-getting-better/

[11] Luke Johnson, 'Lies, Damned Lies and Running a Business', *Financial Times*, http://www.ft.com/cms/s/0/364f2924-47e1-11e4-ac9f-00144feab7de.html#axzz3FH4CKRWx

[12] Marianne M. Jennings, *Seven Signs of Ethical Collapse: How to Spot Moral Meltdowns in Companies … Before It's Too Late*, New York: St Martin's Press, 2006.

13 http://www.scu.edu/ethics/practicing/focusareas/business/bcep/meltdown-signs.html

14 John P. Davis, *Corporations*, New York: G.P. Putnam's Sons, 1905.

15 Baden-Fuller and Stopford, *Rejuvenating the Mature Business*.

16 Harrington Emerson, *The Twelve Principles of Efficiency*, New York: Engineering Magazine, 1915.

Chapter 11

The leaning tower of academe

The seven sins of management don't come from nowhere. Corporate cultures play a large part in creating the environments in which those sins can flourish, but cultures too have their origins, and one of those origins is the education and training people receive which preconditions their views of the world.

The business education and training system has a major role to play in overcoming the problem of managerial incompetence. Unfortunately, that same system has also become part of the problem. In this chapter, I want to try to explain why, to some people outside of academe, the system appears to be both incomprehensible and not fit for purpose, and some of things that (I think) need to be done to reform business education and training.

But the fault does not lie entirely within the system. Businesses, especially in the West, have been complacent in their attitude towards education; they seem to think it should be a free good, delivered to them at need. Business needs to rethink its own attitudes towards education and training and be prepared to invest a lot more in education in particular; not just money, but also time, thought and collaborative effort. The worlds of business and business education overlap too little and too infrequently, and if we are going to tackle the problem of managerial incompetence and management failure, that needs to change.

First, let us remind ourselves of the distinction between training and education. *Training* teaches us how to do things, or to lightly paraphrase the *Oxford English Dictionary*, brings us to a desired standard or level of efficiency. We learn how to perform certain tasks to an optimal standard. Much training is linear; it shows us how to do tasks or solve problems through series of set routines. On the whole this is probably necessary, but it does mean that training has its limits. We can train someone to operate a machine, drive a bus, fill in a spreadsheet, analyse a set of accounts. We cannot train them to make strategy, have vision, think more broadly and thoughtfully about the world, understand values or culture or purpose. (Yes, I know some companies have values training. Teaching people to recite values off by heart is utterly pointless, if they don't *understand* them. You might as well teach the values to performing seals.)

Education, on the other hand, is about understanding. The purpose of education is not to help us learn to *do* things, it is to learn to *think* about things. Education broadens the mind, opens it up to new ways of thinking and makes us see the world in new ways.

This is of course contrary to the established popular view, and every year I hear complaints from MBA students that the programmes they are on are insufficiently practical and they are not learning enough skills. Every year I give the same reply; the purpose of the MBA is not to teach you skills. If you want skills, go do some workshops, or sign up for a MOOC, or for heaven's sake, read a book; name a skill, and there are probably at least half a dozen handbooks out there waiting to teach it to you. The purpose of the MBA is not to help you become more skilled, it is to revolutionize your worldview, stretch your brain, challenge your thinking and send you back out into the so-called real world better able to understand the forces and dynamics of economies, markets and organizations. Learn skills on an MBA? You might as well try to make toast in a blender.

As well as running my own business, I've taught MBA students off and on for twenty years, and been associated with business schools in some way for longer than that. I am a great admirer and respecter of business schools; I think they have the potential to a great force for good in the world. And I am passionate about the MBA. Far from being out of date and irrelevant to modern business, as some critics would have it, I believe that, adapted and refreshed to meet the needs of the twenty-first century, the MBA can become more valuable than ever. However, whether the MBA fulfils that potential will depend on (1) whether business schools can manage that process of adaptation and (2) whether businesses can change their own views about education and see the business education for what it really is.

How business schools turned away from the light

To understand the problem, let's go back to how business schools began. Training institutions, like the medieval Italian *scuole d'abaco* or their Indian equivalents the abacus schools, or the book-keeping colleges that sprang up in nineteenth-century America and educated business luminaries as diverse as Henry Heinz and Frederick Winslow Taylor, have been around for a long time. The first institution that we might recognize as a business school in the modern sense was Hayleybury, the training college established by the East India Company in 1805, where as well as useful skills, such as languages and accounting, trainee managers also learned Indian philosophy and history and tried to understand a little better the country they were about to run.

The École Superieur de Commerce, not connected to any company and open to all qualified students, opened its doors in Paris in 1819. There was then a long gap to the Wharton School in Pennsylvania and the Haut Études Commerciales (HEC) in Paris, both founded in 1881 and both still going strong today. Then came Leipzig Commercial College in Germany and business schools at the universities of California and Chicago in 1898 and finally the institution that for years was the flagship of the business school movement, Harvard Business School in 1908.

The philosophy of Edwin Gay, founding dean of Harvard, is particularly relevant here. Gay did include an element of skills in his syllabus and invited in experts, including Taylor, to lecture on these. But he believed the primary purpose of the business school was to produce graduates who were fit and ready to run businesses. The most important elements were not skills but personal qualities: courage, judgement and sympathy (sympathy in the Darwinian meaning, the ability to work with and understand others; today we might also call it empathy) featured high on his list of desired characteristics. Gay's Harvard Business School also stressed the importance of practical research. For example, Paul Cherington and Melvin Copeland, who set up the first marketing department there, dug into the principles of economics to help explain the workings of markets.[1] Over in Chicago, Walter Scott and his colleagues employed psychology to help understand consumer behaviour.[2]

The key words in the last two sentences are *understand* and *explain*. Neither Cherington nor Scott provided toolkits. They provided knowledge, practical knowledge of the way the world worked. The methods they used to gather knowledge were not always scientific, nor were their findings particularly scientific in nature. The largest research study of the period, the Hawthorne experiments of the late 1920s and 1930s conducted by staff at Harvard Business School, has been shown to be riddled with methodological errors. Yet the truth remains: no single study has taught us more or made us think more deeply about work than the Hawthorne studies.[3] Out of that hothouse of experiment and inquiry came not just a vast range of behavioural approaches to work and organization that persist to this day, but also the beginnings of the quality movement; Walter Shewhart, W. Edwards Deming and Joseph Juran, the founders of quality management, were all employed in some capacity at the Hawthorne works.[4]

However, these advances and developments did not impress the arcane and snobbish world of higher education. British universities flatly refused to have anything to do with business schools; the idea that universities should soil their hands with commerce was unthinkable. American universities put up with business schools but treated them as ugly ducklings. Typical was the attitude encountered by one Harvard law graduate who told his dean that he planned to go on to the business school to take an MBA. 'You are about to graduate from the greatest educational institution in the world', thundered the dean, 'and now you're going to *that* place?'[5]

Following the Second World War, there was a strong effort to 'reform' business schools, beginning in America and gradually spreading to Europe and around the world. The Ford Foundation report of 1959 set the tone. Business schools were required, as a condition of being allowed to stay in the university club, to become more focused on research; empirical, academic research, not the kind of problem-solving fieldwork in which they had specialized before.

The two key words now were 'rigorous' and 'interdisciplinary'. The latter meant that business school research had to abandon its former reliance on disciplines like business economics and psychology and bring in influences from mathematics, computer science, physics and sociology.

What is wrong with that, I hear you ask? In the short run, nothing; there is no doubt that the quality of business research improved as the influence of multiple perspectives was fed in. But in the long term, there were two unexpected consequences. First, this new ideology of business schools convinced business academics that what they were doing was science. The term 'management science' began to be bandied about; by the 1960s, it was commonplace that management was a science and could be studied in the same scientific way as other disciplines. Paradoxically, this mean that interdisciplinarity got squeezed out; because management was a science in its own right, it could draw on its own accumulated body of knowledge without needing to refer to other fields of study.[6]

The second unintended consequence, for business schools, was that their academic staff now began to identify more closely with the university than with their original constituents, businesses and managers. The majority of business academics today see themselves as academics, first and foremost. Fewer and fewer business academics have much in the way of work experience in business, with the result that some of their work betrays a breath-taking lack of understanding of the real-life cultures and politics of business. Fewer and fewer are willing to engage in consultancy work with businesses, which might give them such understanding; consultancy is a distraction from their real work, which is research. Fewer and fewer are willing to publish their work in magazines or newspapers that professional managers might want to read; they concentrate on the peer-reviewed academic journals which, as one colleague suggests, only three people and a dog actually read. It doesn't matter; what matters is the status of being published there. As an editor of professional business magazines, I find it increasingly common for business academics to refuse to publish or share their ideas with business people *at all*; the only audience they are interested in is other academics.

This intellectual onanism,[7] along with the failure to engage with businesses on a practical level, is one of the reasons why the business world has become more sceptical about business schools and business education in recent years. Smaller firms are particularly dubious, and I even hear that desperate old cliché, 'the best education comes from the University of Life', being flogged around the course once more. Businesses aren't the only ones to have lost sight of the purpose of education; business schools have too.

Business schools have, in effect, turned away from the light. They are living in Plato's cave, studying the shadows on the wall and writing papers about them, then passing these papers to each other to read. I honestly believe that we have reached a point where some academics, and some business schools, are frightened of the reality of daylight. They need to find, somewhere, the courage to leave the cave and go back out into the real world.

Switching metaphors, I believe that 'back to the future' is the way forward. Business schools, like businesses themselves, need to go back and look at the reasons why they were founded in the first place. Business schools must rediscover their own sense of purpose, if they are to help businesses maintain theirs.

The fracturing of management thought

A further effect of the scientization of management that has been going on since 1959 is the gradual fracturing of management thought into different sub-disciplines. This is fine on one level; it allows people to concentrate on one aspect of business and study it to its fullest extent. Problems start when it comes time to re-combine all these fractured sub-fields into a coherent whole. Here, business schools struggle. Every business school I have ever been involved with or observed has struggled with the problem of holistic management. General management, once a mainstay of business school curricula, is rarely taught today.

And yet, success in business depends on having a strong core of managers who can manage in the round, think across disciplines and see the business as a coherent whole. But where are those managers to come from?

Not from the training, coaching and consulting industries, which have bought into the fragmentation of management and increased it by an order of magnitude. They have also bought heavily into the ideas of linear thinking, of step-by-step approaches to change management and of tightly defined roles. In the previous chapter I alluded to the separation of leadership and management. This has its origins in academia, in particular in the work of John Kotter and the late Warren Bennis, both widely read and respected.[8] The damage has been done by a generation of leadership consultants who adopted the ideas of Kotter and Bennis uncritically and at face value, and set about convincing two generations of young men and women that they should, as my student said, think of themselves as either leaders or managers but not both.

Heaven forbid that anyone should have to carry out two roles at the same time! But that is exactly what management does require, over and over again, day in and day out. Henry Mintzberg's *The Nature of Managerial Work*, one of five books that I believe should be required reading for every manager,* shows how managers have to switch roles rapidly or adopt more than one role as a matter of routine. But most trainers and consultants are able to or prepared to teach only one role, or one fairly narrow set of roles. They rely on metrics and tools (in fairness, because that is what their clients often expect), thus reinforcing the belief that management is a science, and like Taylor a century and more ago, break down management into the little constituent parts on which they are experts.

The result, too often, is confusion, error, muddle and delay. Specialist consultants appear and disappear seemingly at random. Their advice, well meant and perfectly valid from their own point of view, is contradictory and confusing. Sometimes they leave companies worse off than when they first arrived on the scene.

---

* The other four are Mary Parker Follett, *Creative Experience*, Pablo Triana, *Lecturing Birds on Flying*, Machiavelli, *The Prince*, and LeShan and Margenau, *Einstein's Space and Van Gogh's Sky*. Only two are about business and only one is about management.

Some of my colleagues and friends are trainers, coaches and consultants (I don't have a daughter, so the question doesn't arise). I have myself, in my time, turned my hand to both coaching and consulting. I know the value they can bring; I know the transformational effect that good ones can have, in a very short space of time. But consultants, trainers and coaches must also beware of the seven sins of management, especially short-term and linear thinking, and they too must have a purpose: the betterment of management *as a whole*.

The best consultants and trainers I know are not in it for the money. They are missionaries, zealots, fanatics who believe, like me, that management can be a force for good in the world and that it is the duty of those who can to help improve management and help make it better, so that management in turn can make the world a better place. They want to identify the sources of incompetence and root them out. It is now up to that spearhead of idealists to start dragging the rest of their professions with them. Trainers and consultants, like business schools, must start using their influence and knowledge as forces for good.

Are experts necessarily revealers of truth?

And, of course, businesses have played their own role in the current disconnect what is offered and what is needed. For a start, it really is time businesses stopped regarding the education system as being nothing more than a device for delivering shiny, freshly minted managers and workers who can settle at once into their assigned jobs, all the skills they require perfectly honed and in place. As I said earlier, education doesn't work like that.

What is more, even if we could develop a system that would pop out die-stamped, perfectly formed managers, there are a hundred reasons why we shouldn't. Top of the list is the fact that every company is unique, and every situation it finds itself in is unique. Companies need managers who can adapt to situations, who can think outside the normal parameters and who can draw on experience and networks to solve problems creatively rather than in a box-ticking manner. Producing managers like that is a matter of custom building, not mass production.

Mary Parker Follett begins her great book *Creative Experience* by asking an intriguing question: are experts necessarily revealers of truth?[9] Very often that is how they are treated; as gurus dispensing wisdom from on high. The view that because you hire an expensive consultant you have to agree with what he or she says is both persistent and erroneous; equally erroneous is the view that all business school lecturers know what they are talking about. I am a business school lecturer. QED.

Follett's point is that people themselves often know what is right better than any outside expert. They sometimes need help to identify and fully understand the truth they already possess, but the truth is already there. I have always admired lecturers and consultants who believe that their main purpose is to help people unlock what they already know, rather than forcing new and possibly irrelevant knowledge on them. Businesses can do the same. Search around the business, looking as Nonaka and Takeuchi advise, for both explicit and tacit knowledge. Find out what we already know, what our people know, and create the culture of knowledge sharing that we discussed in Chapter 5.

Finding out what we know enables us to also identify the gaps in our knowledge, what we don't know. Once the gaps in knowledge have been located and their nature understood, only then is it time to turn to the outside world for help. Knowing what we don't know should also enable us to choose the right kind of provider. If we need specific skill sets, good: we can seek out specialist training consultants who will deliver those within the context of the larger business. If on the other hand we need people with more holistic knowledge, people who can develop strategy and vision and, yes, purpose, then that is where business schools come in. The high-level education that they provide will give the company access to networks of knowledge – not skills, remember, but knowledge – that will enable it to broaden its own horizons.

It's not hard. Just find out what you need and then go to the right place to get it. Stop expecting business schools to deliver you cloned managers. Stop expecting MBA programmes to turn young, inexperienced managers into people who can walk on water. Start engaging with the education system and making it work for you, rather than complaining because it doesn't do exactly what you want.

Inherently annoyed

In an interview in *Business Strategy Review*, published in October 2014, business guru Gary Hamel outlined his view of the future of business research; and to my way of thinking, it looked quite a lot like business research in its original form. Hamel called for more active engagement in businesses, citing Harvard Business School and the Hawthorne experiments as he did so, and he also called for a more experimental approach to research with more heuristics, more trial and error. He also called for researchers to be willing to take risks, and to care about what they were researching.

'You have to be kind of inherently annoyed', said Hamel, 'you have to be *au contraire* and you have to challenge what's there. Classic academic training turns you into a kind of intellectual rule-taker. You're reading what the people before you said, you're building on those theories, rather than being an intellectual rule-breaker.'[10]

I agree, but I would expand this point of view beyond just research and apply it to the entire purpose of business schools, and the training, coaching and consulting establishment as well. To the lecturers, trainers and others involved in this whole field of endeavour, I would say: be inherently annoyed! Find something that is really wrong with modern management and then throw your weight into fixing it. Work with businesses to identify the problem, find the solution and then pass that on to as many people as you can. Don't disengage. Don't pigeonhole yourselves. Don't think that the number of papers you publish or the number of clients you have is synonymous with success, because it is not.

I will add, too, that for business academics, getting closer to business is not a nice-to-do, it is a must-do. Since 2008 especially, the chorus of voices asking what business schools are for and whether business education really justifies the investment is growing. It is time business schools stood up and answered those questions, positively. John Davis reminds us that when society tires of an institution, it throws it away. If businesses schools cannot justify their existence, then sooner or later they will begin to disappear.

The tower of academe is leaning; but there is still time to prevent the fall.

On the other side of the coin, you get out of a partnership what you put into it. Businesses should no longer expect to be passively spoon-fed knowledge by the business schools and training establishments. They need to get involved, not just by donations and monetary support but by contributing intellectual resources too. Open your doors to students and let them come in and see how businesses are run in real life. Send your managers to business schools, not just as students but as lectures and presenters of live case studies; come and teach the teachers. And it is a dead certainty that in the process, the businesses and managers too will learn. In twenty years, I have never yet stood in front of a classroom of graduate level students when I did not learn at least one thing from them.

Tackling the problem of management incompetence and failure absolutely requires businesses and educators to work together. Educators provide the raw material that will become the managers and leaders of the future. Businesses know better than anyone what they need, when and where. A partnership between the two, now, could create a new generation of managers full of the necessary passion, purpose and inherent annoyance to get things done.

Let's at least try. Even if we fail, is it really possible to make matters worse?

---

[1] H.K. Heaton, *A Scholar in Action: Edwin F. Gay*, Cambridge, MA: Harvard University Press, 1952; Melvin Copeland, *And Mark the Era: The Story of Harvard Business School*, Boston: Little, Brown, 1958.

[2] Walter Dill Scott, *The Psychology of Advertising*, Chicago: Dodd, Mead & Co., 1913.

[3] Mayo, *The Human Problems*; Fritz Roethlisberger and W.J. Dickson, *Management and the Worker*, Cambridge, MA: Harvard University Press, 1939.

[4] The connection between workplace behaviour and the quality movement at Hawthorne has never been fully explored. It should be.

[5] Anthony J. Mayo, Nitin Nohria and Laura G. Singleton, *Paths to Power: How Insiders and Outsiders Shaped American Business Leadership*, Boston: Harvard Business School Press, 2006, p. 132.

[6] Mie Augier and James G. March, *The Roots, Rituals and Rhetoric of Change*, Stanford: Stanford University Press, 2011, explore this process of drift in much more detail; my account is necessarily highly simplistic.

[7] I first used this phrase several years ago in *A History of Management Thought*. If anything, I think it has become still more valid with the passage of time.

8 Warren G. Bennis and Bert Nanus, *Leaders: Five Strategies for Taking Charge*, New York: Harper & Row, 1985; John P. Kotter, *A Force for Change: How Leadership Differs from Management*, New York: The Free Press, 1990.

9 Mary Parker Follett, *Creative Experience*, New York: Longmans, Green, 1924.

10 http://bsr.london.edu/lbs-article/851/index.html

Chapter 12

High noon in the garden of good and evil

Several years ago I interviewed one of the grand old men of Indian business, R.K. Krishna Kumar, then head of Tata Tea (now Tata Beverages). I was doing research for a book on the Tata corporate brand, and I asked him what he thought the chief attributes of the Tata brand were. I sat confidently expecting to hear him say things like 'trust' and 'responsibility' and 'service'. Instead, he nodded slightly and then looked directly at me. 'This is not a brand story', he said. 'This is a story about good and evil.'

I was, to put it mildly, stunned. I had interviewed any number of CEOs and chairmen of major corporations by this point in my career, and I had never heard any of them use language remotely like this. I had asked a question about branding; his answer took us into the realm of metaphysics. I was also, I admit, uncomfortable. 'Good' and 'evil' are emotive words; was it even appropriate for us to be talking about them in a business context?

The more I thought about it, however, the more I realized that he was right and I was wrong. Business is not a value-neutral activity. No matter what we do in management, we touch the lives of others: the people who work for us, the people in the communities we serve, the people who own businesses and entrust us with their management.

As managers, we are given power and authority over other people. We have a choice: we can use that power and authority wisely and for the benefit of others, or we can use it badly or wrongly or selfishly for the benefit of ourselves. That choice seems clear to me. If you don't like good and evil, choose other less emotive terms; those will do for me.

I said in the introduction to this book that I believe that management is a force for good in the world. So it is; so long as managers believe that it is and act accordingly. In that chapter I also listed some of the negative consequences of bad management. But consider some of the powerful positives of good management: improved health care and better medicines leading to longer lifespans; blink-of-an-eye communications, allowing us to tap into worldwide networks from anywhere on those networks and all the sharing of knowledge and ideas that has resulted; steadily improving forms of alternative energy that are both good for the environment and are driving energy prices down; a higher standard of living for hundreds of millions, even billions of people around the world; goods and services that not only improve physical living conditions but also bolster self-esteem and confidence and make people happy. All that and much more happens because of good management.

How? Managers don't make things, they don't stand in labs and invent things, or build things, or grow things. No; they make it possible for other people to do those things, efficiently and effectively, and then build the architecture of the value chains that bring goods and services into the market where the people that need them can have access to them. If you want to define management in a single word, try this: *facilitation*. Managers make it possible for other people to do what they want to do, what they must do. In economic terms, managers bring the makers and the buyers together, and make it possible for exchange to take place. In purely human terms, managers enable people do things that make them happy and fulfilled, either when consuming or producing, or both.

In the 1970s, Robert Greenleaf elucidated the principles of 'servant leadership', the notion that leaders are servants of the organizations they lead, not the masters.[1] The duty of the leader is to enable the rest of the organization to do what it needs to do to fulfil its purpose. In Greenleaf's thinking, leaders sublimate themselves to the organization, and put its needs before their own. If you accept my admittedly contentious view that managers also lead, then this view can be applied quickly to management positions.

And indeed, does it not make sense? Why else are we as managers given authority over other people? To use them as our playthings? To enslave them into our own service and drive them to help us achieve our own goals, at the expense of theirs? Both happen, of course, as we saw in this book, but is either view morally justified in the modern world? So, if we accept that we are *not* to use other people for our own ends, it follows logically that we are given authority so that we can help them do what they need to do, if the organization is to reach its goals. We are there to work for them, not them to work for us.

I said earlier that managers and leaders don't make things. No; they make things *happen*.

Once you are prepared to accept that premise (which I admit could take some time to digest), the next question is, how do we reconcile this servant–leader/manager posture with the natural pride and ambition that any truly driven manager will have? That pride and ambition, as we saw in Chapter 4, turns easily to arrogance, especially once we have had a sniff or two of success. In the same chapter, I suggested that pride and humility need each other; pride without humility is what makes arrogance happen, while humility without pride leads to unhappiness and loss of confidence.

The balance to be walked between pride and humility is a narrow one, keen as the razor's edge, and many fall from it on one side or the other. The key to maintaining balance is constant self-examination and reminder. Remember what you have done in the past, the successes and the mistakes. Never forget the latter; they are both the anchor to your humility and a never failing source of learning ways in which to do better and improve. Work on those mistakes and eliminate them; and at the very least, try not to make the same mistakes twice (much, much easier said than done). Don't be downcast by your failures, but don't get too carried away by your successes either. Rudyard Kipling had it right:

> *If you can meet with Triumph and Disaster*
> *And treat those two impostors just the same...*

And what is true of individuals is true of companies. Creation of a culture of humility is a sovereign remedy against self-centred focus and arrogance. And how do you create such a culture? By reminding people of purpose. Why are they here? Why do they come to work? What do they hope to achieve? It doesn't matter whether you are working in a lab or down a mine, in a boardroom or in a sewerage works; there is a purpose there, and if you remind employees of it in a language that makes sense to them, most will respond. The others need to go.

We also touched on the 'sin' of ignorance, of people who are simply not up to the job, or else for one reason or another have never been given the mental skills and equipment that they need. This is an area where training and education can play an important role, but at the same time the company also needs to become better at managing knowledge and creating a culture where knowledge is valued and shared. There are several reasons for this. First, without such a culture, much of the knowledge accruing to individual managers through training and education will stick with them and not be shared among others; and if those managers leave, this knowledge will be lost entirely. One of the additional advantages to education in particular is that the knowledge it provides can be spread around the organization; one MBA graduate can share knowledge with five, ten, a dozen, twenty others and improve their effectiveness too.

Second, knowledge helps us to get away from a number of sins, not just ignorance but also linear thinking and short-termism. The more we know about the world around us, the more likely it is that we can break out of path-dependent routines and move on to something new.

And third, there is a moral reason. To repeat, as managers we are given power and authority over other people. But what right have we to direct their efforts or give them orders if we know less than they do? Is there any more pitiable or despised figure, in any walk of life, than an ignorant superior?

There is of course a strong connection between our second sin, ignorance, and the third, fear. Knowledge very often brings confidence, but human nature is such that most of us are fearful of uncertainty. Fear makes us hold back; if arrogance leads us to take too many risks, fear drives us to take too few, and we know that risk is an essential part of business. Fear squeezes and blocks our risk appetite, and that in turn holds back the company from achieving its purpose.

Courage is one of the first attributes of a manager. The very first definition of managerial competences, by St Bernardino of Siena in the early fifteenth century, listed the willingness to accept responsibility and the willingness to accept and assume risk as two of the four qualities every manager should have (the others were that managers should be efficient, and be willing to work hard).[2] Most works on managerial and leadership competence up to the present day have stressed the need for courage in some form. Managers need courage to stand up for what is right and question what they believe to be bad decisions; they need courage to hold fast to their purpose when economic times get rough, and they need even more courage to initiate change programmes when change is needed. They need the courage to tell the truth and not let themselves, or their colleagues, hide behind false beliefs. Sometimes, managers have to be prepared to be the most unpopular people in the room.

Greed, on the other hand, stems sometimes from a lack of fear. Companies like Lehman Brothers were not fearful enough when perhaps they should have been. The main problem with greed, though, is that it takes over from and wipes out the idea of purpose. When companies begin to think that their only purpose is to make money – as again happened at Lehman Brothers – then they lose their central moral core. Greed undermines the company because it turns attention away from the people who matter most, the stakeholders, and focuses attention on the company and its managers.

It is important to set the values in a corporate culture right from the beginning and ensure that those values enshrine the principle that profit and growth are by-products of good business, not ends in their own right; or as Confucius once said to one of his followers, 'virtue is the root, and wealth is only its outcome'. Serve customers well and efficiently and you will make money. Get carried away by the false gods of ever increasing profit and growth and, again like Lehman Brothers, eventually you will overreach yourself and fall.

Lust for power and empire and domination over others, including sexual domination, damages companies in much the same manner as greed, by deflecting attention away from the things that are most important. Replacing cultures of selfish domination by cultures where self-restraint is the order of the day is essential to reducing the risk of failure. In this area in particular, leaders need to lead by example. They should have standards by which they live themselves, before expecting their followers to follow. It is no good having an ironclad policy requiring employees to not say or do anything damaging to the company on Facebook, if your own Facebook page is full of images that you think are amusing but will horrify the rest of the world (I leave it to your own imagination to decide what those images might be; there has been enough bad language in this book already).

We mentioned how linear thinking is in part a result of lack of knowledge, but it is also linked to the scientization of management and the unhealthy yearning for precision. Fragmentation of knowledge and increasing specialization have created a silo effect, but they have also led to a situation where linear thinking is dominant and anything which is not linear and cannot be broken down into steps gets branded as 'intuition' or 'guesswork' (in modern management thought, the two are wrongly seen as equivalent).

The answer is holistic thinking, seeing organizations as integral wholes and a willingness to look outside the framework of the company and its immediate surroundings for any source of learning. Beware the point of view which says that one's own industry, or one's own time and place, or one's own circumstances are completely different from anything elsewhere, or anything that has gone before. No matter where you look, no matter who you talk to, there is always something to learn. Broad holistic thinking must complement linear thinking, not replace it; just as long-term thinking must exist alongside a short-term perspective, not supplant it.

I have dwelt long enough – too long, some might say – on the need for purpose. I'll make just two final remarks on the subject. Purpose expresses the central reason why a business exists; if you don't know what the purpose of the business is, then make it *your* business to find out as soon as possible, and then live by what you have learned.

And, if you cannot find a purpose or do not believe that businesses have purposes, get out of business. Do it now. Quit. Go and do something else, anything else, and let your place be filled by someone who understands. If you don't believe in purpose and you have a management job with power and authority over other people; if your only purpose in being a manager is to have a comfortable job and enrich yourself, then you are dangerous to those other people and to yourself. Sooner or later, your lack of moral core will drag you down, and probably them too. Get out, now.

So, what are the keys to management success? Table 12.1 describes them: humility, knowledge, moral courage, focus on purpose, restraint and broad thinking. These aren't tools; you can't learn these things as steps from a coaching manual. They come from education, experience and intelligence. They need to be cultivated, as Kenichi Ohmae said about strategy, as habits of mind.

Table 12.1 Responses to the Seven Sins of Management

Arrogance	Humility. Remember that others matter more than you do. Remember you and your company are not perfect, and that they can fail. Use that knowledge to restrain your judgement and make level-headed decisions that are good for everyone, not just yourself.
Ignorance	Knowledge. Create a culture where knowledge is valued and shared. Use knowledge as a foundation and shield to build strength and resilience into the business.
Fear	Courage. Accept that risk is inevitable, and help others to accept this too. Turn weaknesses into strengths; help people and the business as a whole confront their fears and address them. Sometimes, out of risk and fear come greatness.
Greed	Remember why the business exists. Don't mistake profit and growth for goals. Remember the true purpose and grow only where it is good for the business. Profit is a by-product of what you do, not an end result.
Lust	Restraint. Self-control is a very useful thing; make sure people know what the concept really means. Set an example of the standards you wish people to adhere too. Develop a culture of respect for others, not one where domination of others is seen as normal and desirable. Crush power blocs and barons, and unify the organization around its central purpose.
Linear thinking	Broad thinking. Introduce multiple ways of thinking and encourage the view that there are many ways to solve a problem. Reduce or eliminate dependence on targets and numerical goals and encourage a culture of achievement. Learn from as many sources as possible and encourage diverse thinking. Linear logic and short-termism should not be discarded, but they should be complemented by other, different mental models. Enrich your mental armour with every tool you can find. Never read your PowerPoint slides in a presentation.
Lack of purpose	Rediscover the purpose, or create a new one. Either way, give the business back its moral core and help it rediscover why it exists and what is meant to do. Persuade managers to think more about the business and less about themselves. Build integrity, honesty and honour back into the culture.

How do you do this? First, by thinking about these things and their importance, all the time, and reminding yourself of how constant vigilance is needed to keep the seven sins of management from taking hold. We saw in earlier chapters how easily they take root, often without people noticing until it is too late. Encourage a degree of introspection, of thinking and critical review of the organization and what it is doing and where it is going. Another paradox: a certain amount of inward focus is necessary for outward focus. We need to think about ourselves and our capabilities if we are to effectively serve others.

Second, of all the key factors, purpose is the most important. Remember the purpose and remind others too. So long as you have the purpose clearly in mind, and act accordingly, everything else will follow.

And finally, remember this point always: management is not about you. It is about other people. It is about helping customers to meet their needs, enabling employees to do their jobs better, delivering value to shareholders, treating suppliers with dignity and fitting into the prevailing mood of society, all these things, all the time. At no point in this cat's cradle of relationships are you, the manager, the most important person. You are the leader; you are also the servant.

So, that's it? All you have to do is to be humble, knowledgeable, brave, self-controlled, a broad thinker who remembers what the business is for, and you will succeed automatically? Well, no. Lots of things can still go wrong, and luck is still there waiting in the wings. And remember, the key issue here is not individuals but cultures. Even if you have all of the above qualities, you might still get dragged down by a hostile culture. So, as well as cultivating your own strengths, endeavour to build a culture that has all these features. If you can do so, you will have a strong and resilient culture which should be proof against anything fortune can throw at it. There is strength in numbers. Alone, we are weak. Together, believing in business as a force for good, we are very strong.

Shouting at imaginary dogs

One of the more memorable characters in John Berendt's *Midnight in the Garden of Good and Evil*, a study of character set in the American city of

Savannah, is William Simon Glover, who walks through the streets every day shouting at an imaginary dog. Years ago, a friend died and left Glover a bequest of ten dollars a week provided Glover would continue to walk his friend's dog. The dog itself died some time ago, but Glover continues to walk around Savannah calling to the dog. By doing so, he has persuaded a judge that he believes the dog is still alive. This in turn allows him to continue to collect the bequest. Of course, it is only a matter of time before another judge looks at the issue and orders the payment to be stopped; meanwhile, Glover collects as much money as he can.

Glover, like most of the characters in Berendt's book, lives in an unreal world of his own making, a world which revolves around himself. His selfishness is so utter that he is prepared to betray even the memory of his dead friend. I thought about Glover while reading the preview for a forthcoming new series of *The Apprentice*, a television programme that stands for pretty much everything I hate about modern business. The culture of *The Apprentice* betrays at some point all of the seven sins of management: arrogance of course, ignorance of even a basic under-standing of what management is, fear of failure, greed for success, lust for control, linear thinking in the step-by-step exercises the contestants are given and above all a complete lack of understanding of any purpose in business except to make money.

Like the characters in Berendt's book, the contestants on *The Apprentice* live in an unreal world. Their efforts to build businesses are like so much shouting at imaginary dogs; they are ultimately short term, meaningless and futile. Their efforts are also emblematic of much of what is wrong with modern management culture. I repeat: I believe in management as a force for good in the world. I think – I hope – most managers still agree with me. But we have been on a long slow slide for some time, away from a belief in purpose and value into scepticism and cynicism. My fear is that one day we will wake up and find the entire managerial class have stopped caring. They are only in it for themselves and what they can get. They are not managing for purpose, they are contestants for some sort of illusory prize in a world of make-believe. They are not managing anything real, they are shouting at imaginary dogs.

Society created businesses, and managers, because it had a need for them, said John Davis. When society no longer wants these institutions or becomes tired of them, it will throw them away. Don't believe me? What has happened to the tobacco industry over the last forty years? Once upon a time tobacco was seen as a beneficial product. Now it is – pardon the pun – under a cloud. Tobacco companies have consolidated, merged or disappeared. Society no longer wants them. It is throwing them away.

And sometimes it goes beyond particular industries. Sometimes, as in Russia after 1918 and China after 1949, it abolishes the very principle of free-market business and nationalizes everything. Managers then became mere administrators, puppets on the strings of the command economy, with no purpose other than to deliver quota. All the good that management could offer vanished. Why? Because society deemed that on the whole, business and management were doing more harm than good. Never mind whether this view was right; it was the view that prevailed.

We're not at the point where society is ready to revolt against business, not yet, but there were some nasty moments after 2008; we came closer to full-scale anti-business demonstrations than most of us would like to admit. The fall of Lehman Brothers did more than just cost job losses in New York; it shook the city's faith. If even a trusted and revered institution like that could be shown to be rotten to the core, what were the rest like? The vehemence of public opinion on both sides of the Atlantic that greeted the phone-hacking scandal is another straw in the wind. Don't get me wrong, Rupert Murdoch and his managers deserved the pillorying they got, but there is a danger that the public will start to see all businesses as being the same.

There is an air of suspicion and scepticism now, including inside business itself. One survey in 2010 suggested that less than a third of people working in the banking industry believed banks could be trusted. More recent polls have shown that we don't trust our politicians either, or the journalists who are supposed to hold them to account. An unpleasant mood is building up, and sometime in the next decade there will be a serious calling to account of our leaders and managers in many spheres, business included. The conditions to create such a showdown already exist; only a sufficient cause is wanting.

The reawakening of moral purpose in management and the consequent elimination of the seven deadly sins needs to aim for more than just the prevention of business failures, though that would be a good start. It should have as one of its aims the rebuilding of public confidence in business, a reawakening of a sense that management is a moral pursuit and that it is on the right side in the struggle for good and evil. In fact, I am not concerned so much by the public view, as I am by the rising tide of belief among managers themselves that management is no longer a force for good. The rot, the hollowing out of the moral core, is beginning.

We're not in real danger, not yet. But the clock is ticking.

The first duty of management

What is the first duty of management? Not to make profits, or grow market share, or increase the share price, or generate value for share-holders, or climb the ladder of promotion, or make yourself rich, no.

That is not to say that these things are forbidden. On the contrary, they are absolutely permissible and laudable, so long as you obey the first rule of management, which is:

> *To leave the world a slightly better place than you found it.*

Not the whole world, or even very much of the world, we must be realistic. But if you can influence the little corner of the world that you control and make things better for the other people in it - customers, employees, fellow managers, shareholders, stakeholders - in a way that *doesn't* actively make life worse for anyone else; and if you can continue to do that in each job you hold as you make your way through your career to your honourable and richly deserved retirement: well then. Get up on that podium, take your bouquet and bow your head while they put the medal round your neck, and I'll cue the band to play your national anthem. Because if you can do that, then you really will have won.

---

[1] Robert K. Greenleaf, *Servant Leadership: A Journey into the Nature of Legitimate Power and Greatness*, Mahwah: Paulist Press, 1977.

[2] Raymond de Roover, *San Bernardino of Siena and Sant'Antonio of Florence: The Two Great Economic Thinkers of the Middle Ages*, Boston: Baker Library, Harvard Graduate School of Business Administration, 1967.

Warning flags

There are exactly fifty warning flags in Chapters 4–10, warning signs that a company may be beginning to develop a culture of incompetence, and there is a risk of failure. Treating these problems quickly and eliminating them should reduce that risk and increase the chances of success.

Look at each of the fifty, going back to the text in the relevant chapter if you wish to refresh yourself as to what they mean, and then ask yourself if you can see any sign of these warning flags in your own company. If possible, answer 'yes' or 'no' to each; if the answer is 'maybe', or 'a little', then probably the true answer is 'yes'. Count the number of 'yes' answers and consult the guide at the end of the list.

Chapter 4

- Leaders who are surrounded by people who are too afraid or too sycophantic to challenge them.
- Top executives who are invisible to the rest of the organization.
- The belief that just because the firm has been successful in the past, it will go on being successful in the future.
- People saying, 'But this is how we've always done it.'
- Executives speaking about stakeholders, especially customers, in derogatory terms.
- People saying, 'That can't happen here.'
- Any manifestation of the belief that, so long as intentions are pure, the end justifies the means.

Chapter 5

- People describing even relatively minor failures as black swan events.
- Significant numbers of people in senior positions who have no prior experience of that role.

- Unrealistic plans and expectations.
- Intolerance of or prejudice against 'people who aren't like us'; casual sexism and/or racism.
- No one ever questions the efficacy of a strategy once it is set in motion.
- Set routines and procedures, the purpose and utility of which are never questioned.
- Constant churn and reorganization; a belief in change for change's sake.
- The presence of large numbers of people who clearly aren't up to their jobs.

Chapter 6

- Absolute reliance on models, in the belief that these always tell the truth.
- Excessive and obsessive planning, which result in plans that no one can read or knows how to follow.
- The widespread belief that the company is responsible for its own destiny, and luck plays no part in its success.
- All-white (or all Indian, or all Chinese), all-male boards and teams.
- The belief that the company can go into foreign countries and do things the same way it does them at home.
- A culture of conformity, where questioning and dissent are discouraged or even punished.

Chapter 7

- A series of rapid acquisitions funded by debt, especially when those acquisitions do not seem to relate to each other.
- A lack of central ideology or belief that unites the various elements of the company.
- A heavy emphasis on profit targets, especially when those targets are linked to rewards and bonuses.
- Any strategy based on market share as the end game.

- Allowing investors to call the shots on strategy. Most investors aren't interested in strategy. Most investors can't spell strategy.
- An excessive focus on competition.

Chapter 8

- A culture where sexual harassment is winked at, or excused along the lines of 'boys will be boys'.
- High divorce rates among senior managers and board members.
- A culture where the formation of personal power blocs and 'fiefdoms' is seen as normal, and where there is a strong cult of personality.
- Celebrity CEOs.
- The prevalent belief that personal bonuses are more important than the company's goals.
- Bureaucracies that control power and information without sharing them.

Chapter 9

- Excessive insistence on conformity to routine.
- The reluctance or refusal to accept new ideas.
- The refusal to accept that things which cannot be measured or valued are important.
- The introduction of metrics which add costs but do not add value.
- Too many targets, and/or targets which are badly defined and set.
- Excessive focus on either the short term or the long term, rather than a balanced view of both.
- Reliance on spreadsheets to make decisions, rather than personal judgement.
- People reading their own PowerPoint slides during presentations.

Chapter 10

- Promoting people on the basis of past performance is common practice.

- Promoting or hiring people for reasons other than competence.
- Under-promotion, or the failure to promote people to a level where they can fully exercise their talents.
- Rituals that must be strictly adhered too, but contribute nothing of value to the business.
- Managers who refuse to take responsibility or accept the burdens of leadership.
- A general inability to distinguish between blame and responsibility.
- Signs of social loafing, people not pulling their weight when working in groups or teams.
- Nodding dog managers, who never voice an opinion of their own but agree with whatever is put in front of them.
- High staff and management turnover.

If the number of 'yes' answers is...

0 warning flags: Really? Try again.

1–5: Excellent; despite a few flaws, you would appear to have a strong and purposeful corporate culture. However, do not rest on your laurels. Look at the 'yes' answers and think again. How significant are the problems? What would it take to fix them? And remember, times change and so do cultures. Keep running this exercise at intervals and be alert to new problems as they arise.

6–10: Not so good. Start work at once on identifying the source and nature of the problem and find out why these warning flags have come up. Your corporate culture is not in danger yet, but the drift has begun.

11–15: Not good at all. The company and its managers are losing touch with reality on a steady basis. Go after each of those warning flags, find out the causes of each and eliminate them. Prioritize them only if you must; all are important.

16–25: The rot has set in. Does the company still remember what its purpose is, why it is in business? This number of answers suggests the answer is no. Start reminding it, quickly and forcibly, and start getting other managers and staff on side. Be ruthless; get rid of people whose entirely selfish behaviour is holding the company back. There is still time to save the business, but there is a lot of work to do.

26+: This is a zombie company. Run. Get out, now. Find another job somewhere else, where you can save your self-respect, your dignity, your mental health and quite possibly your personal freedom.

Index